Dada is a part of the *Pegasus Movements in Literature* Series under the General Editorship of Ulrich Weisstein, Indiana University.

MANUEL L. GROSSMAN

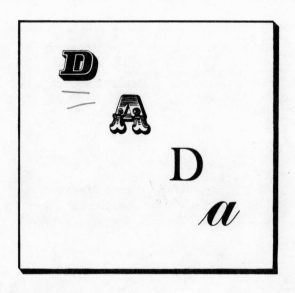

PARADOX,

MYSTIFICATION,

AND AMBIGUITY

in European Literature

PEGASUS · NEW YORK

A Division of THE BOBBS-MERRILL COMPANY, Inc.

Publishers

TO THE OTHER JARRY

Now, we are trying to revive Dada. Why? Who cares? Who doesn't care? Dada is dead. Or is Dada still alive? We cannot revive something that is alive just as we cannot revive anything that is dead.
Is Dadadead?
Is Dadaalive?
Dada is.
Dadaism.

MAN RAY

CONTENTS

ACKNOWLEDG-MENTS

On acknowledging those who supported me in this project, I would like to express my gratitude to Roger Shattuck, who helped make the project possible, and Michel Sanouillet, whose comments about Dada helped me to understand the movement. I would also like to thank Stephen Landrigan, my able assistant, Kay Jaffe, the Librarian at Boston College, and the Graduate Office at Queens College. I am also grateful to Ulrich Weisstein, the editor of this series, for his guidance and valuable comments. And finally, I would like to thank my wife Rochelle for her inspiration, support, and advice.

The author and publisher wish to thank the following for permission to reprint:
From: the English translation of Tristan Tzara's poem "Maison flake." Reprinted with permission of the Black Swan Press, Chicago, Ill. from Tzara's *13 Poems*, F. Rosemont, ed.

From: *The Dada Painters and Poets*, ed. by Robert Motherwell (Documents of Modern Art 8), George Wittenborn, Inc., New York, N.Y. 10021.

From: the poem "Kaspar Is Dead," pp. 217-218 of *On My Way* by Jean Arp, George Wittenborn, Inc., New York, N.Y. 10021.

And special thanks to Horace Marston of French Reproduction Rights, Inc. for blanket permission to quote from various French authors.

Dada aimed to destroy the reasonable deceptions of man and recover the natural and unreasonable order. Dada wanted to replace the logical nonsense of the men of today by the illogically senseless. That is why we pounded with all our might on the big drum of Dada and trumpeted the praises of unreason. Dada gave the Venus de Milo an enema and permitted Laocoon and his sons to relieve themselves after thousands of years of struggle with the good sausage Python.

JEAN ARP

ONE OF the most interesting of the recent occurrences in the arts has been the gradual reemergence of Dada into the contemporary consciousness. Plagued by the constant atmosphere of war and the increasingly rigid constraints of a technological society, artists and intellectuals have begun to listen to the strident voices of the Dadas, a group of young revolutionaries who were among the first to challenge the status quo. As a result of this renewed interest, the Dada movement has emerged from the shadow of Surrealism, where it had remained for more than twenty years.

Echoing Dada's spirit of revolt, such diverse phenomena as Existentialism, the Theater of the Absurd, and Abstract Expressionism have helped to establish its importance as an underground force. But, perhaps even more significant, the advent of Pop Art and other forms of so-called Neo-Dada have brought this force to the surface and have provided an indication of the full extent of Dada's influence on the modern artist.

Recognized not only as a seminal influence in the arts, but also as a meaningful parallel to today's life style, the Dada movement, perhaps even more than Surrealism, is increasingly regarded as a model for contemporary experience.[1] This emphasis upon their contemporary relevance helps to give the Dadas the prominence they deserve, but at the same time makes it all the more difficult to put their movement into historical perspective.

There is a tendency to dismiss the Dada movement as a forerunner of today's protest movements and to see the Dadas as little more than an earlier version of our "hippies," "yippies," and "peaceniks." Admittedly, as Jacob Korg has pointed out in an essay entitled "The Literary Aesthetics of Dada," these groups "mingle anti-militarism, extreme humanism and opposition to convention with a thoroughgoing irrationalism, just as Dada did. . . ."[2] But this is far from the whole story. Regardless of the attitudes they expressed or the techniques they used, the Dadas were, above all, artists, and it is this factor which seems to distinguish their behavior from that of the youthful protesters of today. As we shall see, their idea of revolution—in apparent contrast to that of the other groups mentioned above—was almost always expressed in artistic terms.

The attempt to find contemporary equivalents for Dada, especially in movements not primarily concerned with the arts, fails to do justice to its essential complexity. Pointing up this characteristic, a reviewer for *The Times Literary Supplement* asked in 1953, "How is one to define, let alone confine, a movement which cannot be identified with any one personality or place, viewpoint or subject, which affects all of the arts, which has a continually shifting focus and is moreover intentionally negative, ephemeral, illogical and inconclusive?"[3] More than fifteen years later, after all the books and articles that have been written about Dada—many of them by former Dadas—this question remains the basic one for anyone trying to understand the movement. For it is still virtually impossible to reconstruct the events, untangle the web of mystifications, ambiguities, and paradoxes, or in any other real way come to terms with the history of this movement. The Dadas' aversion for dates (best expressed by Arp: "Only morons and Spanish professors can be interested in dates."[4]) has compounded this problem considerably. But, chronological difficulties notwithstanding, the most vivid symbol of Dada's remarkable elusiveness, as well as a source of its power, is the term itself. While there is general agreement that the word *Dada* was discovered, or invented, in Zurich, sometime in 1916, how it happened and who was responsible for the discovery has never been fully determined. And, as one might expect in a group of strong-willed individuals, this mystery has been the source of bitter recrimination.

The main protagonists in this controversy, which grew more and more heated as the movement itself began to fade, were Richard Huelsenbeck, the principal spokesman for Berlin Dada, who claimed that he and Hugo Ball had discovered the term while looking through a French-German dictionary, and Tristan Tzara, the self-proclaimed leader of the international Dada movement, who had his own version of the event. At one time or another, nearly every member of the movement was embroiled in this controversy. When his version was challenged by Francis Picabia and André Breton, who were contesting his leadership, Tzara even went so far as to cajole his friend Jean Arp—who had previously refused to participate in all of this petty bickering—to corroborate his claim. In a style which was obviously tongue-in-cheek and a parody of the pompous manner in which important births are announced, Arp finally made the following declaration: "I hereby declare that Tzara invented the word Dada on 6th (sic) February 1916, at 6 p.m. I was there with my 12 children when Tzara first uttered the word . . . it happened in the Café de la Terrasse in Zurich, and I was wearing a brioche in my left nostril."[5]

This explanation naturally satisfied no one, with the possible exception of Tzara himself. And even after the last traces of the movement had faded, what Huelsenbeck, with uncharacteristic self-irony, has called "the battle of the Dada greybeards" continued to smolder.

Trying to determine what Dada stands for is a task which, while difficult enough under ordinary circumstances, is made virtually impossible by the Dadas' fondness for mystification. Tzara's account of the origin of the word, which ridicules Huelsenbeck's more elaborate explanation, illustrates this perfectly. As part of his authorization for Marcel Duchamp and Man Ray to use the title *New York Dada* for their magazine, Tzara wrote that "in Switzerland I was in the company of friends and was hunting the dictionary for a word appropriate to the sonorities of all languages. Night was upon us when a green hand placed its ugliness on the page of Larousse—pointing very precisely to Dada—my choice was made. I lit a cigarette and drank a demitasse."[6]

The disdain Tzara felt for anyone trying to make sense out of Dada was made especially clear in his famous "Dada Manifesto of 1918" in which he provided the following definition:

DADA MEANS NOTHING

If you find it futile and don't want to waste your time on a word that means nothing. . . . The first thought that comes to these people is bacteriological in character: to find its etymological, or at least its historical or psychological origin. We see by the papers that the Kru Negroes call the tail of a holy cow Dada. The cube and the mother in a certain district of Italy are called: Dada. The hobby horse, a nurse both in Russian and Rumanian: Dada. Some learned journalists regard it as an art for babies, other holy jesusescallingthelittlechildren of our day, as a relapse into a dry and noisy, noisy and monotonous primitivism. Sensibility is not constructed on the basis of a word; all constructions converge on perfection which is boring, the stagnant idea of a gilded swamp, a relative human product.[7]

In poking fun at the idea of definition, Tzara called attention to the Dadas' scorn for systems of thought and codifications of experience. "The true Dadas," he later wrote, "are against Dada."[8] With this in mind perhaps, they carefully avoided using the term *Dadaism*, with its unmistakable connotations of a coherent system or school of art, in their pronouncements and writings.

This brief excursion into the topsy-turvy world of the Dadas may help to explain why, until quite recently, critics have tended to overlook the significance of their movement. While this situation has begun to change in the plastic arts,[9] the critics of literature have still, for the most part, failed to grasp Dada's significance, passing it over either as a visual-arts movement or as an unimportant phenomenon.[10]

Contrary to this view, Dada was a movement of poets as well as painters. Just how important a role these poets played in its development is evident to anyone who studies its Paris and Zurich phases. It is hard to dispute that Paris Dada was primarily literary; and even in Zurich, where many of its breakthroughs occurred in the plastic arts, far-reaching literary experiments were also carried out.

The literary significance of a movement which was instrumental in the development of such poets as Paul Eluard, Louis Aragon, Jean Arp, Tristan Tzara, and Francis Picabia—poets who not only put into question what have been termed man's "consoling myths," but also influenced the later attempts by modern writers to explore new realms of feeling and form—must not be dismissed quite so lightly.

We may never know the whole story of the movement. But, as a result of memoirs and of authoritative studies such as Michel Sanouillet's *Dada à Paris,* we now have enough background to approach these experiments with some understanding. With this in mind, I have divided my book into five chapters. The first two chapters provide a discussion of the artistic and intellectual climate that led to the founding of Dada and its most important precursors. Chapter One focuses on the role of Alfred Jarry, Arthur Cravan, and Jacques Vaché as precursors of the Dada movement, and Chapter Two examines the contributions of Marcel Duchamp, Francis Picabia, and Man Ray to pre-Dada in New York. The third chapter is a survey of the movement itself from its origins in Zurich to its demise in Paris. This is followed in Chapter Four with an analysis of the literary experiments of the Dada poets and anti-poets, with particular emphasis upon such largely overlooked works as Tzara's "Maison Flake," Picabia's *Jésus-Christ Rastaquouère,* and Aragon's *Anicet.* The concluding chapter of the book assesses Dada's overall importance as a literary phenomenon. Unless otherwise indicated, the translations used in this book are my own.

CHAPTER ONE

THREE PRECURSORS OF DADA

After Stéphane Mallarmé, after
Paul Verlaine, after Gustave Mo-
reau, after Puvis de Chavannes,
after our own verse, after all our
subtle colour and nervous rhythm
. . . what more is possible? After
us the Savage God.

WILLIAM BUTLER YEATS

THE DADA REVOLT against language and logic followed
on the heels of a sharp and widespread reaction
against applied science and its mundane vision of the
world. In the eyes of many modern thinkers, science
had become little more than what Paul Valéry has
termed a set of "successful recipes." What good were
its marvelous inventions—wireless telegraphy, the mo-
torcar, the flying machine, and the moving picture—
these men asked, if they resulted in such spiritual im-
poverishment? Led by Max Planck and Albert Einstein,
who attacked Newtonian physics and advanced new
concepts of time and space, these thinkers began to
question the conventional reality which was the basis
for all of this "progress." Epistemologists postulated new
conditions for knowledge, psychologists explored the
unconscious mind, and mathematicians devised non-
Euclidian geometries.

The focal point for these new ideas about reality, especially as they apply to the arts, was the philosopher Henri Bergson. In a series of lectures presented at the Collège de France—to which all of Paris flocked—Bergson sharply criticized mankind's blind worship of reason and intelligence. He proposed that modern man's obsession with controlling his environment had caused him to lose touch with the forces of intuition, the "vital impulse," which made it possible for him to respond to "the cosmic vibration and the rhythm of the universe."[1]

Bergson's teachings provided a philosophical framework for those writers who, following in the path of Baudelaire, Rimbaud, and Lautréamont, had already begun their own revolt against reason. Some of these younger poets, such as Charles Péguy and Paul Claudel, expressed their reaction against conventional reality through their writing alone, while others, such as Alfred Jarry, made the irrational the guiding principle of their lives as well.

The current of irrationalism, which developed in the wake of these widespread reactions against reason, was electrified by World War I and the resultant breakdown of established values. In the arts in general and poetry in particular, the revolt, which had been more or less submerged, broke through to the surface. Following Jarry's example, disillusioned young writers began to question even the most basic aspects of human existence. If man's life must culminate in the blood and horror of a war like this, they asked, how worthwhile can it be? It was out of this kind of questioning that the Dada movement developed. Capping a long period of revolt, Dada naturally had many precursors. But, in marked contrast to the Surrealists, who proudly proclaimed that their genealogy included such men as the Marquis de Sade and Lautréamont, the Dadas tended to play down the roles of even their most radical predecessors. Unlike the Surrealists, who were concerned with continuing what they considered the most significant trends in the arts, the Dadas often expressed a desire to break with all previous traditions, no matter how revolutionary they might seem.

That this revolutionary spirit, in itself, makes them part of a viable literary tradition is hard to dispute. Even Tzara himself ultimately acknowledged this when he distinguished between two kinds of poetry—"poetry as a means of expression" and "poetry as an activity of the mind."[2] He did not elaborate upon this crucial distinction until 1931, but he offered hints of it in his earlier writings. For example, in his famous manifesto of 1918 he alluded to two types of literature in what was for him, a remarkably straightforward manner. The first is the kind of literature in which "the writers who teach morality and discuss or improve psychological foundations have, aside from a hidden desire to make money, an absurd view of life, which they have classified, cut into sections, channelized. . . ." In contrast to this, he proposed, *"there is a literature that does not reach the voracious mass It is the work of creators, issued from a real necessity in the author, produced for himself. It expresses the knowledge of a supreme egoism, in which laws wither away."*[3]

Tzara's attitude toward these two types of writing was made clearer in his "Essay on the Situation of Poetry" which was published in 1931 in *Surrealism in the Service of the Revolution:*

> Let us immediately denounce a misunderstanding that claimed to classify poetry as *a means of expression.* The poetry which distinguishes itself from novels only by its external form, the poetry which expresses either ideas or sentiments no longer interests anyone. To it I oppose poetry as an *activity of the mind.* . . . It is perfectly evident today that one can be a poet without ever having written a line, that there exists a quality of poetry in the street, in a commercial performance, anywhere, the confusion is great, it is poetic.[4]

Moreover, Tzara traced aspects of poetry as an "activity of the mind" back to Hugo, Baudelaire, Huysmans, Mallarmé, and Saint-Paul Roux: men who, realizing that it was futile to try to express the mysteries of life through words alone, had rejected the idea of poetry as "a means of expression." Even more important, according to Tzara, were the extreme revolutionaries of modern poetry—Gérard de Nerval, Lautréamont, Rimbaud, Jarry, and Apollinaire—who had affirmed poetry not as a written product, but *"une manière de vivre."*[5]

Tzara's retrospective discussion of its various precursors provides ample evidence that the Dada movement emerged out of a literary tradition, albeit a highly revolutionary one. A detailed look at three of Dada's most radical and most immediate predecessors—Alfred Jarry, Arthur Cravan, and Jacques Vaché—indicates that what might be called the Dada spirit was very much in the air even before the movement developed.

Alfred Jarry: Destroyer of the Ruins

Jarry's role as a precursor of Dada is nicely summed up in the foreword of his play *Ubu Bound* when Ubu speaks about the need to destroy and build anew:

> Hornsboodle, we should never have knocked everything down if we hadn't meant to destroy the ruins too. But the only way we see of doing that is to put up some handsome buildings.[6]

Following his own character's advice and using literature and theater as his weapons, Jarry blasted away at the very ruins of his society. With unmistakable admiration, Breton attested to the success of Jarry's tactics when, in his *Anthology of Black Humor*, he wrote that "literature, from Jarry on, is dangerously booby-trapped like a mine field."[7]

The destructive side of Jarry's nature is embodied in Ubu, a character who most vividly expresses the ferocity of the poet's revolt. Although Jarry admitted that Ubu "represented for him everything in the world that is grotesque,"[8] he was fascinated enough with this horrible creature to weave a cycle of plays around his terrible exploits and develop him into one of the most notorious antiheroes in literature. Regardless of whether he is a usurper King *(King Ubu)*, an unwelcome guest *(Ubu Cuckolded)*, or a willing slave *(Ubu Bound)*, Ubu stands, in Jarry's words, "for the power of the base appetites."[9]

As a result of one of the strangest transformations in literary history, Jarry's own personality and that of his character Ubu somehow became entwined. And, by a curious twist of fate, Jarry gradually became inseparable from Ubu. The legend which surrounds this mysterious metamorphosis has made it impossible, even today, to determine whether Jarry assumed this role to carry his revolt behind the enemies' lines and make his every gesture an affront to society or whether he was simply the victim of his own imagination. Perhaps, as the poet Georges Clancier has said, both hypotheses are equally valid since it is virtually impossible to tell the victim from the hangman in Jarry's life.

In any event, Jarry played the role of Ubu to the hilt and, in the process, helped erase the traditional distinctions between art and life. Assuming the guise of his own monstrous creature, King

Ubu, he adopted a pompous style of speech which was worthy of a usurper King, the wind becoming "that which blows" and a bird "that which chirps." To add to this incongruous picture, Jarry dressed in one of two ways, appearing either as a bicycle-racer (tight sweater, short coat, old pants tucked into his socks) or as a kind of imaginative hobo (dirty canvas suit, paper shirt and inked-in tie). In addition, he spoke in a staccato manner which, according to André Gide, sounded the way you would imagine a nutcracker to sound if nutcrackers could talk. Among Jarry's other accoutrements were his bicycle, a prized possession which he naturally spoke of as "that which rolls," and his trusty firearms.

A chapter in Jarry's legend has grown up around his exploits with guns. Supposedly, he was always armed to the teeth, with a carbine on his shoulder and two pistols at his belt. Judging by Breton's comments in his *Anthology of Black Humor,* this aspect of Jarry's character, whether legendary or real, proved especially fascinating to the Dadas. Cleverly making use of Jarry's own technique, Breton referred to him as *"celui qui revolver"*[10] and went on to cite his penchant for guns as a primary example of black humor. Pointing out Jarry's fondness for drawing his revolver in unlikely places—at literary gatherings, at the circus, and on the bus—Breton alluded to what must go down in the annals of black humor as a classic incident. One day Jarry was taking target practice in the backyard of a summer house in Corbeil which he shared with Alfred Vallette, the publisher of the *Mercure de France,* and his wife, the novelist Rachilde. Some of the shots began to go astray and land in a neighbor's garden. The terrified woman, who feared for the lives of her children playing in the yard, rushed next door to complain to Madame Rachilde. Overhearing their conversation, Jarry came back into the house and, with all of the pompousness he could summon up, assured her that "if that should ever happen, *Ma-da-me,* we should ourselves be delighted to get some new ones with you."[11]

So much, then, for Jarry's efforts to carry out the first part of Ubu's dictum—to destroy everything, even the ruins. The paradoxical thing about all this destruction, however, was that often at the same time he was also carrying out the second part of Ubu's dictum—constructing handsome buildings. Through his absurd posturing, Jarry carried the fusion of art and life far beyond anything envisioned either by Rimbaud or Oscar Wilde. In the process, he discovered an entirely new universe of the imagination.

The symbol of this visionary side of Jarry's nature was Dr.

Faustroll, "savant, pataphysician, imperturbable logician." Dr. Faustroll made his appearance in Jarry's posthumous novel *Exploits and Opinions of Doctor Faustroll Pataphysician,* an account of a supernatural voyage, which he refused to publish until he had "acquired sufficient experience to savor all its beauties."[12] Subtitled "a neo-scientific novel," this work points up Jarry's ability to combine provocative humor with the most rigorous logic. Both of these qualities are illustrated in the following deadpan description of Dr. Faustroll:

CONCERNING THE HABITS AND BEARING
OF DOCTOR FAUSTROLL

Doctor Faustroll was sixty-three years old when he was born in Circassia in 1898 (the 20th century was (-2) years old).

At this age, which he retained all his life, Doctor Faustroll was a man of medium height, or, to be absolutely accurate, of $(8 \times 10^{10} + 10^9 + 4 \times 10^8 + 5 \times 10^6)$ atomic diameters; with a golden-yellow skin, his face clean-shaven, apart from a sea-green mustachios (*sic.*), as worn by King Saleh; the hairs of his head alternately platinum blonde and jet black, an auburn ambiguity changing according to the sun's position; his eyes, two capsules of ordinary writing-ink flecked with golden spermatozoa like Danzig schnapps.[13]

The perfect synthesis of rationality and absurdity that Jarry achieved in this writing is again illustrated by Faustroll's description of his boat, a large sieve which is virtually unsinkable. After describing the sieve at great length and providing minute scientific details that account for its seaworthiness, Faustroll concluded on the following note: "The skiff is not only propelled by oar blades but also by suction disks at the end of spring levers. I am all the more convinced of the excellence of my calculations and of its insubmersibility in that, as is my invariable habit, we shall not be navigating on water but on dry land."[14]

Throughout the book, which describes how Faustroll and his crew—including a curious baboon Bosse-de-Nage, a creature who can express himself only by using the monosyllables *Ha Ha*—travel to marvelous lands, Jarry made it a point to comment on various aspects of the scientific and artistic traditions of his time. Equally important, he also sketched the outlines of pataphysics, an idea that represented the crowning achievement of his life of reversed values. Defining pataphysics as *"the science of imaginary solutions, which symbolically attributes the properties of objects, described by their virtuality, to their lineaments,"*[15] he pointed out how this "science of the particular" puts in question some of the premises of the scientific method:

> Pataphysics will examine the laws governing exceptions, and will explain the universe supplementary to this one; or, less ambitiously, will describe a universe which can be—and perhaps should be—envisioned in the place of the traditional one, since the laws that are supposed to have been discovered in the traditional universe are also correlations of exceptions, albeit more frequent ones, but in any case accidental data which, reduced to the status of unexceptional exceptions, possess no longer even the virtue of originality.[16]

Jarry not only explored the meaning of pataphysics in his writing, but also made it the guiding principle of his life. Even the circumstances of his death—now, like so many of his other exploits, become legendary—seemed to affirm this. After lying in a semicoma, feebly repeating the phrase, "I am looking, I am looking," he awoke briefly to request a toothpick. His friend Dr. Saltas, who was at his bedside, ran out and got some. With the toothpick in his hand, a change came over Jarry ("as if he were suddenly filled with a great joy as on the days he went off fishing or on a canoe or bicycle trip,"[17] Saltas later wrote) and he died. This was in 1907, almost ten years before the advent of the Dada movement. But the uncompromising destructiveness of Jarry's revolt, the pataphysical paradoxes of his life, and his curious fusion of art and life anticipated and prepared the way for Dada.

Arthur Cravan: Poet, Boxer, and Deserter of Five Nations

Although Jarry's spirit of mystification was an important source of inspiration to the Dadas,[18] his style calls to mind the artful pretense and "comic innocence" of the Banquet Years rather than the overtly provocative manner of Dada. For an expression of the cruder, more self-conscious style which was to become the trademark of Dada, we must look to Arthur Cravan, who stands alongside Jarry as an important precursor of the Dada movement.

Cravan, whose real name was Fabian Lloyd, was the son of English parents who were living in Lausanne, Switzerland. Temperamentally unsuited for life in Switzerland, he left home in 1903, at the age of sixteen, and traveled to the United States, where he barely managed to support himself by boxing and doing various odd jobs. Soon growing tired of this, Cravan returned to Europe and, after settling for a brief time in Berlin—where he frequented the sleaziest bars and associated with drug addicts, hustlers, and prostitutes—he moved on to Paris. Living in the artistic capital of the world, Cravan quite naturally became interested in art and literature. He began to hang around places like the Closerie des Lilas and to make friends with some of the leading figures in the avant-garde, men like Kees van Dongen, André Salmon, and Blaise Cendrars.

Claiming to be the nephew of Oscar Wilde, Cravan also engaged in public performances, which brought him some notoriety. A typical example of these took place at the Salle des Sociétés Savantes on July 5, 1914. The handbill announcing his appearance read as follows:

> COME TO THE—Salle des Sociétés Savantes—8 rue Danton—
> TO SEE—The Poet—ARTHUR CRAVAN–(Nephew of
> Oscar Wilde)–Boxing Champion, weight 105 kilos, height
> 2 meters.–THE BRUTAL CRITIC–WILL SPEAK–BOX–
> DANCE–The new 'Boxing Dance'–THE VERY BOX–in
> conjunction with the sculptor MAC ADAMS — Other eccentric numbers—NEGROES.BOXERS.DANCERS–Sunday July
> 5th, 9 o'clock in the evening—Ticket prices: 5 fr., 3 fr., 2
> fr.[19]

An account of the actual proceedings was published in *Paris-Midi* under the headline "The Nephew of Oscar Wilde." According to this report, Cravan not only danced and boxed, but also fired several rounds from a pistol.[20] In his lecture, he vented his wrath upon the art world, declaring that "athletes, homosexuals, thieves trom the Louvre, and madmen were superior to artists,"[21] and hurled insults at his audience.

Cravan's reputation was not limited to public performances. He also made his literary mark by publishing *Now*, a vehemently anti-intellectual review which has been recognized as an early forerunner of Picabia's *391*. Although *Now* lasted for only three years, from 1912 to 1915, everything about it—its method of distribution, its format, and its philosophy—was distinctive. This magazine, which was coverless and resembled the later Dada periodicals in the disjointedness of its format, was distributed in a novel way: Cravan sold it from a kind of wheelbarrow, like a pushcart vendor. Primarily a vehicle for expressing his love of primitive spontaneity and scorn for traditional art and literature, *Now* anticipated the Dada magazines in philosophy as well as format.

Cravan was not a prolific poet, but in *Now* he published a few poems which pointed up his fascination with the exotic, his overwhelming enthusiasm for physical pleasure, and his desire for every kind of excess. Characterized by these traits and written in an extraordinarily free-wheeling style, these poems invariably call to mind the style of Blaise Cendrars:

I yearn to be in Vienna and Calcutta,
To take all the trains and all the ships,
To fuck all the women and gulp down all the food.
Man of the world, chemist, whore, drunkard, musician, worker, painter,
(acrobat, actor,
Old man, child, swindler, street arab, angel, and rake,
millionare, bourgeois, cactus, giraffe or crow;
Coward, hero, negro, ape, Don Juan, pimp, lord, peasant,
(hunter, industrialist,
Flora and fauna
I am all things, all men, and all animals![22]

In his disdain for orthodox poetic structure and in his preoccupation with curious juxtapositions of words and images, Cravan also seems to resemble Tzara. Cravan often makes use of those long strings of seemingly unrelated words and phrases with which Tzara later became so fascinated. For example, the opening section of Cravan's poem "Exercise No. 4" reads as follows: "Country, juvenile, the aquatic plants, viaduct, signals, the West; the parrots, tender, prairies, awaken the bushes, charcoal, coke, coal, chic; toward the new cycle-tracks; the tennis. . . ."[23]

But, its resemblance to Cendrars and Tzara notwithstanding, Cravan's poetry has a distinctive style of its own, based on a feeling for simple things. "Nature," Cravan wrote, expressing his almost pantheistic view, "I am your servant."[24] And it is this spirit, embodied in the recurring descriptions of untamed nature and the images of large, majestic jungle animals—"languorous elephants," "timid giraffes," and fierce tigers—which gives his poetry a simple, masculine lyricism:

> I dreamt of a bed which would float on the water and more commonly to sleep on tigers—I frequent the paths—I follow the movement of mists on the theater of plains and valleys where plants in rectangles of radishes and cabbages form like tombs. . . .[25]

Cravan's provocative sense of humor was also communicated through, the pages of *Now*. Among other things, he provided an amusing portrait of André Gide upon which Breton later lavished praise because it helped young writers like himself to measure the distance between Gide and his creation, Lafcadio. But far and away the most devastating illustration of Cravan's type of "insult humor" was his critique of the Independents Exhibition in Paris which was, in Breton's words, "the master piece of humor applied to art criticism."[26]

After declaring that art is for people "without imagination," Cravan posed the obvious question: why should someone so disdainful of art even bother to criticize it? His answer—to exasperate people and gain some notoriety—was simple and to the point. Having made his intentions clear, he went on to heap abuse upon the world of art and literature. He proposed that the exhibit tent might have had some of the charm of Barnum's circus tents if it were not filled with such arty types ("painters with long hair, writers with long hair; painters with short hair, writers with short hair; ragged writers").[27]

Warming up to his task, Cravan mounted a brutal attack not only upon the paintings in the exhibition, many of which he had not even seen, but also upon the painters themselves: Maurice Denis, Suzanne Valadon, Alice Bailly, Kasimir Malevich, and Robert Delaunay, among others.

Not content with merely belaboring Delaunay and his paintings, Cravan even went so far as to insult his former friend's Russian wife in an unprecedented example of gratuitous slander:

> He married a Russian, yes, Virgin Mother! a Russian woman, but a Russian woman to whom he's afraid to be unfaithful. For my part, I should rather practice indecency with a professor of philosophy at the Collège de France— *Monsieur Bergson* for instance—than to go to bed with most

Russian women. I do not say that I shall not fornicate some day with *Madame Delaunay,* because, like the vast majority of men, I am a born collector and consequently it would give me a cruel satisfaction to debauch a kindergarten teacher, especially as at the moment of breaking her, I should have the impression I was smashing an eyeglass.[28]

Cravan was no less sparing of Marie Laurencin, declaring that she "needs to have her skirts lifted up and to get a sound . . . some place, to teach her that art isn't a little pose in front of the mirror."[29]

Despite his penchant for destructive criticism, Cravan's remarks were not all negative. Substituting what might be called a form of "physical euphoria" for Rimbaud's famous "disorder of all the senses," he offered his own prescription of what the artist and his art should be. "The first requirement for an artist," he proposed, "is to know how to swim."[30] He went on to advise the would-be artist to "take a few pills and purge your spirit; do a lot of fucking or better still go into rigorous training: when the girth of your arm measures nineteen inches, you'll at least be a brute, if you're gifted."[31] And he concluded this regimen with the following suggestion: "Go and run in the fields, gallop across the plains like a horse; jump rope, and when you're six years old, you won't know anything any more, and you'll see mad things."[32]

Once the artist has achieved this state, he must, according to Cravan, take pride in it. "If you have the good fortune to be a brute," he wrote, "you've got to keep on being one. Everyone will understand that I prefer a big stupid Saint Bernard to Mademoiselle Fanfreluche who knows how to dance the gavotte and, at any rate, a yellow man to a white man, a black man to a yellow man and a black boxer to a black student."[33]

Only in this way, Cravan continued, can the artist overthrow the idea of art spelled with a capital A and become involved with life again. For, as he so sternly reminded Marie Laurencin, "painting is walking, running, drinking, eating and fulfilling your natural functions."[34] In poking fun at Laurencin's work, Cravan anticipated the anti-art attitudes of the Dadas:

Art, with a capital A, is on the contrary, dear Mademoiselle, literally speaking, a flower (oh, my dear child!) which blooms only in the midst of contingencies, and

> there is no doubt that a turd is just as necessary to the
> formation of a masterpiece as your door-knob, or, to use a
> figure that will really strike your imagination, is just as
> necessary, I say, as the deliciously languorous rose which
> adorably casts the perfume of its languidly pink petals over
> the virginally pallid surface of your delicate, tender and
> artistic mantelpiece (baby hair!).[35]

When war was declared in 1914, Cravan's short-lived publishing venture came to an end, and he was forced to leave Paris.
Fearful of conscription, he left the French city in 1915 and began
a curious game of hide-and-seek with the authorities of several
countries that wanted to make him a soldier. After traveling
through Central Europe and miraculously crossing all kinds of
borders without being captured, he finally ended up in Barcelona
in 1916, where he joined a circle of expatriates and the like who
had gathered around Francis Picabia.

But, unable to stay in one place for any length of time, Cravan
quickly grew bored with life in Barcelona and traveled to New
York in 1917. For a brief period he was forced to sleep in Central
Park with various other fugitives. The nature of Cravan's nomad
existence was poignantly captured in a remark that he made to
Picabia a propos of his nights in Central Park: "The squirrels
have become my friends, they sleep in my pockets. And like all
friends, I must leave them."[36] Cravan's prediction came true soon
afterwards when the United States entered the war, and he was
compelled once again to flee the draft. This time with the aid of a
dead friend's identity papers he traveled through Canada to New-
foundland.

Throughout this period of dodging the authorities, Cravan was
embroiled in many intrigues and involved in numerous adventures. One of these was a boxing bout with Jack Johnson, the
former heavyweight champion of the world, in Spain in 1916.
Like Cravan, Johnson, who had left the United States to avoid
prosecution for an alleged violation of the Mann act, was living
in Spain as a fugitive. In order to keep himself in trim and earn
some needed cash, Johnson, still recognized as the European
champion, was engaging in exhibition bouts.

The fight between the two men was clearly no contest.
Johnson—one of the great boxers of all time—made quick work of
Cravan, who "in anticipation of the inevitable result . . . had
arrived in the ring reeling drunk."[37]

Cravan's strangest adventure, however—his disappearance in Mexico—was yet to come. The danger of conscription passed, he had returned to New York from the Far North. Still wandering rather aimlessly, he had continued on to Mexico, where he engaged in a variety of activities, including prospecting for silver. But once again he drifted back to boxing, this time as the proprietor of a boxing academy, which he opened sometime around 1918. This venture was dealt a financial blow, however, when one of the local fighters defeated Cravan in a bout. And it was on the heels of this financial disaster and the affront to his pride that Cravan vanished mysteriously, never to reappear.

As with Alfred Jarry, it is difficult to separate the real from the legendary Arthur Cravan. Even after the disparate elements of his life have been pieced together, we are left with an inexplicable ambivalence. On the one hand, Cravan was a man who lived up to his slogan that "all great artists have the sense of provocation," delivering scandalous lectures, expressing a complete scorn for art and literature, and embodying Rimbaud's declaration—"I don't understand laws; I don't have a moral sense, I am a brute . . . I am a beast, a Negro"—in his every action. On the other hand, he was a man who, even in his most brutal moments, confessed to the sensibility of the poet ("I am enough of a brute to give myself a belt in the teeth and subtle to the point of neurasthenia");[38] a poet who makes us feel life's sadness:

The curtain raises itself in the afternoon wind
And the day strips before dying away
And my maturity already seems to complain
At the edge of the settings of deepening reddish mud
Which gently sinks in and slowly grows larger.[39]

What André Breton has called "the signs before the runners of Dada" are unmistakable in Cravan. He anticipated the Dadas' provocative sense of humor as well as their preoccupation with the spontaneous and the primitive and their uncompromising attacks against art. And beneath his bravado and braggadocio, one catches a glimpse of the modern malaise, a mood which Jacques Vaché expressed so poignantly and which always seems to have been at the opposite pole of Dada's most free-wheeling gestures.

Jacques Vaché: Pataphysician in the Void

Whereas Cravan had, in the tradition of Alfred Jarry, based his revolt upon the provocative gesture and the openly destructive act, Jacques Vaché, the third precursor of Dada, expressed his in terms of a kind of "paralyzing irony" which, interestingly enough, also derives from Jarry. Vaché's guiding principle—what he himself referred to as "Umour"—was, in large part, a variation on Jarry's pataphysics. But, unlike Jarry—who, harking back to the spirit of the Banquet Years, seemed to take great pleasure in his absurd view of life—Vaché's form of pataphysics was *without joy*. Thus, he defined "Umour" as "a sense of the theatric and joyless futility of everything, when one is enlightened."[40] Making the connection with Jarry even clearer, Vaché declared that Ubu's destructive approach played a major part in his concept of "Umour."

As was the case with Jarry's pataphysics, Vaché's "Umour" was more than just a theoretical construct; it was the basic ingredient of his life, much of which was spent as a soldier at the front. Swept up in the terror of World War I, Vaché experienced the "joyless futility of everything" in a very real way. But, faced with the arduous task of day-to-day survival, this strange young soldier, behind the virtually impenetrable facade of his "Umour," actually found a way of triumphing over circumstances. And it was this triumph which called forth the admiration of Breton and his colleagues, transforming Vaché into an early symbol of their Dadaist revolt.

Breton's writings provide the most detailed account of Vaché's life during the war. The two men met for the first time in Nantes in 1916 where Breton, having been mobilized, was serving as a provisional intern at the Neurological Center, and Vaché, a former student at the Ecole des Beaux-Arts, was in the hospital recovering from a wound in his calf. Recalling that Vaché shared none of his own enthusiasm for art and literature, Breton noted that he detested Rimbaud, hardly knew Apollinaire, and scorned Cubism. The single exception to this sweeping condemnation of modern writers was Jarry, whose work Vaché knew and admired.

After a period of convalescence, Vaché left the hospital and, while he was still recuperating, began to assume the eccentric postures and engage in the curious activities which were characteristic of him. He worked as a stevedore unloading coal by day and made the rounds of the movie houses and bars of Nantes by night. Dressed like a dandy, he would wander from movie house to movie house, usually leaving after only a few minutes. He also haunted the seediest bars where, according to Breton, he could sit and watch the "glaborous faces" and "hieratic postures" of the regulars.[41] For these nightly vigils, Vaché would sometimes don the uniforms—that of an English officer, an aviator, or even a doctor—which were his favorite disguises.

During this period, Vaché also began to experiment with various little games that ridiculed the amenities and conventions of daily living. For example, he introduced Breton as André Salmon, refused to say hello or goodbye even to his best friends, and stopped answering his mail. Moreover, he acted out the role of a kind of modern-day Marquis de Sade with Louise, the young girl who lived with him, forcing her to stand in a corner for hours without moving or speaking while he entertained his friends.

Judging by his *Letters of War*, Vaché continued to live his "Umour" and to ridicule social conventions even after he had returned to the front. Between 1916 and 1918, he sent letters to Breton, Aragon, and their friend Theodore Fraenkel in which he documented his attempts to amuse himself despite the trying conditions of war. In a letter to Breton, he informed his friends that he had been made an interpreter for a British unit, a position which, while it had its advantages, failed to relieve the monotony of life at the front. After praising the tea and light tobacco of the British, he poignantly expressed the tedium that sensitive young men like himself could not help experiencing in this situation:

> But all the same, all the same, what a life! Of course, I have no one to talk to, no books to read, and no time to paint—In short *terribly* isolated—I say, Mr the Interpreter—Will you . . . Excuse me, the way to? Have a cigar, sir?—supply train, inhabitants, mayor and billeting paper—A shell which affirms and the rain, the rain, the rain, rain—the rain—the rain—two hundred heavy trucks one after another, one after another—one after another. . . .
>
> Thus, I am seized again by the terrible boredom . . . of things without any interest. . . .[42]

Escaping from this intolerable situation, Vaché retreated into his imaginary world of "Umour." First, he pretended that he was actually on the German side, then, he imagined that one of the English officers, suddenly transformed into a winged hermaphrodite, danced the vampire's dance while drinking a cup of tea with milk.

Surrounded by the miserable conditions of war, it is not surprising that Vaché continued to express the scorn for art and literature which had made such a strong impression on the young Breton in Nantes. In one of his letters, he questioned the importance of Apollinaire and Rimbaud, two of Breton's most cherished heroes, but reaffirmed his admiration for Jarry.

In still another letter, he elaborated on his disdain for modern literature and its most important spokesmen. Although he was aware that his words might wound Breton, Vaché spared him nothing. Declaring that he liked "neither ART, nor artists," he explained that "we ignore MALLARMÉ without hatred, but he's dead—But we don't know Apollinaire, nor Cocteau any more—For—we suspect them of too consciously creating art, of fixing up romanticism with telephone wire. . . ."[43] After extending his attacks to certain other literary idols, i.e., Baudelaire, Pierre Reverdy, and Max Jacob, Vaché made one final blanket condemnation in which he summed up all of his animosity toward art and literature: "ART IS A SILLY THING."[44]

Vaché's *Letters of War* show how his concept of "Umour" affected his attitudes and way of life, but they are important for another reason as well: perhaps better than any abstract discussion, they convey a vivid impression of the impact of a senseless war on the minds of the young men involved. Despite his ironic way of looking at war—or perhaps more precisely *because* of it—Vaché poignantly expressed the feelings of boredom, dehumanization, and hopelessness of the men at the front. "I am extremely bored behind my glass monocle," he wrote; "the disembraining machine moves with a great noise, and not far away, I have a stable of TANKS—a very UBUESQUE animal, but without joy."[45] Continually resorting to the language of King Ubu, he even touched upon what must have been the unexpressed fear of these poor soldiers—the fear of dying young. He wrote to Fraenkel: "I would be bored to die so younggggg. Ah! then MERDRE."[46]

A member of Paris Dada only in spirit, Vaché died soon after the Armistice on January 6, 1919, in Nantes. His death is shrouded in mystery. The official report of the police and the medical authorities stated that Vaché and one of his friends died of an accidental overdose of opium. But Breton, noting that Vaché was an experienced opium user, has advanced the possibility that he deliberately took an overdose of the drug and in dying committed one last *"fourberie drôle"* at the expense of his unsuspecting friend. Reinforcing this interpretation, Breton recalled that Vaché not only objected to dying in the war, but also made the terrifying declaration: "I would die with someone. It's too boring to die alone. . . . By preference, one of my 'best friends.' "[47] As a result of these speculations, Vaché's death has become legendary, and along with Jarry's famous deathbed request for a toothpick and Cravan's mysterious disappearance, has gone down in the annals of black humor.

Unlike Jarry, and to a lesser extent Cravan, Vaché left little more than his letters to judge him by. Epitomizing their antiliterary ideal, he thus evoked the unqualified admiration of Breton and his group. In recalling that the time they had spent together in Nantes was "nearly enchanted," Breton has affirmed that Vaché's influence was the most important in his life and the one which paved the way for Dada. "Without him," Breton wrote, "I would, perhaps, have been a poet; he frustrated in me that conspiracy of obscure forces which causes us to consider something as absurd as a vocation."[48] Summing up Vaché's role as a precursor of Dada, Breton noted that his "good fortune is to have produced nothing. He always kicked aside the work of art, that ball and chain that hold back the soul after death. At the very moment when Tristan Tzara was sending out a decisive proclamation from Zurich, Jacques Vaché, without knowing it, verified its principal articles."[49]

Despite Breton's declaration, there is some question as to whether or not Vaché's attitudes toward literature were as truly uncompromising as they seem. That Vaché may have had literary pretensions of his own, in spite of his seemingly outright condemnation of literature, is evidenced by the fact that he was willing to submit a poem "White Acetylene" and a fragment of a novel *The Bloody Symbol* to Breton to publish in one of the Dada magazines. Moreover, there is some indication that, in spite of Breton's denial, Vaché may not only have known about Zurich Dada, but even may have been influenced by it. It is hard to believe that he would have ignored a movement, so close to his own interests, which had existed in Zurich since 1916, and which had been recognized soon afterwards in Paris. Although no document has yet turned up which can settle this question with any certainty, there is a letter from Soupault to Tzara dated January 17, 1919, eleven days after Vaché's death, which indicates that he, Soupault, had read Tzara's Dada manifesto of 1918 to three of his friends: Breton, Aragon, and Vaché.[50]

As for Breton's contention that Vaché was unaware of what he was doing, his *Letters of War* seem to tell another story. For someone not interested in creating literature, Vaché seems all too self-conscious about his writing style. For example, in one of the letters he sent to Breton, Vaché confessed that he had had a great deal of difficulty deciding exactly how he should phrase his ideas and therefore had waited until the right moment arrived before writing.[51] This would hardly seem to be the style of the type of man Breton has pictured.

Vaché may not have completely lived up to his own high ideal or that of his hero Lafcadio, whom he admired because he "doesn't read or produce except in amusing experiences,"[52] but he still stands as an important precursor of Dada. For it was Vaché's anti-art attitudes and pataphysical submissiveness that provided the model which young men like Breton needed, in order to cope with the miseries of war, transcend the boundaries of traditional literature, and triumph over the dictates of conventional reality.

CHAPTER TWO

PRE-DADA IN NEW YORK

These games of exploration in an inaccessible dimension and in unexplored regions of being, this climate of invention which has never since been retrieved, seem to have contained all the germs of what later became Dada. . . .

GABRIELLE BUFFET-PICABIA

Even before the ideas of Jarry, Cravan, and Vaché had come to fruition in Paris and the term Dada, which was to become the rallying cry for the movement, had been discovered in Zurich, New York was the center for what, in retrospect, might be called pre-Dadaist activity. Marcel Duchamp and Francis Picabia, two artists who, like Cravan, had fled Paris to escape the war, provided the major impetus. Returning to an earlier scene of triumph, Duchamp and Picabia arrived in New York in 1915. Two years before, they had both participated in the Armory Show (Duchamp contributing *Nude Descending a Staircase* and Picabia *Procession to Seville)* and, as a result of the scandal their paintings provoked, they had gained a reputation as leaders in the rebellion against traditional art. Now that they themselves had moved to New York, it is not surprising that they became the focal point for the avant-garde.

Prior to the arrival of Duchamp and Picabia, the photographer Alfred Stieglitz and his circle of artists and writers, who were the prime movers of the Armory Show, had begun to explore certain Dadaist ideas in their lavish magazine *Camera Work*, which featured photographs, reproductions of paintings, and philosophical articles. Benjamin De Casseres, an ardent disciple of Nietzsche, contributed an essay entitled "Modernity and Decadence" to *Camera Work* in 1912, celebrating "the indefinite, the uncertain, the paradoxical":

> In poetry, physics, practical life there is nothing . . . that is any longer moored to a certainty, nothing that is forbidden, nothing that cannot be stood on its head and glorified. The indefinite, the uncertain, the paradoxical, is the scarlet paradise of intellectual intoxication. . . .
> Anarchy? No. It is the triumph of discrimination, the beatification of paradox, the sanctification of man by man.
> . . .
> Nothing which lasts is of value. . . . That which changes perpetually lives perpetually. . . . Incessant dying and renewing, incessant metamorphosis, incessant contradiction. . . . I desire as many personalities as I have moods . . . I desire to be ephemeral, protean . . .
> I find my supremest joy in my estrangements . . . I desire to become unfamiliar with myself . . . I cling to nothing, stay with nothing, am wed to nothing, hope for nothing. I am a perpetual minute.[1]

In another essay, De Casseres attacked logic and rationality. He wrote: "Sanity and simplicity are the prime curses of civilization . . . a kind of lunacy wherein a fixed idea blankets the brain and smothers the admirable incoherence of life to a smug symmetry and proportion. . . ."[2] His solution for this problem, like his diagnosis, was truly Dadaist: "We should mock existence at each moment, mock ourselves, mock others, mock everything by the perpetual creation of fantastic and grotesque attitudes, gestures and attributes."[3]

Picabia had already had some contact with Stieglitz's circle as early as 1913, when he had visited New York for a brief period in conjunction with the Armory Show. At that time, he had not only become friends with Stieglitz, De Casseres, and Marius de Zayas, but had also contributed to their magazine *Camera Work*. Himself a great admirer of Nietzsche, Picabia seems to have found a "kindred spirit" in De Casseres. Some idea of the mutual respect in which these two held each other emerges from De Casseres's remark that Picabia was "a descendant of Heraclitus, for whom the irrational, chance, and constant change were principles of existence."[4]

Back in New York once more, Picabia naturally gravitated to Stieglitz's circle. As a member of this group, he collaborated in the publication of a new magazine, entitled *291*, which superseded *Camera Work*. Among other things, he published his famous "object portraits," e.g., the *Portrait of an American Girl in the State of Nudity* in the form of a sparkplug.

Another intellectual center in New York in 1915 was the salon of Water Conrad Arensberg, a wealthy businessman, art collector, and sometime poet who liked to surround himself with interesting people. Arensberg's informal gatherings, which provided such amenities as food and chess, were characterized by a free-wheeling atmosphere that was bound to attract many of the European artists and writers who had come to New York to avoid the war (Albert Gleizes and his wife Juliette Roche, Edgar Varèse, Jean Crotti, Arthur Cravan, etc.), as well as their American counterparts (William Carlos Williams, Amy Lowell, Joseph Stella, Margaret Anderson, Isadora Duncan, Alfred Kreymborg, Mina Loy, Arthur Dove, Man Ray, etc.).

Both Picabia and Duchamp (the latter, no doubt, because of his love for chess) were drawn to this group from the start and, along with Man Ray, they soon became its fulcrum. Ray's connection with a New Jersey colony of artists, socialists, and anarchists that include Max Eastman, Alfred Kreymborg, and Alexander Berkman, as well as his deep involvement with the avant-garde generally, made him a perfect partner for Duchamp and Picabia.

Soon after they met, these three men became the nucleus of a loosely organized group of painters who were primarily interested in following up Duchamp's Paris experiments. To his category of the "ready-made" (unaltered manufactured object), they added the "ready-made assisted" (an object altered by the artist). Contributing his photograph of the Mona Lisa complete with goatee, mustache, and the letters L.H.O.O.Q.;[5] and *Why Not Sneeze,* a bird cage which, instead of birds, contained lumps of sugar made of white marble, Duchamp proved as much a master of the "ready-made assisted" as he had of the "ready-made." Ray's *The Gift,* an iron with a row of tacks soldered on to its flat side, was also noteworthy.

In addition to these variations upon the "ready-made," these artists also began to explore a form of machine art which, in contrast to the Futurists' attempts to glorify the machine, recognized its dehumanizing qualities. Once again, the prototype was a work by Duchamp, *The Bride,* a clever juxtaposition of mechanical and biological elements. Continuing in the vein of his "object portraits," Picabia created mechanical forms in a kind of blueprint pattern. Ray also made some important contributions to this genre, the most notable of which were his *Danger-Dancer,* a visual comparison of the movements of a ballerina with the meshing of gears, and *Hermaphrodite,* a shiny "mechanical demon."

Although the United States had not, as yet, entered the war, there was an unmistakable prewar atmosphere in New York during the period when these "anti-art" experiments were taking place. Picabia's former wife Gabrielle recalls this period vividly:

> No sooner had we arrived than we became part of a motley international band which turned night into day, conscientious objectors of all nationalities and walks of life living in an inconceivable orgy of sexuality, jazz, and alcohol. Scarcely escaped from the vice of martial law, we believed at first that we had returned to the blessed times of complete freedom of thought and action. This illusion was quickly dissipated. The famous American neutrality was indeed nothing but seething slag from the furnace that raged beyond the ocean.[6]

Duchamp, the epitome of the anti-artist, fit nicely into this foreboding atmosphere. Declaring that "we are all playing a miserable game,"[7] he abandoned art completely and preoccupied himself instead with creating "strictly useless and anti-aesthetic" mechanical devices and playing chess. With this decision, he was not only following in the tradition of Rimbaud, but also, perhaps, revealing the influence of Vaché's concept of "Umour."

Picabia did not fare so well in New York. Caught up in the city's driving rhythm, he drank heavily, smoked opium, and, in general, lived such a dissipated life that he soon developed a nervous condition which was so serious that it forced him to leave New York for Barcelona. He and his wife landed in Barcelona in August of 1916 and immediately became part of a strange circle of ex-Parisians, deserters, and pacifists who were sitting out the war. Among this group were Marie Laurencin, who had been forced to leave Paris when she married the German citizen Otto von Watgen; Albert Gleizes and his wife, both of whom were pacifists; Maximilien Gauthier (Max Goth), a poet who was avoiding the draft; and Arthur Cravan.

Since Barcelona did not have Paris' café society, most members of this group, characteristically, spent their time reminiscing about Paris, a pastime with which Picabia quickly became bored. To stave off this boredom and "to celebrate the unforseen reunion . . . of a few specimens of prewar artistic life, who had been outlawed from the world by their military incompetence and the tragic circumstances of the era,"[8] he decided to publish a journal which he named *391*. Aside from its title, which may have been Picabia's way of recalling those happier days with Stieglitz's circle, *391* had nothing in common with the magazine *291*. Begun in Barcelona as a collaboration between Picabia and his friends, *391* was to appear in New York, Zurich and Paris as well and to become one of the most significant Dada journals, ranking with Tzara's *Dada* as the most representative publication.

From January to March of 1917, four issues of *391* appeared; this proved to be a periodicity that Picabia would never again achieve with his journal. These issues included poems and machine art by Picabia, various writings by other members of the group, and a unique section consecrated to what have been referred to as "false news reports." These tidbits of questionable information about the comings and goings of prominent people from the arts became Picabia's way of poking fun at his friends and enemies.

The poems which Picabia published in the Barcelona issues of *391* foreshadow certain themes that were to preoccupy him during his entire lifetime. Like Tzara, he was beginning to break with all traditional formulae for creating poetry. This is illustrated, in particular, by "Magic City," which vividly captures the cynical, virtually nihilistic thoughts that were constantly running through Picabia's mind:

MAGIC CITY
A dangerous and tempter wind of sublime nihilism
pursues us with a prodigious gaiety.
    Unexpected vision.
    Destroying equilibrium.

Increasing debilitation.

Emancipations.

Everywhere men and women with a music which pleases me
in public or in secret

giving vent to their sterile passions.

Opium.

Whisky.

Tango.

Spectators and actors
more and more subtle

rise above the gross satisfactions.

Women less strong
more beautiful and more unconscious.

The men with a silent hidden motive
look back at their pleasure.

Years of genius and oriental sun.

1914–1915[9]

Despite the distraction of his journal, Picabia was soon fed up
with the provincial atmosphere of Barcelona, which he later
described in one of his most sarcastic "false news reports." "Like
all unpleasant cities," he noted, "Barcelona is full of crab lice and
intellectuals, the intellectuals here are cold-blooded; they prefer
onanism to rape, dirt to a bath, and the subtle sport of contradictory insinuations to the perilous affirmation."[10]

By the end of March, 1917, Picabia and his wife had decided to
return to New York. Arriving on April 4, the very day the United
States entered the war, they were once again thrown into the
middle of the turmoil. Picabia's return also coincided with the
American Independents Exhibit, a show patterned upon its Paris
counterpart, which was designed to focus the attention of the
public and the critics on the experiments that were being carried
out in New York. This exhibition had opened in March; its
committee of judges included John Covert, Walter Pach, Albert
Gleizes, William Glackens, as well as Duchamp himself.

To test the intentions of the officials sponsoring the show,
Duchamp, under the alias "Richard Mutt," tried to enter his most
famous "ready-made," an ordinary urinal which he had baptized
Fountain. It was, of course, refused, and Duchamp resigned as a
judge. This act served to increase the separation between him,
Picabia, and Ray and those who failed to see Dada as anything
more than another form of modern art.

Another incident, which was connected with the American Independents Exhibition and which underscored the increasing militancy of the group, was a lecture delivered by Arthur Cravan, who like Picabia had grown tired of Barcelona. The night of this lecture, a chic Manhattan audience, anxious to be initiated into the mysteries of modern art, gathered. Cravan—very drunk—arrived late and began elbowing his way through the crowd. He was so drunk that, at first, he had difficulty reaching the lecture platform. When he finally succeeded, he began gesturing wildly, ripping off his jacket and undoing his suspenders. He was moving about so spastically that he almost bumped into a canvas which was hanging behind him. The surprise that all of this had created in his bewildered audience quickly gave way to indignation when Cravan leaned over the lecturn and began vilifying them with the most insulting epithets. At this point, the police, sensing that something was wrong, hurried up to the stage, attacked Cravan from behind, and quickly handcuffed him. With the crowd in an uproar, Cravan was roughed up and taken off the stage.

By injecting some of the scandal that dogged his every step, Cravan had thus helped to impress upon the public that Dada was not just another school of modern art. In resuming publication of *391* in New York, Picabia further strengthened this impression. He and his collaborators Arensberg, Varèse, Marius de Zayas, and Max Jacob, who contributed news about European art and literature from Paris, engaged in an increasingly bitter attack upon the traditional notion of art.

Picabia's own outlook on life became more and more jaded. Back in New York he was again indulging in excesses which aggravated his condition and made him nervous and irritable. He quarreled with everyone and in general lorded over *391*. The "false news reports," which reflected Picabia's quarrelsome nature as much as anything else, began to take on that militant, belligerent tone that was to become the characteristic mark of the magazine. In these New York reports, Picabia goaded De Zayas, Isadora Duncan (with whom he later had an affair), Albert Gleizes, Henri Bergson, and Leo Stein. His vituperative attack upon Stein, in particular, was a masterpiece of insult humor: "Like the Cuban Fish, he blows up when one tickles him."[11]

The poems, which continued to appear in these New York issues of *391*, expressed Picabia's cynical, rootless, and, above all, nihilistic view of life. These qualities were vividly captured in a poem entitled "Idéal Doré par l'Or," the last part of which contained his "nomad philosophy:"

> One must pass through life, red or blue, completely nude, with the subtle music of a fisher, ever ready for the celebration—Alas, it's the opposite; everything is a chorus of chatter—Beautiful uselessness.
>
> Infusoria, Protozoa, dogs, rabbits, what solitude of monarchs honest people, solitude poisoned under cannon fire.
>
> Poor artists alienists without passion or spirit or charm italian race horses like the moon.
>
> Males and females of today no rough frontiers enough of the laying out of the silly misfortune—Woman don't look back any longer at the man in the brutality don't cry in the desert which grows larger.[12]

In the hectic atmosphere of New York, Picabia's health became progressively worse, and this, coupled with the change in the moral climate that occurred once the United States entered the war, convinced him to leave for good. He departed for Lausanne, Switzerland, where he hoped to cure his nervous condition, in the fall of 1917.

Duchamp, in the meantime, began to devote much of his time to experiments with language. He traces his involvement with language, which goes back to the period when he was living in Paris, to two men: Jean-Pierre Brisset, a writer who undertook a philological analysis of language based on a kind of network of puns, and Raymond Roussel, an eccentric playwright whose self-produced play *Impressions of Africa*—which Duchamp, Picabia, and Apollinaire saw in Paris in 1911—became a model for their cool, absurdist form of humor.

Starting out where Brisset and Roussel had left off, Duchamp engaged in word experiments which were designed to revitalize a language that in most cases had lost all but its utilitarian meaning. By destroying the previous content of certain everyday words, he was able to liberate them from prior restraints and provide them with an entirely new spirit. Under the pseudonym RROSE SELAVY he published an amazing series of puns and word games in the various Dada magazines. The following are among the most noteworthy of these untranslatable bits of Dada wisdom:

Un mot de reine; des maux de reins[13]
Nous nous cajolions (nounou; cage aux lions)[14]
OH! DO SHIT AGAIN! OH! DOUCHE IT AGAIN![15]

Between 1919 and 1920, Duchamp traveled to Paris where he met the French Dadas. Indications are that this was the first real contact between the New York and European movements. Although Picabia, who had become acquainted with Tzara and the Zurich group while he was in Switzerland, may have written of their activities to his friends in New York, no trace of this appeared in their publications until Duchamp's return in February, 1920.

Inspired perhaps by the publicity that the Paris Dadas were receiving, Duchamp and Ray decided to collaborate in making New York into an "official" center for the movement. The only significant result, however, was the publication in April, 1921, of a fascinating review, *New York Dada,* which in typical fashion lasted but one issue.

Among other things, this issue contains a portrait of Baroness Elsa von Loringhoven, who according to Georges Hugnet, the author of "The Dada Spirit in Painting," was "a woman whose whole life was Dada."[16] Hugnet has provided the following description of the Baroness: "Dressed in rags picked up here and there, decked out with impossible objects suspended from chains, swishing long trains, like an empress from another planet, her head ornamented with sardine tins, indifferent to the legitimate curiosity of passers-by, the baroness promenaded down the avenues like a wild apparition, liberated from all constraint."[17]

Another feature of *New York Dada* was a section entitled "Pug Debs Make Society Bow," a takeoff on the chic fashion magazines' descriptions of coming-out parties. In this case, the party in which Mina Loy was to present the Marsden Hartleys and the Joseph Stellas reads more like a boxing match; the couples are referred to as "Queensberry proteges" and the event is to take place in "Madison Square Garden." While "Master Marsden" is to be decked out for this affair in "a neat but not gaudy set of tight-fitting gloves and will have a v-back in front and on both sides, Master Joseph . . . will affect the six-ounce suede glove with hard bandages and a little concrete in em if possible."[18]

Combining the satirical and the zany, this single issue of *New*

York Dada—perhaps more than anything else that they did—expressed the kind of absurd humor the New York group delighted in. But lively as it was, *New York Dada* signaled the end of Dadaist activities in that city. A variety of events brought this about: the war had ended, and many of the artists who contributed to the movement had gone back to their own countries; Stieglitz had closed his gallery and with his wife, the painter Georgia O'Keefe, had gone into retirement on Lake George; and, Arensberg's financial affairs had shifted, forcing him to move to Los Angeles. The final blow came when first Duchamp, in May, 1921, then Ray, in July of the same year, left New York to join the Dada movement in Paris.

During this period, when artists and writers were leaving the United States in large numbers and the central focus of the Dada movement was on Europe and specifically on Paris, little magazines such as *Broom, Secession, Transition,* and especially *The Little Review* kept the American public informed about the fortunes of Dada and published the works of its most significant exponents.

Having discussed the events in New York in some detail, we might now consider their significance. In what ways, for example, did the developments in New York anticipate what was happening in Europe generally? Even though the New York and Zurich activities had decidedly different tones and there was no real contact between the two groups until 1920, in at least one essential way they were similar: they expressed the same willfully iconoclastic spirit, the same irreverent attitude toward modern art and life. In his own humorous way, Jean Arp has alluded to this oneness of spirit, while at the same time suggesting its basic differences:

> In 1914, Marcel Duchamp, Francis Picabia, and Man Ray, then in New York, had created a *dada* (hobby-horse) that left nothing to be desired. But great was their distress, for they found no name for it. And because it was nameless, we in Zurich knew nothing of its existence. But when in 1916 we engendered our Dada and it was born, we—Hugo Ball, Tristan Tzara, Richard Huelsenbeck, Emmy Hennings, Marcel Janco, and I—fell rejoicing into each other's arms and cried in unison: *"Da, da ist ja unser Dada"* ("There, there's our Dada").[19]

While the Zurich Dadas discovered a slogan for their revolt and organized a program around it, albeit a loosely structured one, the events in New York, deriving as they did from the spontaneous, almost gratuitous attitudes and gestures of men like Duchamp, Picabia, and Ray, lacked even this much structure. And, as Gabrielle Buffet-Picabia has pointed out, it is this quality of New York Dada which in large part accounts for its impact both in the United States and Europe:

> Without other aim than to have no aim, it imposed itself by the force of its word, or its poetic and plastic inventions, and without premeditated intention it let loose, from one shore of the Atlantic to the other, a wave of negation and revolt which for several years would throw disorder into the minds, acts, works of men.[20]

CHAPTER THREE

THE DADA MOVEMENT IN EUROPE

Who on earth, in those days of collapse, was still ready to believe in "eternal values," in the "canned goods" of the past, in the academies, the schools of art? The cry of "dada" became universal—to hell with beauty! In those days dada was in the air everywhere. A spark, and all was afire: New York, Amsterdam, Barcelona, Berlin, Hanover, Paris and so on.

MARCEL JANCO

Having developed simultaneously and independently in Zurich and New York, the Dada movement, between 1915 and 1923, spread throughout the European continent. Countries such as Holland, Belgium, Italy, Spain, Yugoslavia, Czechoslovakia, Rumania, Poland, and even Russia were the scene of Dadaist activities. Growing out of the revolutionary spirit of the young, the Dada movement thus was not restricted to any one place; by and large, its most interesting manifestations and the events which determined its spirit occurred in the cities of Zurich, Berlin, Cologne, Hanover, and Paris. It is to these European centers that we must turn our attention.

Zurich

The Dada movement in Zurich grew up around a group of artists who had been displaced by the war. On the surface, this placid old University town, which had become prosperous as the banking center of Switzerland, would seem to be as unlikely an atmosphere for Dada to flourish in as one could imagine. But Switzerland had remained neutral during the war and had become something of an oasis for those who were fleeing from its terror—"a haven of refuge amid the sea of fire, of iron and blood."[1]

Hans Richter has spoken of Zurich as "the peaceful dead-centre of the war."[2] In some ways this was true. Zurich carried on its normal peacetime pursuits: the shop windows were clean and well lighted; there were modern bookshops and art galleries; and, the streets were filled with healthy young people wearing sports clothes instead of uniforms. As Stefan Zweig wrote in *The World of Yesterday,* a trip to Zurich from "walled-in and half-starved" Germany was "like stepping from a closely suffocating room into invigorating and snow-filled air."[3]

But with the war going on all around Switzerland, Zurich was also a place of refuge for famous writers, would-be revolutionaries, and spies whose activities were bound to disturb the city's illusory peace and quiet. Thus, the same city which housed such writers as James Joyce and Romain Rolland also became the main focus for some of the ideological conflicts that had generated the war: the place of exile for Russian Socialists like Lenin and Zinoviev; the gathering spot for German Expressionists like Ludwig Rubiner and Leonhard Frank, and a center for German propaganda. The Germans maintained about a dozen newspapers and magazines in Zurich which also circulated in France. One of these newspapers, *Paris-Genève,* which even went so far as to publish a false report that France contemplated an invasion of Switzerland, was ultimately suppressed by Swiss authorities.

In addition to established figures like Joyce and Rolland, there was a group of younger expatriate artists and writers in Zurich at this time who came mostly from Germany and the Eastern European countries. Out of this group the nucleus of the Dada movement—Hugo Ball, Jean Arp, Marcel Janco, and Tristan Tzara—emerged. The pivotal figure around whom these diverse personalities gathered was Ball. A deserter from the German army, Ball had fled to Switzerland with his girl friend, a former cabaret singer named Emmy Hennings.

Ball was a tall, thin, soft-spoken man whose face was slightly pock-marked and whose wobbly gait has been compared to that of a praying mantis. Like so many of the young men of his generation, he had become immersed in Nietzsche's idea of human freedom. His admiration for the great nineteenth-century philosopher was made especially clear in a dissertation entitled "A Polemical Treatise in Defense of Nietzsche" which he wrote while a student at the University of Munich between 1906 and 1910. Among other things, this study, which Ball never completed, but continued to work on even after he had left the University, demonstrates his fascination with Nietzsche's dionysiac theory of art. Ball not only agreed with Nietzsche's contention that society could be regenerated only through a return to the forces of instinct and emotion and a repudiation of Socratic rationalism, but, perhaps even more important, was sympathetic to the iconoclastic philosopher's call for a revolt against traditional morality and a denunciation of the Church, the state, and any other external authority which might interfere with individual freedom.

Inspired by Nietzsche, Ball became virtually obsessed with a desire to destroy the old order and replace it with something that was based on the dark, mysterious, instinctual forces of the unconscious. And, considering this attitude, it is not surprising that he turned to that force which represents the very fountain of Nietzsche's philosophy: the theater. This was not a completely new preoccupation for Ball; before he became a student, while slaving away in a leather factory at his parents' insistence that he learn a trade, he had studied dramatic literature and had even written plays in his spare time.

But now the theater began to loom up as more than a mere pastime for Ball, who was convinced that it was the only institution capable of bringing about the conditions he so fervently desired. Possessed with this idea, he left the University and enrolled in Max Reinhardt's School of Dramatic Arts in Berlin in September, 1910. When his parents objected to this sudden decision, he wrote them a letter expressing his almost fanatical hope for the theater as a means of changing society.

More convinced than ever of the value of theater, Ball found further confirmation of his ideas in the plays of Frank Wedekind with their unmistakable Nietzschean overtones. In a passage in his diary in which he celebrated Wedekind's awesome power,

Ball wrote that "my strongest impression was the one made upon me by the terrible, cynical theater of the poet Frank Wedekind. . . . His approach consists of dissolving into nothingness the last remains of a civilization deeply rooted in the theater and in himself."[4]

The practical reality of studying theater, however, was a disappointment for Ball. Despite his persistence, he was unable to prove himself as an actor and turned instead to critical writing and stage management. Presumably fed up with the inflated egos of his fellow students and his own lack of progress, Ball left Reinhardt's school in the fall of 1911 and took a job as a stage manager at the Municipal Theater in Plauen (Saxony). This job, which had the added disadvantage of keeping him in a virtual state of poverty, proved too prosaic to allow him to carry out his grand designs for the theater; so in 1913, he moved to Munich, where he assumed the role of *Dramaturg* for the Münchener Kammerspiele, a combination of critic, playwright, and jack-of-all trades to which the young Bertolt Brecht would later aspire.

Perhaps even more important than Ball's day-to-day activities at the Kammerspiele was the way in which he spent his free time. He began frequenting the cafes where alienated but zealous bohemians and artists like himself gathered in the evenings to drink and discuss their grandiose schemes for changing the world. It was at one of these gathering places, the Café Simplizissimus, that Ball met his future wife, Emmy Hennings. And at another, the *Café des Westens* in Berlin, he came in contact with the fiery young poet Richard Huelsenbeck, who later followed him to Zurich.

Most of the people who frequented these cafés were drifting toward Expressionism. Sharing their horror of modern man's dehumanization, Ball discovered a certain kinship with these revolutionary artists and writers. Having worked in a leather factory, he could speak from firsthand experience about the evils of the modern industrial state. Following the example of Georg Trakl, Johannes Becher and Jacob van Hoddis, Ball began to write poems which vividly attacked the corrupt practices of this mechanized society. Moreover, he made friends with some of the most avant-garde painters in Germany, men such as Paul Klee, Oskar Kokoschka, Franz Marc, and Wassili Kandinsky.

Especially impressed with Kandinsky's ideas for the fusing of the arts into one sovereign form, or *Gesamtkunstwerk*, Ball praised the Russian artist for "the loftiness and purity" of his conception as well as for his courage in breaking new ground. He went on to say that he was seriously considering Kandinsky's ideas as a model for a new approach to theater:

> In 1914, when I was thinking over the plan for a new theatre, I was convinced of this: a theatre which experiments beyond the realm of day-to-day preoccupations. Europe paints, composes and writes verse in a new way. A fusion, not merely of all art, but of all regenerative ideas. The background of colours, words and sounds must be brought out from the subconscious and given life, so that it engulfs everyday life and all its misery.[5]

The war cut short these speculations before Ball had any real chance to test them out. At first, in an attack of patriotic fervor he decided to enlist, but when it was discovered that he had a slight heart condition that would delay, but not cancel, his military service, he began to change his mind. After hanging around for some time with a packed suitcase prepared to be re-called, he decided to travel, as a civilian, to the front to see for himself what it was really like. In November, 1914, he arrived at the Belgian border, where the fighting was going on, and remained there for two weeks. What he saw there—the horrors of war which were so much greater than he could possibly have imagined—shocked and unnerved him, causing him to reconsider his decision. Accompanied by Emmy Hennings, he fled to Zurich. He later expressed his change of heart in one of his poems:

> I had no love for the death's head hussars,
> Nor for the mortars with the girls' names on them,
> And when at last the glorious days arrived,
> I unobtrusively went on my way.[6]

In the strange city of Zurich, cut off from everything that was familiar, Ball and Hennings had a very difficult time of it; they lived a poverty-stricken life and were on the verge of suicide. But eventually they managed to eke out a meager living as entertainers. Ball played the piano for The Flamingo, a traveling theater company, and his wife worked as a performer in a nightclub.

While he was living on the fringes of society, Ball—perhaps as a kind of escape from a world that was too much with him—began delving into the writings of the mystics; he read the works of Medieval German philosophers such as Meister Eckhardt and the occult writings of the Hindus. This caused him to believe more and more firmly in the magical and the irrational and to sharpen his already uncompromising attack against rationalistic science.

With the view of liberating man from the restraints of industrial society and bringing him in contact with the forces of the unconscious still uppermost in his mind, Ball began to write a novel *Laurentius Tenderenda* in which he explored certain linguistic, vocalic, and rhythmic devices. He also corresponded with Filippo Marinetti, who was carrying out similar experiments.

Despite his poverty, Ball never lost sight of his ideal of a dionysiac theater. But it was not until he had made the acquaintance of a group of like-minded individuals, which included Janco, Tzara, and Arp, that he had the opportunity to realize his intentions. At Ball's suggestion, these men decided to organize an artistic cabaret, the Cabaret Voltaire. Some idea of the rationale underlying this decision was provided by Richard Huelsenbeck, who later joined the group himself, when he noted that the name Cabaret Voltaire "was not chosen accidentally, but out of veneration for a man who had fought all his life for the liberation of the creative forces from the tutelage of the advocates of power."[7]

Before discussing the activities at the Cabaret Voltaire, we must look more closely at the personalities who, in addition to Ball and Emmy Hennings, now comprised the fledgling Dada movement in Zurich. Janco was a tall, friendly, young architect and painter who wore his hair in "gypsy curls" and loved to talk. Reduced by the war to abject poverty, he had been forced to leave his native Rumania and come to Zurich, where he was able to earn his living by singing folk songs, accompanied on the piano by his brother.

In Rumania, Janco had been deeply interested in avant-garde art, especially in Cubism and Futurism, and together with Tzara he had worked on a review entitled *Simbolul*. While a member of the Cabaret Voltaire, he continued to experiment with various forms of modern art; he was responsible for the exotic decorations of the Cabaret and became famous for his terrifying masks. Unlike many other members of the group, who moved further and further away from art toward anti-art, Janco retained his faith in more traditional painting. As Arp has affectionately noted, "secretly, in his quiet little room, Janco devoted himself to a 'naturalism in zigzag.'"[8] Because of his genial personality and strong sense of loyalty, Janco, even in the roughest times, was able to avoid the internecine strife that plagued the movement.

This was not the case with Tristan Tzara, his strong-willed compatriot. Poet, philosopher (or, more precisely anti-philosopher) and cosmic public relations man, Tzara had been in the thick of virtually every Dadaist donnybrook. Like Janco, Tzara, whose real name was S. Rosenstock, had left Rumania and traveled to Zurich in order to get away from the war. While involved with *Simbolul,* he had written poetry whose delicate imagery called to mind the Symbolists and gave little hint of the anti-art style that he was later to develop.

Ball was the prime mover who brought Zurich Dada into being, but it was Tzara's enthusiasm and energy which kept its "creative flame" burning. He was a little man, but, like Napoleon, he more than made up for his diminutive stature by his dominant personality, his nervous energy, his great ingenuity, and his militant posture. Dressed in a conservative suit, his appearance seemed to belie his overpowering abilities, and the curious but precise description that Janco has provided of his fellow Rumanian belies it even more. Janco wrote: "His walking with short quick steps like a girl was an expression of his distrustful nature. His mocking little eyes, the eyes of a circumspect rodent, shone behind his glasses."[9]

Jean Arp—the third member of this newly formed group—was perhaps the most complex character of the three, combining in the same personality a shy, reserved manner and a fun-loving spirit, a childlike naïveté and a sophisticated outlook. With the advent of the war, Arp, an Alsatian artist who had been in the forefront of modern art in Paris, was placed in a precarious situation; for even though his background was French, he was technically a German citizen.[10] To avoid the unpleasantness these divided loyalties might have caused, as well as the war itself, he and his brother had left Paris in June, 1915, for Zurich, where their mother was already living.

As a result of his mysticism, his creative imagination, and his love of magic, Arp became, in Janco's words, "the high priest of Dada." Befitting this role, he managed to remain somewhat anonymous, seldom appearing at the Cabaret or taking part in the "antibourgeois activities" for which the Zurich group became notorious.

Arp's congenial manner allowed him to avoid much of the bitterness which later befell the movement. Even during the period when Huelsenbeck was attacking everything about Zurich Dada, he was careful to exempt Arp. The qualities that kept Arp out of these disputes have been summed up by his old friend Hans Richter. "I don't think that Arp ever had an enemy," Richter wrote. "Friendly, polite, unchanging and without any pretensions he always made good company. He gave DADA a slightly ironic, olympian touch. He took DADA immensely seriously, but laughed about it happily."[11]

Guided by the spirits of Ball, Janco, Tzara, and Arp, the Cabaret Voltaire began to take shape. On February 2, 1916, Ball published an announcement in a Zurich newspaper informing the general public that the Cabaret Voltaire, "a center for artistic entertainment," was being formed by a group of young artists and writers. Three days later, he noted in his diary that an overflow crowd had packed the Cabaret. This was the first of many such crowds.

What did the inhabitants of Zurich, many of whom had had no previous contact with "the new aesthetics" think of the Cabaret Voltaire? The Cabaret had a normal seating capacity of between thirty-five and fifty people, with fifteen to twenty tables, and a stage of about one hundred square feet; its walls were covered with the most provocative contemporary art, which had either been borrowed from friends or donated by the participants: posters by Slodki, etchings by Picasso, paintings by Arp, Modigliani, Kandinsky, Klee, Jawlensky, Léger, Matisse, all of which were set off by Janco's "opulent Archangels."

The performances, which lasted until the early hours of the morning and often caused friction with the neighbors and unpleasantness with the police, were a potpourri of cabaret songs, balalaika music, dramatic readings of plays, novels, and poems, and recitations of simultaneous poetry. This last activity, which was designed to create "a nonsensical but sonorous effect," consisted of the simultaneous reading of three unrelated texts in three different languages. These simultaneous readings became the most popular activity for the Zurich Dadas, but the Cabaret's policy of humoring anyone who wished to participate in the performances often interfered with the readings. In this regard, Janco noted that "sometimes a young man would get up on the rostrum and read his poetry, sometimes there might be a group asking for permission to give a balalaika concert. We suffered them all in patience and then imperturbably got on with our simultaneous poems."[12]

As time went on, entire programs were devoted to the most daring literary experiments conducted in the various countries. The most noteworthy of these was the French evening which featured readings from the works of Apollinaire, Max Jacob, André Salmon, Jarry, Jules Laforgue, and Rimbaud. The poems of Blaise Cendrars, Jacob van Hoddis, Else Lasker-Schüler, and Ferdinand Hardekopf were read during other programs.

In addition to the various forms of dramatic readings, a series of improvised performances, often inspired by Marcel Janco's grotesque masks, gave the Cabaret Voltaire another dimension. In describing the performances which grew out of the masks Janco brought to the Cabaret one evening, Ball provided a vivid indication of the amazing kind of "mask play" which he and his colleagues had devised:

> The effect was strange. Not only did each mask seem to demand the appropriate costume; it also called for a quite specific set of gestures, melodramatic and even close to madness. Although five minutes earlier none of us had had the remotest idea of what was to happen, we were soon draped and festooned with the most unlikely objects, making the most outlandish movements, each out-inventing the other. The dynamism of the masks was irresistible. In one moment we became aware of the great importance of such masks in mime and drama. The masks simply demanded that their wearers should start up a tragico-absurd dance.[13]

As Ball described them, the dances themselves were filled with that marvelously absurd quality which characterizes Dada at its best:

> One of the dances we called "Flycatching." This particular mask went with clumsy, tentative steps, long-armed snatching gestures and nervous, shrill music. The second dance we called "Cauchemar." The dancer unfolds from a stooping posture, at the same time moving straight forward. Her mask has a wide open mouth and a broad, twisted nose. The performer's arms, menacingly raised, are lengthened by means of special tubes. We called the third

dance "Festive desperation." The arms are curved to form an arch and from them dangle long golden cut-out hands. The figure turns several times to the left and to the right, then revolves slowly and ends by suddenly collapsing into a heap before slowly returning to the first position and starting again.[14]

Infused with the spontaneity of the popular theater, yet imbued with an indefinable sense of magic, these masked performances in which, in Ball's words, "the paralyzing horror which is the backcloth of our age is . . . made visible,"[15] were perhaps the closest he ever came to realizing his dream of a dionysiac theater.

The free-wheeling atmosphere of the Cabaret Voltaire made it a "meeting place of the arts;" from all over Zurich the weird assortment of characters which the war had brought together—"painters, students, revolutionaries, tourists, international crooks, psychiatrists, the demimonde, sculptors, and polite spies on the lookout for information"[16]—flocked to it.

On February 29th, Richard Huelsenbeck joined the group, thus further intensifying the already spirited tone of the performances. Tzara fittingly celebrated the arrival of the man who was to become his toughest adversary: "HUELSENBECK ARRIVES—bang! bang! bangbangbang."[17] A young, energetic poet who knew and admired Ball, Huelsenbeck had come to Zurich, like the others, to escape the war. As he himself put it, "I had escaped by the skin of my teeth from the pursuit of the police myrmidons who, for their so-called patriotic purposes, were massing men in the trenches of Northern France and giving them shells to eat."[18]

Huelsenbeck's appearance at the Cabaret Volatire coincided with the increasingly primitive tone that was developing. While continuing to experiment with simultaneous poetry, the group had begun to explore new kinds of rhythm, sound effects, and the potential of the human voice. Ball, in particular, had spent much of his time attempting to transcend traditional language through "phonetic" and sound poems. Expressing a love for "Negro rhythm," Huelsenbeck recited his poems to the beat of a drum or marked out their rhythm by cracking a riding whip in the air. In commenting upon this technique, Ball wrote, with admiration, that "he wanted the rhythm *reinforced:* he would have liked to drum literature into the ground."[19]

These "Negro rhythms" became so popular that the Zurich group organized African nights in which the entire program would be devoted to the cult of the primitive. Presided over by Jan Ephraim, who had spent some time in Africa, they consisted of poetry readings and African chants performed to the accompaniment of little side drums.

The group's fascination with the primitive also led them to explore the idea of "bruitism," a form of "noise music" which had originated with the Futurists Marinetti and Luigi Russolo. The members of the Cabaret Voltaire punctuated their performances with drums, gongs, howls, sirens, and cow-bells. Ball even went so far as to compose a complete bruitist concert, a nativity play which featured such instruments as shawms, little bells devised especially for the purpose, and babies' rattles. Later, in their "provocation-demonstrations," they provoked the audiences by jangling keys for hours and banging tin cans together.

Aside from their shared intention "to make the Cabaret Voltaire a focal point of the 'newest art,'"[20] these artists, who were often so different and sometimes so incompatible, had one basic attitude in common which helps account for this agitation: their abiding hatred for the war. Huelsenbeck summed up their feelings in his essay "En Avant Dada: A History of Dadaism," when he wrote:

> None of us had much appreciation for the kind of courage it takes to get shot for the idea of a nation which is at best a cartel of pelt merchants and profiteers in leather, at worst a cultural association of psychopaths who, like the Germans, marched off with a volume of Goethe in their knapsacks, to skewer Frenchmen and Russians on their bayonets.[21]

Somewhere in the midst of this "half artistic, half revolutionary" atmosphere, the Zurich group discovered the word *Dada*, the term that was to become the umbrella for their most provocative actions. Having found a name for their movement, they began to vary their activities and branch out into other areas. In June, 1916, for example, they published their own journal, a thin pamphlet edited by Hugo Ball and appropriately titled *Cabaret Voltaire*. Subtitled "A Literary and Artistic Miscellany," it was both eclectic and cosmopolitan in spirit: poems by Marinetti, Jacob van Hoddis, Apollinaire, and Cendrars[22] appeared alongside those by Ball, Tzara, and Huelsenbeck and the graphic art of Picasso, Modigliani, and Kandinsky was exhibited next to that of Arp and Janco.

To underscore its international character, Ball affixed the following note: "In order to avoid a nationalistic interpretation, the editor of this miscellany declares that it has no connection at all with the 'German mentality.' "[23] In the tradition of avant-garde publications, *Cabaret Voltaire* lasted for only one issue, but it was a prelude to even greater activity.

Some of this activity centered on the establishment of the "Dada Collection," a publishing venture under whose auspices Tzara brought out his *First Celestial Adventure of Mr. Antipyrine* and the prolific Huelsenbeck published two volumes of poetry: *Fantastic Prayers* and *Schalaben Schalomai Schalamezomai*. But the events which, above all, attracted the attention of the public were the high jinks and "provocation-demonstrations" which the Dadas organized to "épater le bourgeois." On the surface, these were not new. The performances at the Cabaret Voltaire were always provocative and, as Janco has noted, "we made our good fellow-citizens roar like lions,"[24] Huelsenbeck was even more explicit about these provocations; he proudly declared that the Cabaret performers "did not neglect, from time to time, to tell the fat and utterly uncomprehending Zurich philistines that we regarded them as pigs."[25]

What was new, however, were their attempts to extend the battlefield beyond the confines of the Cabaret Voltaire to the Zurich newspapers, where "false news reports" became a favorite weapon of the Dadas, and to larger halls, where massive "provocation-demonstrations" became the order of the day. The Zurich "false news reports" were characterized by a spirit of absurdity that was sometimes lacking in those that Picabia published in *391*. For example, in one report they announced that they had Marinetti imprisoned in "a Public Urinal." In another, they told of an imaginary duel between Arp and Tzara, supposedly fought with pistols.

The account that appeared in the local newspaper was particularly amusing because it implicated one J. C. Heer, a sentimental poet who was very popular at this time. Heer was alleged to be one of the seconds. The next morning he published a disclaimer stating that he had been out of town during the event, but a disclaimer of this disclaimer said otherwise: first, it reassured the public (although such reassurance was probably the last thing they wanted to hear) that neither adversary had been hurt since both had fired in the same direction—away from the other; then, it quoted two witnesses to the effect that Heer had been in attendance after all. These witnesses noted, in passing, that they could well understand why a respected figure like Heer would not want to be implicated in "the stormy quarrels of youth," but that their duty demanded that they should not lie. The witnesses, of course, turned out to be Dadas and the entire affair proved to be false.

The climax of this age-old conflict between bohemian and bourgeois, which had broken out anew in Zurich, came during the various demonstrations the Dadas staged in an effort to enrage and taunt the public. The first of these was "The Dada Night," a wild mélange of nihilistic poetry, raucous music, and unadulterated rowdyism which was held on July 14, 1916. Tzara's description of this demonstration, which, among other things, featured the first public reading of his *The First Celestial Adventure of Mr. Antipyrine*, shows how overpowering this confrontation must have been:

> In the presence of a compact crowd Tzara demonstrates, we demand we demand the right to piss in different colors, Huelsenbeck demonstrates, Ball demonstrates . . . the dogs bay and the dissection of Panama on the piano on the piano and dock-shouted Poem-shouted and fighting in the hall, first row approves second row declares itself incompetent the rest shout, who is the strongest, the big drum is brought in, Huelsenbeck against 200, Ho osenlatz accentuated by the very big drum and little bells on his left foot—the people protest shout smash windowpanes kill each other demolish fight here comes the police interruption.[26]

In many ways, this demonstration was a turning point for the Zurich movement: it marked the end of the initial stage of Zurich Dada, the end of the Cabaret Voltaire, and the beginning of new leadership and a new spirit. Six months after it had begun its hectic existence, the Cabaret Voltaire closed its doors. Exhausted by the physical strain of nightly performances and the mental anguish of the internal bickerings that were constantly going on among this headstrong group, Hugo Ball decided to close down the Cabaret and take Emmy Hennings to Vira-Magadino, a small village in the Italian part of Switzerland, for a much-needed rest. A leadership struggle between Ball and Tzara seems to have been the immediate impetus behind this decision. Natural adversaries because of their radically different temperaments—the one quiet and thoughtful, the other loud and boisterous—the two men were moving further and further apart in their vision of what Zurich Dada should be. For Ball, Dada symbolized the magical world of the child; a world in which man, having regained his childlike simplicity, could recapture the direct contact with the unconscious that the adult world had lost. Through the power of Dada he thus hoped to create a kind of "constructive anarchy." He admitted that "it may be imperative to strive with all one's might for chaos and the ruthless extirpation of faith," but ultimately he looked for "a thorough reconstruction . . . made on a changed basic faith."[27] This was a far cry from the openly nihilistic and methodically destructive philosophy of Tzara.

These differences in outlook and temperament seem to have finally resulted in an open conflict which proved too much for Ball,[28] who left sometime in August, 1916.

Ball's self-imposed exile was only temporary, however. More anxious than ever to experiment with ways of creating a *Gesamtkunstwerk,* he returned to Zurich in 1917. Once again, reunited with Tzara, he helped found the Dada Gallery, which opened its doors on March 8, 1917. A combination of art gallery and cabaret, the Dada Gallery became a center for Expressionist, Futurist, and Dadaist art, showcasing such painters as Klee, Kandinsky, De Chirico, Kokoschka, and Max Ernst, and featuring music, poetry, drama, and lectures. Its performances took place on a bi-weekly basis rather than the frenetic nightly schedule of the Cabaret Voltaire.

The Dada Gallery, which was, among other things, the scene of his famous "O Gadji Beri Bimba" recital, provided Ball with the opportunity to continue his experimentation with language and exploration of the *Gesamtkunstwerk.* But this was no longer enough for him. Under the influence of such mystics as Paracelsus, Jacob Böhme, and Nostradamus, in whose writings Ball had become deeply immersed, he realized that he must change his approach to life and be more in tune with nature. At the heart of this realization was the seemingly sudden awareness that the dionysiac experiences, in which he had put so much faith, had placed him "in contradiction to nature."[29] This, coupled with the fact that his temporary absence had allowed Tzara's increasingly militant and iconoclastic attitudes to come to the fore, apparently made Ball realize that he must break with Dada. Declaring that "I have examined myself carefully, and I could never bid chaos welcome,"[30] he left Zurich, this time for good, in the summer of 1917.

Ball's search for a harmony with nature was to take him far afield from the hectic atmosphere of Zurich Dada. Traveling first to Berne, where he worked for a time as a journalist and political adviser, he finally settled in Ticino in southern Switzerland, where he lived a simple life as a devout Catholic.

With Ball gone, Tzara's conception of Dada became even more dominant. He himself expressed the change that came over the movement in a passage in his "Zurich Chronicle":

> Slowly the young girls departed and bitterness laid its nest in the belly of the family man. A word was born no one knows how DADADADA *we took an oath of friendship* on the new transmutation that signifies nothing, and was the most formidable protest, the most intense armed affirmation of salvation liberty blasphemy mass combat speed prayer tranquillity private guerilla negation and chocolate of the desperate.[31]

Undermining the eclectic spirit of the earliest days of Zurich Dada, which was symbolized by the Futurist, Expressionist, and Cubist paintings that studded the walls of the Cabaret Voltaire, Tzara took it upon himself to break completely with modern art. Although the masks, costumes, and bruitist concerts which the Dadas had borrowed from the various modern art movements were still in evidence, they served a different purpose: they became part of the Trojan horse technique that Tzara used for breaking down the audience's resistance and making it all the more susceptible to the provocations to follow. Tzara declared that "Dada isn't modern" and proved it by lumping avant-garde artists and writers with the bourgeois. "Down with cubism and futurism," he wrote, "each phrase an automobile horn let us mix friends and colleagues the bourgeois salad in the eternal basin is insipid and I hate good sense."[32]

Tzara had the chance to exercise this inconoclastic spirit in demonstrations, such as the one which took place on July 14, but an equally important vehicle for his new philosophy was the periodical *Dada.* Founded in 1917, it became, under his leadership, the official organ of the Zurich movement. Its first two issues, published in July and December respectively, indicate that Tzara was still trying to find his true voice. As it was to be more or less a continuation of *Cabaret Voltaire,* they retained the subtitle, "A Literary and Artistic Miscellany," the same international flavor, and the same stress upon Futurism, abstract art, modern French poetry, etc.

But the third issue, published in December, 1918, was something quite different. Based on the principles of complete liberty and spontaneity, *Dada* III attempted to overthrow all previous aesthetic conventions: all forms of punctuation, including the use of capital letters, were systematically done away with; none of the pages were numbered; and the typography was violently disjointed, combining texts and illustrations in a perfectly arbitrary manner. The revolutionary intentions underlying these experiments were symbolized by a Descartes quote which appeared in slanted style across the top of the journal's cover: "I don't even want to know that there were men before me."[33] Another important feature was Tzara's dynamic "Dada Manifesto of 1918," a document which increased his international reputation considerably.

Aside from symbolizing the movement's new tone, *Dada* III was important for another reason; among its collaborators, it included several new names: Paul Dermée, Vincent Huidobro, Pierre Reverdy, and, above all, Francis Picabia. The Spaniard, who was still recuperating from his nervous condition in Lausanne, was to become Tzara's staunchest ally.

Prompted by Tzara, who had enthusiastically read his poetry and exchanged letters with him since August, 1918, Picabia arrived in Zurich in January, 1919. The meeting between Tzara and Picabia was another turning point in the history of the Zurich movement as well as a significant development in the lives of both men. Sharing a revolutionary attitude toward art and a nihilistic approach to life, these two had a strong influence upon each other. In its timing alone, Picabia's appearance in Zurich was crucial: it helped fill the vacuum which had existed since Huelsenbeck's return to Berlin in January, 1917, and Ball's departure that summer. With the absence of these two key figures, a period of relative inactivity had set in. But now, with the help of Picabia, Tzara was able to get things going once again. Contact with Tzara, whose exuberance made him forget his neurasthenia and yearn once again for a life of action, was equally beneficial for Picabia.

To celebrate their new relationship in fine style, Picabia published the eighth issue of *391* and Tzara the No. IV-V issue of *Dada.* The Zurich issue of *391* clearly illustrates the kind of artistic partnership that was developing between the two men: half of the material was written by Picabia, and the other half by Tzara.

One page even contained two untitled prose poems—one by Picabia, the other by Tzara—which were placed in opposite directions in such a way as to form a unique simultaneous poem.

The traditional false news page, containing real or imaginary information about events in New York, Paris, Zurich, and Barcelona, was also noteworthy. Among the choicest items was a statement that Duchamp had left for Buenos Aires to organize "A Health Service of Public Urinals" and a scoop that Marie Laurencin was in love with a toreador in Barcelona. The section on Zurich contained a notice that the forthcoming issue of *391* was to be devoted to the memory of art and some high-class grafitti, the kind one sees on subway walls in university areas: "Allah is great but Flake is greater."[34]

Dada IV-V, the so-called Dada Anthology, which was also, in large part, the result of the collaboration of Tzara and Picabia, appeared in May, 1919, in two versions, one in French, the other in a combination of French and German. Characterized by the same turbulent style as *Dada* III, the unusual format of this issue pointed up the contributions of more new stars in the Dada galaxy—André Breton, Philippe Soupault, Louis Aragon, and Georges Ribemont-Dessaignes.

Another contributor, who deserves special mention, was Walter Serner, an Austrian poet and revolutionary. Having joined the group toward the end of 1916, just before the demise of the Cabaret Voltaire, he became one of those most adept at distilling its new spirit. A shadowy figure who "took root in anything that was extraordinary," Serner had formerly published a nihilistic periodical entitled *Sirius*. According to Hans Richter, Serner, "the incarnation of revolt," was "the cynic of the movement, the declared anarchist, an Archimedes who meant to lift the world off its axis and let it hang."[35]

Serner's ability to enrage an audience was revealed in a demonstration which took place on April 9, 1919. This demonstration, which, by Tzara's estimate, attracted more than a thousand people, was a kind of climax of the Dada movement in Zurich. Serner's appearance was preceded by a simultaneous poem written by Tzara and performed by twenty people; an address by Richter entitled "Against, Without, For Dada"; a reading by Arp of his newest poetry; and a series of dances by Suzanne Perrotet to the music of Schönberg. Tzara's poem, in particular, had riled up the audience. Commenting on their response, Tzara himself noted that "the scandal assumes menacing proportions islands spontaneously form in the hall, accompanying, multiplying underlining the mighty roaring gesture and the simultaneous orchestration. Signal of the blood. Revolt of the past, of education."[36] But Tzara's recital ended the first part of the program and the audience had a chance to calm down during the brief intermission.

Now, as they awaited the next event, they were beginning to grow restless. Suddenly, Serner, carrying a headless dummy, made his entrance. Placing the dummy down, he went back behind the curtain and returned bearing a bunch of artificial flowers which he motioned for the dummy to smell. Laying the flowers at the dummy's feet, he then proceeded to sit in a chair in the middle of the stage with his back to the audience and to recite from his nihilistic tract "Final Dissolution."

For some reason, these strange goings-on set the audience off. Hans Richter, who himself took part in the demonstration, has provided a vivid description of what happened:

> The tension in the hall became unbearable. At first it was so quiet that you could have heard a pin drop. Then the catcalls began, scornful at first, then furious. "Rat, bastard, you've got a nerve!" until the noise almost entirely drowned Serner's voice, which could be heard, during a momentary lull, saying the words "Napoleon was a big strong oaf, after all."
>
> That really did it. What Napoleon had to do with it, I don't know. He wasn't Swiss. But the young men, most of whom were in the gallery, leaped on to the stage, brandishing pieces of the balustrade (which had survived intact for several hundred years), chased Serner into the wings and out of the building, smashed the tailor's dummy and the chair, and stamped on the bouquet. The whole place was in an uproar.[37]

In attempting to sum up all of the wild goings on of "Dada Night," Tzara called attention to the central concept in his approach to Dada: what he later called "the cretinization of the public." He wrote that "Dada has succeeded in establishing the circuit of absolute unconsciousness in the audience which forgot the frontiers of education of prejudices, experienced the commotion of the NEW."[38]

Despite the stir it created, this was to be the last massive Dada demonstration in Zurich. Split by internal dissension and a thinning of its ranks, the Zurich movement was beginning to break up. The end of the war had made it possible for many of the artists who were in the movement to return home to their native lands. Picabia himself took this opportunity to return to Paris.

With Picabia gone, a combination of circumstances began to draw Tzara away from the city: for one thing, Picabia was constantly urging him to come to Paris, where the young poets of the *Littérature* group were preparing a hero's welcome for him; for another, the departure of many of the artists and revolutionaries from Zurich had allowed the city to return to its prewar bourgeois atmosphere. By the middle of January, 1920, Tzara made the break. He left Zurich and went to live with Picabia in Paris, a decision which, for all intents and purposes, proved the final blow to Zurich Dada.

It should be noted in passing that Tzara had paved the way for this shift in operations through his role as public-relations man for the Zurich movement. Throughout his stay in Zurich, he had kept in close contact with the artistic leaders in Rome, Berlin, and Paris. Thus, even before he arrived in Paris, he had established relations with influential men like Paul Guillaume, Jean Cocteau, Paul Dermée, Pierre Albert-Birot, Philippe Soupault, André Breton, Louis Aragon, and Apollinaire.

Berlin

When Richard Huelsenbeck returned to Berlin in January, 1917, he discovered an atmosphere that bore little resemblance to the one he had left behind in Zurich. He recorded his impressions in "En Avant Dada" in 1920.

> I felt as though I had left a smug fat idyll for a street full of electric signs, shouting hawkers and auto horns. In Zurich the international profiteers sat in the restaurants with well-filled wallets and rosy cheeks, ate with their knives and smacked their lips in a merry hurrah for the countries that were bashing each other's skulls in. Berlin was the city of tightened stomachers, of mounting, thundering hunger, where hidden rage was transformed into a boundless money lust, and men's minds were concentrating more and more on questions of naked existence.[39]

The conditions Huelsenbeck described were the result of the

war which was to have resulted in "a new and better Germany." The Germans had naively welcomed this war. "Crowned with flowers and with oak leaves on their helmets," wrote Stefan Zweig in *The World of Yesterday,* "[the German soldiers] marched jubilating on their way to shambles through streets that rumbled and sparkled as if on a holiday."[40] Proudly proclaiming, "We'll be home at Christmas," they went off to war.

While the soldiers were preparing for their "baptismal of fire," those at home marshaled the powerful forces of propaganda that would be needed to support the men at the front and turn Germany into a great war machine. Bellicose philosophers extolled the Teutonic mind and praised Germany's art and culture, while denigrating the achievements of France and England. Not to be outdone, doctors, clergymen, and artists added their strident voices to the warlike cries, calling for "a bath of steel" that would cleanse the world.

Led by the august Gerhart Hauptmann, even famous writers fell into line; their patriotic writings were designed to inspire and inflame the heroic young warriors. Stefan George, a poet who at this time was virtually worshipped by the young, sent his proud "Siegfrieds" off to fight a "holy war":

Tens of thousands must be struck by the holy madness,
Tens of thousands must be swept by the holy sickness,
Tens of thousands by the holy war. . . .[41]

And Thomas Mann wrote: "My puny work, however mortal and merely half-good it may be—if there is in its parables some vital share in that which in one of to-day's. catch-words is termed 'German Militarism,' then it has honour and reality, then reality has something of its honour and of its spirit."[42]

Patriotic fervor ran so high that people began to feel guilty if they had not been wounded or lost a leg in battle. Some idea of the militaristic spirit which took hold of the country comes from a particularly grotesque anecdote related by George Grosz. Returning from the front in 1917, with an ailment which was diagnosed as shell-shock—but which he himself admitted was the result of his complete disillusionment with the war—Grosz was sent to a special asylum for the shell-shocked and the insane. "In the asylum, or hospital," he recalled, "there was a great factory for artificial arms and legs. From my cell window, I could see the competition of legless soldiers. It was very German. Great generals would come and give prizes for the best cripples. The ones who could best eat with their steel claws or best jump with their artificial legs."[43]

But neither the propaganda nor the faith of the Germans in the rightness of their cause could protect the people from the true horrors of war. After a series of initial victories by the German army, a period of war-weariness began to develop. As the casualties from the bloody trench warfare mounted, the morale both at home and at the front began to sink; the soldiers were going through unimaginable misery and the people at home were beginning to look at the war more realistically. Graft by the officialdom, exploitation of the peasants and laborers, and shameless war profiteering—all of these caused the Germans to take a second look at what they and the other peoples of Europe had wrought. They did not like what they saw.

An allied blockade of Germany aggravated the already existing food shortages, and as food became scarcer, unscrupulous "middlemen" profited from the people's misery. To add to their problems, other necessities of life—coal, textiles, leather, etc.—were becoming harder to get, all of which was compounded and made worse by governmental mismanagement and black-market operations. The bloodletting, the exploitation, and the corruption exacerbated the growing antiwar sentiment among the German people: their slogan changed from the proud "God punish England" of the early stages of the war to the defeatist "only a bad harvest can save us."[44]

Huelsenbeck's decision to come back to these intolerable conditions was, for the most part, prompted by his loss of faith in Zurich Dada. In particular, he accused Tzara of turning Zurich Dada into just another form of abstract art. Just how bitter Huelsenbeck felt about this is illustrated by his retrospective description of the Dada Gallery. "As I think back on it now," he wrote, "an art for art's sake mood lay over the Galérie Dada—it was a manicure salon of the fine arts, characterized by tea-drinking old ladies trying to revive their vanishing sexual powers with the help of 'something mad.' "[45]

In order to be successful in Germany, he went on to say, we will have "to discard our patent leather pumps and tie our Byronic cravats to the doorpost."[46] And, echoing the words of Arthur Cravan, he condemned the artist and thinker, calling instead for men of action, men who would be willing "to make literature with a gun in hand."[47]

Huelsenbeck presumably found men of this kind among a group of Berlin artists and writers who were led by Raoul Hausmann, a versatile young Czech who wrote phonetic poetry, painted, and carried out experiments with photomontage, and Franz Jung, a German writer whose published works had already brought him a measure of success. The members of this group, which had begun as an offshoot of Expressionism, had, like most of Berlin's avant-garde, gotten their start with *Der Sturm,* the influential magazine of Herwarth Walden and his exotic wife Else Lasker-Schüler. Among other things, this magazine had published poetry by August Stramm, essays by Strindberg, and plays by Kokoschka, as well as sponsoring exhibitions for Kandinsky, Chagall, and Marc.

With the start of the war, however, Hausmann's and Jung's group had drifted away from *Der Sturm* toward *Die Aktion,* a radical review edited by Franz Pfemfert, who expressed his social-revolutionary spirit by publishing antiwar literature. Instrumental in this change was Walden's political orientation, which was bound to disturb anyone who did not wholeheartedly support the war. Walden's slogan was: "Let everyone be a Prussian after his fashion—after his fashion—but let him be one! For in earthly things the Prussians are artists."[48] Guided by this curious sentiment, he and his wife supported the war effort and hobnobbed with state officials, military officers, and the secret police.

The antiwar attitudes of this Berlin group apparently derived as much from their vague feelings that life was absurd as from any specific political beliefs.[49] The most vivid expression of this aspect of their philosophy was Franz Jung's *Imbecile's Book,* a series of fantastic stories written in 1913, whose overriding theme, as the title implies, was the absurdity of existence. Possessed with a firsthand knowledge of Zurich Dada, Huelsenbeck had a strong impact upon the group's philosophical orientation. Above all, he brought back with him what Hausmann later referred to as "a magic word," the term Dada, which became the catalyst that helped them focus their feelings into a program of action.

The first public meeting of the Club Dada, as the group now called itself, took place at the New Secession Hall on April 12, 1918, with the featured event being a reading of a Dada manifesto by Huelsenbeck. Among other things, he expressed his solidarity with the international Dada movement, attacked Expressionism, Cubism, and abstract art, and extolled the manifesto as the most effective way in which Berlin Dada could communicate its ideas.

69

Soon after this meeting, Huelsenbeck and his cohorts became involved in their first collective venture: the publication of a pamphlet entitled *Club Dada*. Edited by Huelsenbeck, with the assistance of Jung and Hausmann, this magazine, which characteristically appeared for only one issue, was modeled upon those of Zurich Dada; on its last page it even advertised an upcoming soirée which, like the Zurich demonstrations, was to feature simultaneous poetry, bruitist concerts, and cubist dances. But, while its format resembled the Zurich publications, there were certain political overtones in *Club Dada* that indicated that the Berlin group was beginning to develop a spirit of its own. These were perhaps best symbolized by the phrase, "The disappointed hopes of the German Revolution," which was engraved in big, red letters across the top of the magazine.[50]

This new political consciousness was a natural response to the increasingly desperate socioeconomic climate in Germany. Rather than bringing relief, the end of the war had, if anything, worsened the situation. When the German Empire collapsed and Wilhelm II fled to Holland, the stage was set for a bitter struggle between the majority Social Democrats (the SPD), who were basically interested in creating a "middle-class republic," and more radical groups like the Spartacists. Led by Karl Liebknecht and Rosa Luxemburg, both of whom had ties with the leaders of the Russian Revolution, the Spartacists demanded a condemnation of the imperialistic bourgeoisie and the launching of a great civil war that would prepare the way for "the dictatorship of the proletariat."

With no way of reconciling these two ideologies, civil war was inevitable. In Berlin it began just before Christmas, 1918, when bloody street fighting broke out between the Spartacists and the government's security forces, and lasted until the first months of 1919. Although these battles were short-lived, they were especially intense in certain sections of the city. Thus George Grosz recalls that the symbol in the neighborhood where he lived was "a broken chair with blood on it."[51]

The Spartacist insurrection was broken in Berlin when government forces captured its two leaders. Some idea of the fury which this brief but violent confrontation generated may be gained from the fact that both were executed without a trial; Rosa Luxemburg's body was found months afterwards at the bottom of a canal.

Before the Spartacists were crushed, the Berlin Dadas, whose hatred of the bourgeois acted as a common bond, were drawn to their cause. One can speculate that the Spartacists, for their part, at least in the early stages of their struggle, recognized the value of an alliance. As evidence of this, they entrusted Richard Huelsenbeck with certain cultural responsibilities in Berlin.[52]

In any event, regardless of how important they were to the Spartacists, the Berlin Dadas' brief involvement with the practical aspects of revolution in 1918 and 1919 changed the tone of their movement. With a burst of energy, the group began publishing a series of new magazines—*Der Dada, Everyman His Own Football, Bankrupt, Adversary,* and *Deadly Earnest.*

The two most representative of these publications were *Der Dada* and *Everyman His Own Football.* Edited solely by Raoul Hausmann, *Der Dada* appeared for three issues in 1918. The first of these—a crazy-quilt of Hebrew inscriptions, absurd slogans, woodcuts, and phonetic poetry—established the style of the magazine. All of this "intentional disorder" was further reinforced by its unusual typography; its letters were printed in every conceivable size, shape, and thickness. In its next two issues, *Der Dada* not only continued in this vein, but added some new twists: newspaper collages, faked photographs, and crude "ready-mades."

Der Dada also expressed the growing international spirit of the Berlin movement. Contributions by Tzara and Picabia appeared alongside those of the Club Dada members and allusions to Charlie Chaplin, Erik Satie, and Marcel Duchamp were made in some of the texts. In addition, advertising space was provided for the Dada periodicals that were being published throughout Europe.

Overshadowing even these things, however, was *Der Dada*'s preoccupation with social revolution, the bluntest expression of which was a manifesto entitled "What Is Dadaism and What Does It Want in Germany." Written by Huelsenbeck and Hausmann, this manifesto interspersed serious demands for revolutionary social reforms with seemingly tongue-in-cheek suggestions for making the world more Dadaist. Among other things, it called for the establishment of the simultaneous poem as the "Communist state prayer" and the use of churches for bruitist, simultaneist, and Dadaist performances.

In true Dada fashion, the second of these magazines, *Everyman His Own Football,* appeared for only one issue, and even that was confiscated by the Berlin police. Despite this misfortune, enough copies had been sold, according to Walter Mehring—one of those involved in the venture—to make the phrase "every man his own football" a symbol of disdain for authority in Berlin's argot. Mehring's description of how this magazine was distributed illustrates how resourceful the Berlin Dadas were becoming, while at the same time calling to mind the political events of this bloody period.

> We hired a char-a-banc of the sort used for Whitsuntide outings, and also a little band, complete with frock coats and top hats, who used to play at ex-servicemen's funerals. We, the editorial staff, paced behind, six strong, bearing bundles of *Jedermann sein eigner Fussball* instead of wreaths.
>
> In the sophisticated west end of the city we earned more taunts than pennies, but our sales mounted sharply as we entered the lower-middle class and working class districts of north and east Berlin. Along the streets of dingy grey tenements, riddled by the machine-gun fire of the *Spartakus* fighting and sliced open by the howitzers of the Noske [the Minister of the Interior who directed the government forces] régime, the band was greeted with cheers and applause as it played its two star pieces, which were the sentimental military airs *Ich hatt' einen Kammeraden* and *Die Rasenbank am Elterngrab.*[53]

Before the magazine could become "a best-seller," however, it was confiscated by the police on the grounds that it was not only insulting the military, but that it was also obscene. This last charge seems to have stemmed from Mehring's "Der Coitus im Dreimaderlhaus," a poem which satirized the kind of fluff which was enjoying the greatest popularity among bourgeois theater audiences in Germany. It was directed specifically at the *Dreimäderlhaus*, an operetta celebrating its one-thousandth performance in Berlin.

The polemic tone of this magazine may also have had something to do with the authorities' decision to take it off the streets. In addition to the usual ready-mades and photomontages, it offered protests against the government and uncompromising political cartoons. The lead article was an attack against the National Assembly. This was followed by a political cartoon by Grosz which left no doubts as to where that artist stood in the conflict that was then going on in Germany. Two of the leading figures in the government, the Chief Minister and the Chief Press

Officer, are depicted as puppets of the Pope, and a figure representing the Bourgeois is shown as a ruthless murderer who, armed with grenades, is destroying the city. In case there was any question about the meaning of this, the last page of the magazine—which was a warning to the Bavarian revolutionaries, who evidently had not yet joined the struggle—cleared it up; it read: "The revolution is in peril. Close ranks around your flag and arm for the fight against the White Terror of Berlin."[54]

Between 1919 and 1920, the Berlin Dadas, like their Zurich counterparts, engaged in a series of direct confrontations with the public, which took place at the Neumann Gallery, Meister Hall, and the theater *Die Tribune*. According to Grosz, these evenings were little more than great insult sessions in which the Dadas and their public took turns at vilifying each other. He recalled that while one of the Dadas was on the stage reciting something "very ridiculous," he would go down into the audience to intimidate, cajole, and even threaten the spectators into giving him money for the Club. If anyone objected, Grosz had a technique for making them come around; he would remind them of their silence during the war: "Shut up!" I'd say. "You kept your mouths shut for four years. Now keep them shut a little while longer."[55]

Grosz also remembered that their belligerent skits were often alcohol-induced. Drinking heavily before the performances, the Dadas would soon get into drunken brawls which, once the curtain rose, they would simply continue on stage with the audience. This would invariably lead to hand-to-hand fighting between the spectators and the performers, and just as inevitably the police would be on hand to break up the scandalous proceedings.

These Berlin soirées were such a success at the box office that three of the Dadas—Huelsenbeck, Hausmann, and Johannes Baader—decided to organize a tour of Germany and Central Europe. In the early part of 1920, they traveled to Dresden, Hamburg, Leipzig and Prague, giving lectures and performances and, in general, introducing the public to the rare delights of Dada.

Forewarned by their local papers about the nature of Dada activities, the people came to these performances determined to provoke trouble. This attitude was reinforced in the German cities where reports of the connection between the Berlin movement and the Spartacists inflamed the middle-class citizens. Thus, the audiences in cities like Dresden and Hamburg were convinced that the Dadas were their sworn enemies and took every opportunity to vent their wrath upon them.

Hausmann recalled that it took considerable courage to appear before audiences like these which sometimes numbered more than 2000. He illustrated his point with an amusing anecdote: At a demonstration in Leipzig in February, 1920, a police officer decided to mount the stage before the Dadas made their appearance in order to calm the already unruly crowd. The spectators, however, mistook him for a Dada in disguise, and he never managed to speak: first, he was greeted with derisive shouts and laughter; then, with a torrent of rotten eggs and potatoes which the audience had been saving up for the occasion. Under this assault, he quickly gave up and ignominiously fled the stage.

When the three itinerant Dadas were permitted to perform, they would engage in a variety of activities; in addition to presenting the usual lectures and manifestos, they would recite phonetic poems such as Hausmann's "Automobile Souls." Sometimes, a very young lady dressed in black would accompany them on the piano. At other times, the group would perform dances similar to those presented at the Cabaret Voltaire. If the crowd became particularly unruly, Hausmann mentioned that he would begin to perform a charming little dance, which he named the "sixty-one-steps." This would usually calm them down.

Not long after Huelsenbeck and Hausmann had returned to Berlin (Baader had developed stage fright and left them in the lurch in Prague), their movement began to disintegrate. By the end of 1921, Dada in Berlin, for all intents and purposes, had come to an end; Huelsenbeck left Berlin, Hausmann retreated into his own private art world, and Grosz moved off in other directions. There is no adequate explanation of why this happened, but, in commenting on the sudden changes that took place in the Berlin movement, Sanouillet speculates as to whether things would have been different if the Communist Party had triumphed in Germany. How long, he asks, would the Communists have tolerated "the esoteric Dadaist experiences" which were so often in contradiction with the doctrine of Socialist Realism? Putting this question another way, we might ask: were the Berlin Dadas really committed to the kind of program advanced by the Spartacists and, if so, what was the nature of this commitment?

The problem of the political orientation of Berlin Dada is a central one for anyone who wishes to understand the movement. Those who have wrestled with it have invariably come up with two distinctly different but equally slanted views: they have either overemphasized the Dadas' involvement or denied it entirely. Georges Hugnet, the French poet and historian who chronicled the Dada movement, represents the first position. In his essay "The Dada Spirit in Painting" he proposed that after 1918 the works of the Berlin Dadas were little more than "monuments of pure revolutionary propaganda" and concluded that in Berlin "politics absorbed Dada."[56]

The opposing position was espoused by Hausmann. In his book *Dada Courier,* a combination of personal reminiscences and philosophic speculations which he published in 1959, he attempted to answer Hugnet's arguments. He declared that, with the exception of Johann Herzfeld, none of the Berlin Dadas was a member of the Communist Party, stressing, moreover, that they did everything in their power to safeguard their freedom of thought and action. Hausmann also took exception to Hugnet's contention that the creations of the Berlin Dadas were designed solely as propaganda: he cited the fact that he wrote abstract poems such as "Automobile Souls." As further evidence, he discussed the Dada performances in cities such as Leipzig and Prague, which were apolitical except perhaps for the audiences' use of politics to taunt the performers.

Hausmann's comments provide a much-needed corrective to Hugnet's single-minded analysis, and it would be tempting to accept them at face value. After all, he was a participant. But, in his zeal to censure Hugnet, Hausmann tends to pass over certain aspects of his own political involvement. For example, he failed to mention that on April 20, 1919, he published an article in the magazine *Unique* which not only attacked the German middle class (a favorite pastime of the Berlin Dadas), but also called for Bolshevism to destroy its corruption and pave the way for the kind of values that the as yet uncorrupted masses would bring to the fore. And, in another article published in *The Young Art* in 1919, he wrote that now that the masses were on the move, the middle class was doomed.[57]

Interestingly enough, Hausmann was not alone in these attempts to "tone down" traces of political activism among the Berlin Dadas. His colleague Walter Mehring went so far as to write a vehement letter of protest to the editor of the *Times Literary Supplement* concerning an article which appeared on June 9, 1961, proposing that the Dadas were following the Bolshevists' line in Berlin.

Faced with so many unanswered questions, one cannot help but conclude that neither of these two rather doctrinaire views—the one represented by Hugnet, the other by Hausmann—does justice to the complexities that surround the Berlin movement's relationship with politics. That the truth is somewhere in between can perhaps be seen in a review of the development of Berlin Dada and a discussion of its makeup.

Despite Huelsenbeck's reaction against Zurich Dada, the Berlin movement, at its outset (between 1917 and 1918), seems to have been more of an extension of the Zurich movement than an independent entity with its own spirit. Among other things, the Club Dada's initial emphasis on certain techniques that were associated with Zurich Dada—bruitism, simultaneous poetry, and theatrical dances—seems to bear this out. But, as Berlin Dada continued to develop, the volatile political situation in Germany, coupled with the recruitment of younger, more militant members, like George Grosz, tended to alter its tone.

Grosz joined the Berlin movement in 1918 just after he was released from the army. Having volunteered for the infantry during the period when patriotic fervor was at its peak in Germany, he soon discovered that war meant nothing but misery and horror. But, like Jacques Vaché on the French side, Grosz seems to have been disturbed as much by the tedium as by the horror of war. He wrote: "The initial frenzy and enthusiasm . . . were quickly dissipated, leaving nothing behind for most of us but a vast emptiness. The appeal of gun and helmet soon wore off, and war represented only the grim and the horrible. It came to mean filth, lice, idiocy, disease, and deformity."[58]

Unlike Vaché, however, Grosz did not retreat into a world of pataphysical fantasy. He fought back against the inanities of military life. In describing his desperate struggle with the regimentation and dehumanization that was all around him, he vividly expressed the demoralization and the pessimism that was taking hold of the young men of his generation:

> The fight was literally one to the finish. It was sheer self-defense. I was not defending any ideals or beliefs, I was defending myself. Beliefs? Ha, ha! In what? In German heavy industry? In the big capitalists? In our glorious generals? In my beloved Fatherland?[59]

Returning home to a Berlin beset with social, economic, and

political troubles, the pessimistic young Grosz realized that he had to do something to "extricate [himself] from absolute nothingness."[60] He joined a group of disillusioned intellectuals, artists, and workers—all of whom hated reactionary thought and militarism. Using his art as a weapon in the struggle for social revolution, he mercilessly satirized and caricatured the military, the bourgeoisie, the profiteers, and anyone else who stood in the way of social change.

Grosz's militant attitudes toward the middle class and the values it represented made him especially ripe for Berlin Dada. The poems he wrote prior to becoming an official member of the movement indicate that he was already something of a Dada. In 1916, for example, he published the following bit of Dadaist self-mockery in *The New Youth,* the left-wing magazine in which his first drawings appeared:

> Look out! Here comes Grosz.
> The Saddest man in Europe . . .
> Derby hat on his head. No weak dog!
> By the beard of the high school teacher Wotan!
> Coated with decay, perfumed with stench.
> Grosz sniffs it. *Parbleu!*
> Here is the smell of roasted children . . .
> The Anti-Christ come back, he wears the common suit.[61]

It was from this poem that Grosz gained his famous sobriquet— "the saddest man in Europe." Mehring noted that when he first met Grosz on the terrace of the Cafe Groessenwahn he was "dressed in a loud-checked jacket, with face powdered white like a circus clown, posing as 'the saddest man in Europe.'"[62]

Grosz fit nicely into the Berlin Dada movement. Extolling Dada as "the organized use of insanity to express contempt for a bankrupt world,"[63] he immediately assumed the role of "Propagandada," a position for which he was eminently qualified. In this new capacity, he would walk the streets—dressed in all manner of outlandish costumes—advertising the activities of Berlin Dada. He carried a huge calling card with an artificial eye on one side and the slogan "How do you think tomorrow?" on the other. Instead of a hat, he wore a papier-mâché death's head.

Grosz also became notorious for the sticker slogans he made up and the novel ways he invented for distributing them. Some of his favorites were: "Dada today, Dada tomorrow, Dada forever," "Dada über alles," "Dada kicks you in the behind and you like it."[64] He would plaster these all over shop windows, coffee-house tables, and doors in Berlin.

Because of Grosz's resourcefulness, these Dada stickers must have been as omnipresent as the famous World War II slogan, "Kilroy was here." But Grosz's imagination was not limited solely to his efforts as "Propagandada": he engaged in all sorts of other bizarre antics as a member of the Dada movement. Many of these derived from his antimilitary attitudes. For example, he fashioned an effigy of Von Hindenburg from a store dummy to which he added certain significant details: a stove pipe, a chamber pot, and false teeth. Moreover, during this period he was dubbed "Field Marshal Grosz" because he wore a military uniform complete with a gigantic iron cross made out of cardboard.

The combination of these antimilitary gestures and the satiric attacks against the army in his drawings made Grosz the scourge of the German military. His life was threatened more than once by army officers who had been offended by his attitudes. But even this could not stop this intrepid young man. Quite to the contrary, he would go out of his way to encounter high-ranking military men in order to tease and provoke them.

In addition to these belligerent gestures, Grosz indulged in certain actions which call to mind the mystifications of the Parisian Dadas. He adopted the style of the dandy, carrying a cane with a skull on it, pouring his liquor from a bottle with a skull on it, and drinking out of glasses that were made from skulls. Guests to his apartment—especially if they were important personages—were first greeted by a skeleton in the hall and then confronted by a "corpse" in black tights and derby hat, which was draped over the couch. To add to the effect, Grosz would often enlist the support of his friends who, hidden from view, would make blood-curdling sounds.

Grosz's political leanings and weird imagination help to account for the change of tone which began to occur in Berlin Dada after the war. But the influence was not all one-sided. His drawings and caricatures, already filled with images of hate and violence, under the influence of Dada became a significant symbol of the horror and degradation that possessed Germany from 1916 to 1920.

While men like Grosz brought a new political awareness to the Berlin movement, their influence was tempered by people like Huelsenbeck and Baader. The question of Huelsenbeck's political orientation is complex, but there is evidence that for all of his clamor about the value of Bolshevism in art and his fiery manifestos attacking bourgeois attitudes he was not really much of a political activist. What did the slogan "Bolshevism in art" mean to this ironic young poet? It certainly did not connote orthodox Communism. In his essay "En Avant Dada," Huelsenbeck, referring specifically to Lenin and the Communists, went so far as to question the value of collective action in changing society. He wrote: "Though the real political thinker (such as Lenin seems to be) creates a movement, i.e., he dissolves individualities with the help of a theory, he changes nothing. And that, as paradoxical as it may seem, is the import of the Communist movement."[65] And, in the same essay, when he declared that "Dada is German Bolshevism" he seemed to be doing little more than reaffirming the idea that middle-class attitudes toward art must be abolished. "The bourgeois must be deprived of the opportunity to 'buy up art for his justification,'" he proclaimed. "Art should altogether get a sound thrashing, and Dada stands for the thrashing with all the vehemence of its limited nature."[66]

With Baader, there is even less of a question of a political orientation. Not only was he distinctly apolitical, but his actions contributed to the spirit of absurdity that was at the opposite pole of Berlin Dada's involvement with politics. Born in 1876, Baader was older than the other members of the group. A writer and architect of sorts, he had been introduced to the Berlin movement by Raoul Hausmann. Sporting a bushy black beard and possessed of boundless energy, he distinguished himself by his offbeat gestures and lack of inhibitions.

According to Hausmann, Baader thought of himself as "Jesus Christ returned from the clouds of heaven."[67] It was this delusion which, in 1917, prompted Jung and Hausmann—anxious to create a stir among the masses—to talk him into founding the "Anonymous Society of Christ." Baader was to recruit members at a fee of fifty marks. Anyone who paid this would not only become a Christ, but also be free from temporal authority and exempt from the army. A great procession through the streets of Berlin was planned; but it fell through, along with the entire scheme.

Undaunted by this failure, Baader continued his bizarre exploits. In 1918, for example, right in the middle of services at the Berlin Cathedral, he managed to sneak up to the pulpit and deliver an impromptu sermon. Before the shocked and disbelieving parishioners, he proclaimed that Dada would save the world. Not long after this, at the inauguration ceremonies for the Republic, which were held at the Weimar State Theater, he stood in the gallery and threw bunches of leaflets bearing the title "The Green Cadaver on Dada's White Horse" down to the surprised dignitaries below. In these leaflets, Baader nominated himself "PRESIDENT OF THE GLOBE."[68]

Because of his eccentric, uninhibited behavior and his spontaneous actions, Johannes Baader became an imposing figure in the Berlin movement. His antics—more in the tradition of Alfred Jarry or Erik Satie than in that of the Berlin Dadas—played an especially important part in the movement. Living in what Richter has called "a constant state of euphoria," he was able, through his provocative acts and gestures, to create the kind of publicity that the Berlin movement needed in order to make its impact.

With personalities such as Huelsenbeck and Baader playing decisive roles in its development, Berlin Dada—even during its most political phase in the immediate postwar period—was prevented from expressing the kind of "ideological commitment" that some of its members would have wanted. Writing about the movement in 1925, four years after it had broken up, Grosz underscored this very point: he noted that the Dadas had discovered the relationship between art and the class struggle, but had failed to really explore art as a revolutionary weapon. He went on to say that he looked forward to the time "when the artist will be no longer the spongy bohemian anarchist, but a lucid and healthy worker in the collective society."[69]

Cologne

While Berlin Dada was developing its unique characteristics, an independent movement, led by Max Ernst, Johannes Baargeld, and Jean Arp was evolving in Cologne. Struck by the same patriotic fervor as Grosz, Ernst had joined the army and seen combat as an artilleryman. Finally demobilized in the early part of 1919, he returned to his native Cologne, filled with the same hatred of the war and pessimism about life that Grosz had felt. "A horrible and stupid war," Ernst later said in an interview, "had deprived us of five years of our lives. We had seen everything we held as right, beautiful and true collapse into ridicule and shame."[70] The Cologne to which he returned was a city which, like postwar Berlin, was plagued by economic, political, and social unrest; the British Occupation Army was still in command in that area, and the people shared the young artist's feelings of demoralization.

Not long after he arrived in Cologne, Ernst made friends with Alfred Grunwald, the son of a government official, who divided his time between writing, painting, and acting as head of the local Communist Party. Grunwald's disdain for the German middle class, which had prompted him to found the Rhineland wing of the Party, was symbolized by his pseudonym Baargeld—"Cashmoney." Along with his scorn for the bourgeoisie, Baargeld was violently antimonarchistic, antipatriotic, and oriented toward Communism. He expressed these feelings in *The Ventilator,* a journal which he published during this period.

Beyond the fact that *The Ventilator* was ultimately seized by the British military authorities—presumably for being subversive and revolutionary—little is known about it. Before it was confiscated, Ernst recalled, he and Baargeld used to vend it in the streets and at the entrances to factories. Distributed in this novel way, it was well received by the downtrodden people of Cologne and at the time of its demise, its circulation had reached twenty thousand copies.

A few months after the meeting between Ernst and Baargeld, the third member of the trio, Jean Arp, traveled to Cologne from his refuge in Zurich to visit Ernst, whom he had known since before the war. They had met in 1913 when both were preoccupied with Expressionism. Since that time, in accordance with their different temperaments, the two artists had drifted away from Expressionism: Ernst under the spell of De Chirico, and Arp under the influence of Kandinsky and Klee.

Coincidental with Arp's visit to Cologne, the subversive activities of Baargeld and Ernst, which seem to have been initiated as part of the left-wing revolutionary movement that was taking place in Germany between 1918 and 1919, began to take on a new form. Ernst gradually became convinced that he could express his revulsion toward society more effectively through aesthetic rather than political involvement and Baargeld, while still remaining a Communist, began to distinguish more carefully between his political and his artistic gestures.

It is impossible to say for certain why they tempered their revolutionary zeal in this way, but there are two factors which help to explain it. First of all, there is some indication that Ernst and Baargeld, having come in contact with the periodicals that were being published by Berlin Dada, were disturbed by what they considered their openly propagandist tone.[71] Determined not to submerge their artistic instincts in political propaganda, the two Cologne artists may have searched for a means of expression that would more effectively fuse their desires for poetic and social revolution.

The second factor was that Arp's appearance in Cologne may have been more than coincidental with the changes that occurred in the attitudes of Ernst and Baargeld. Arp had already demonstrated his commitment to a spiritual revolution in Zurich. Moreover, he had, along with Tzara, chosen to emphasize aesthetic, as opposed to political or social ideas. Arp's dominant personality, reinforced by the insights about Dada, which he brought back with him, was bound to have an influence on the other two men.

With Arp now a member, the Cologne group branched out into other areas; they experimented with collages, organized art exhibits, and published periodicals. The most significant of these was *Die Schammade,* a magazine whose title is an untranslatable neologism, but whose subtitle translates as "Wake Up, Dilettantes."

Vividly expressing the new spirit of Cologne Dada, *Die Schammade* avoided all allusions to politics. Close to the Zurich publications in both style and content, it not only contained woodcuts, designs, and objects by Baargeld, Ernst, and Arp, but, in a bow in the direction of the international Dada movement, it included texts in French and German as well as sketches by such diverse figures as Ribemont-Dessaignes, Picabia, Tzara, Paul Eluard, Huelsenbeck, Breton, Aragon, and Serner. The appearance of so many Parisian Dadas is noteworthy, for it illustrates the connections that were developing between Cologne and Paris.

The high point of the Cologne movement came in April, 1920, when the group staged a demonstration in the downtown section of the city. Those who attended this demonstration, which was set up in a small glass-enclosed courtyard, had to walk through a café to reach it. The mode of entrance—directly through the café's urinal—foreshadowed the scandalous proceedings. But, just to put the spectators off their guard, they were first greeted by a series of innocent blue posters with dove and cow designs which Ernst had made. The complacent mood created by these posters did not last long, however. A little girl, dressed as if she were making her first communion, opened the demonstration by reciting some obscene poems.

The setting in which this reading took place underscored its shock value: the walls were covered with drawings and the floors filled with all sorts of mysterious and foreboding objects which, in Ernst's words, "were not meant to attract [but] to make people scream and shout."[72] In one corner of the room stood Baargeld's *Fluidoskeptrik,* an aquarium which was filled with red fluid and contained an alarm clock, a polished wooden arm protruding out of the water, and a head of silky woman's hair floating to the top. Next to Baargeld's bizarre creation was an object which Ernst had fashioned out of hard wood. He had attached a hammer, and his instructions were that anyone who wished could use it to destroy the object. This was all the encouragement that the beer-drinkers from the café needed: they smashed the objects and broke the *Fluidoskeptrik,* scattering the red liquid all over the floor. The ensuing turmoil brought the police, who had already received a complaint that the exhibition was obscene.

The Cologne Dadas engaged in other demonstrations (one of which took place in a downtown washroom and featured a statue of Hindenburg pierced with nails and splattered with red paint), but the April, 1920, one marked the climax of their movement. By the end of 1921, Cologne was no longer a center for the Dada movement. Max Ernst, who had made contacts with the Parisian Dadas and had been invited by Breton to exhibit with them, left for Paris in 1922. He would have left earlier, but he was refused a passport by the authorities because of his Dadaist activities. As for Baargeld, a mysterious fate befell him: he disappeared in an avalanche in 1927.

Hanover

One of the last artists to carry on the Dada tradition in Germany was Kurt Schwitters. Born in Hanover in 1887, Schwitters had followed the typical path of the modern German artist from figurative painting to Fauvism and Cubism. Like many of those connected with the Dada movement in Germany, he was influenced during the war by the group of Expressionist artists that centered around *Der Sturm.* In 1918, however, while studying at the Institute of Technology, Schwitters began to move away from these styles and evolve a new and unusual approach. He created collages from discarded objects that he found in the streets: ticket stubs, scraps of old newspapers, and other assorted odds and ends. The collages he fashioned from these materials Schwitters referred to as "Merz," a name at which, significantly, he had arrived by chance; the term "Merz" came from the middle syllable of "KomMERZiell," a word which appeared on a scrap of paper in one of his collages.

The word "Merz"—a term which he used to characterize his art until his death in 1948—was very important for Kurt Schwitters. He was not adverse to exhibiting with the Dadas from time to time, but his use of the word "Merz" instead of "Dada" symbolized the separation he felt from their movement. In an essay he wrote about the concepts of "Merz" in 1920, Schwitters went to great pains to clear up a misunderstanding which he thought had been created by the use of the term Dada on the jacket of *Anna Blume,* his collection of poems. "On the same jacket," he explained, "is a windmill, a head, a locomotive running backwards and a man hanging in the air. This only means that in the world in which Anna Blume lives, in which people walk on their heads, windmills turn and locomotives run backwards, Dada also exists."[73]

But his attitudes toward individual Dadas were something else. He distinguished between what he called "the kernel Dadas and the husk Dadas."[74] The leader of the husk Dadas, a group which had, in his words, "peeled off from this original kernel," was Richard Huelsenbeck. Schwitters had nothing but disdain for this group, which had oriented Dada toward politics and away from art, and its leader who, in his words, espoused *"kitsch."* [75] For the kernel Dadas, among whom he included Tzara, Arp, Picabia, and Ribemont-Dessaignes, he expressed admiration and respect.

The hostility Schwitters felt toward Huelsenbeck was mutual. Some of this was simply a matter of temperament: as Huelsenbeck said himself, "he disliked my fighting ways, and I liked his static, smug middle class world even less."[76] Underlying this, however, was a basic philosophical disagreement. Just as the apolitical Schwitters had been scornful of what he considered Huelsenbeck's political orientation, Huelsenbeck was, in turn, angered by what he considered Schwitters' fanatic commitment to art which left no room for "the remodeling of life" which the Berlin Dadas regarded as their primary aim.

The animosity between these two men can be traced back to 1918 when Schwitters, wearing a high collar and dark tie, came to the *Café des Westens* in Berlin, requesting to be a member of the Club Dada. Raoul Hausmann was fascinated by him, but Huelsenbeck, for what seemed at that time to be an unknown reason, vetoed his membership. Calling attention to Schwitters' great independence, Hausmann later noted that this decision did not seem to faze him in the least. Hausmann also remarked that from that time on he and Schwitters were drawn to each other; this despite the fact that Schwitters continued to be involved with the hated journal *Der Sturm* and its Prussian editor Walden.

In spite of the good relations that were developing between Schwitters and Hausmann—relations that would culminate in their fruitful collaboration after Berlin Dada had broken up—the antagonism between Schwitters and Huelsenbeck continued to grow. One incident, in particular, fed the fires. Huelsenbeck, who was in Hanover discussing the publication of his work "En Avant Dada," stopped off to visit Schwitters and his family. Evidently, the Berlin poet was so disturbed by the middle-class domesticity he encountered that he insulted Schwitters, which only served, Huelsenbeck recalls, to increase the tension between them.

Schwitters's abbreviated meeting with another of the Berlin Dadas—George Grosz—is worth noting, for it illustrates a great deal about both men's character. Having expressed a desire to meet Grosz, Schwitters was brought to his apartment by Walter Mehring. When Schwitters rang the bell, Grosz appeared, and the following scene, transcribed by Hans Richter, occurred:

> "Good morning, Herr Grosz. My name is Schwitters."
> "I am not Grosz," answered the other and slammed the door. There was nothing to be done.
> Half way down the stairs, Schwitters stopped suddenly and said, "Just a moment."
> Up the stairs he went, and once more rang Grosz's bell.
> Grosz, enraged by this continual jangling, opened the door, but before he could say a word, Schwitters said "I am not Schwitters, either." And went downstairs again.
> . . . They never met again.[77]

Having made a few tentative attempts at becoming a member of the Berlin group, the independent-minded Schwitters decided to remain a loner. Although he contributed in November, 1919, to *Der Zeltweg*, the last publication of Zurich Dada, and was a good friend of Arp (a friendship which developed because, in Richter's words, "they spoke the same language, a kind of sophisticated schizophrenic dialect, a German raised above all conventions."[78]), Schwitters never really belonged to the Zurich movement. Nor did he have any connections with Cologne or Paris Dada; the Dadas seem hardly to have heard of his work in Paris.

Strangely enough, it was only in New York, where Duchamp energetically publicized his collages, that Schwitters was accepted.

In addition to symbolizing Schwitters' independence from the Dada movement, the term "Merz" became the umbrella for his most imaginative and far-reaching ideas concerning the essential interrelationships of the arts. Like Kandinsky and Ball, Schwitters envisioned the creation of a *Gesamtkunstwerk*, which, in his case, was a combination of sculpture, architecture, theater, and poetry that he called composite "Merz" art. A logical extension of his collages, which were often arranged in such a way as to stress their word poetry, this new approach would incorporate all of the arts into one composite unit, erasing the traditional boundaries between them. The energy and thought Schwitters gave to this idea allowed him to exercise an extraordinary creative freedom, much of which stemmed from a principle that he articulated in his 1920 essay on "Merz": "The medium is as unimportant as I myself. Essential is only the forming."[79] With this as his guiding principle, Schwitters engaged in a variety of experiments, using many different artistic forms.

Some of the most interesting of these experiments were conducted in the realm of written and spoken poetry. Schwitters' most famous poem "Anna Blume" was published by *Der Sturm* in 1919. The following excerpt provides an idea of its flavor:

> Red bloom, red Anna Blume, what do people say?
> Prize question: 1) Anna Blume has a bird.
> 　　　　　　　 2) Anna Blume is red
> 　　　　　　　 3) What colour is the bird?
> Blue is the colour of your yellow hair.
> Red is the cooing of your green bird.
> You simple girl in a simple dress, you dear
> green beast, I love your! You ye you your,
> I your, you my.—We?
> This belongs (by the way) in the chest of fires.
> Anna Blume! Anna, a-n-n-a, I trickle your
> name. Your name drips like softest tallow.[80]

Schwitters arrived at this curious mélange of clichés, newspaper headlines, romantic gibberish, advertising blurbs, and popular expressions by riding on streetcars and listening to the gossip of his fellow passengers. Beneath its seemingly gratuitous nonsense, this poem is a trenchant satire upon sentimental poetry. But perhaps more important for us today, "Anna Blume" vividly illustrates the disassociated sensibility of modern life. Anna experiences life in a jumble of colors and exists in a topsy-turvy world where "people walk on their heads, windmills turn and locomotives run backwards."

In addition, Schwitters experimented with phonetic poetry. His earliest efforts in this genre were simple recitations of letters, either in sequence or alone. He would alternate between dramatic readings of the alphabet and demonstrations of a more mysterious nature. "In one of these demonstrations," Moholy-Nagy wrote, "he showed to the audience a poem containing only one letter on a sheet:

W

Then he started to 'recite' it with slowly rising voice. The consonant varied from a whisper to the sound of a wailing siren till, at the end, he barked with a shockingly loud tone. This was his answer not alone to the social situation but also to the degrading 'cherry-mouthed'-'raven-haired'-'babbling-brook'-poetry."[81]

As time went on, Schwitters, perhaps influenced by Hausmann's approach, began to develop more complex forms of phonetic poetry. Thus, in 1923, he created his celebrated "Ursonate" or "Primordial Sonata," a phonetic poem in four movements which was scored much like a musical composition. In writing about Schwitters' "Ursonate," Hans Richter has said that much of its power came from the manner in which its author recited it. As an illustration of this, Richter related the circumstances of Schwitters' first public reading of the poem. This reading, which took place at the home of one Frau Kiepenheuer in Potsdam, was given before an audience whose tone was predominantly Prussian: retired generals, ex-monarchists, and high-ranking members of Potsdam society. When Schwitters began to perform his "Ursonate," "complete with hisses, roars, and crowings," the audience, who had never experienced anything like this before, were first shocked, then convulsed: at first they tried to restrain themselves out of respect for their hostess—but finally they could hold out no longer; two generals, who had tried very hard to keep from laughing, cracked up, and this set everybody else in the room off. Now, Richter recalled, "the dignified old ladies, the stiff generals, shrieked with laughter, gasped for breath, slapped their thighs, choked themselves."[82]

But none of this fazed Schwitters. He simply increased the volume of his stentorian voice and, in Richter's words, "swamped the storm of laughter in the audience."[83] As if by some strange magic, the mood now began to change abruptly, and an evening which had started off with insane laughter ended on an evangelistic note. Amazingly enough, according to Richter, "the same generals, the same rich ladies, who had previously laughed until they cried, now came to Schwitters, again with tears in their eyes, almost stuttering with admiration and gratitude. Something had opened up within them, something they had never expected to feel: a great joy."[84]

While the movements in Berlin and Cologne were fading into memory, Kurt Schwitters continued to engage in Dada-like activities in Germany. He and Hausmann gave a recital entitled "Anti-Dada and Merz" in Prague in September, 1921. This performance featured recitals of Schwitters's "The Great Revolution in Revon" and Hausmann's "The Cigar." The audience had, as usual, come in the expectation of a scandal, but according to Hausmann, they were disarmed by the "novelty and perfection of our program."[85]

In 1923, Schwitters traveled to Holland at the invitation of Theo van Doesburg. His appearance in Holland was to be part of what van Doesburg had planned as a Dada Congress, but, according to the Hanover artist, the Dadas were a bit leery about the reception they would get from the Dutch, so he was the only one who showed up. At the inaugural lecture, which was held in The Hague, it was decided that van Doesburg would explain Dada and Schwitters provide an example of it. Sometime during the lecture, van Doesburg was to stop for a drink of water and that would be Schwitters' cue. Everything went off as planned. Just as van Doesburg started to drink, Schwitters—a perfect stranger sitting in the audience—began barking wildly. The next demonstration was scheduled in Haarlem; the house was packed by the curious Dutch, who had flocked to see these strange goings-on. The two men went through their routine, but this time Schwitters did not bark. The next night, this time in Amsterdam, the audience, which could hold itself in check no longer, took over: people laughed hysterically while others raged at the crowd.

As we look back upon Schwitters' activities, it is certainly paradoxical that this eccentric artist from Hanover, who often went to such efforts to distinguish his work from the Dadas, should be one of the last true representatives of the movement in Germany; it is even more paradoxical that Schwitters—an artist who chose to follow a banner he called "Merz" rather than that of Dada—is today the man who, in the words of Michel Sanouillet, "incarnates perhaps better than anyone else the fiercely individualistic, anarchistic, and fantastic spirit of Dada."[86]

Paris

In Paris, as in the German cities, Dada was ushered in by the war. Like their German counterparts, the young French soldiers marched off to do battle in an exalted, almost Byronic spirit. It was not until the first savage encounters, which left the fields of Belgium strewn with corpses, that the real meaning of war became clear to these "incorrigible romantics."[87] During the battles of Lorraine, the Ardennes, and Charleroi, the French Army alone suffered more than 140,000 casualties. And Verdun, where, as one observer remarked, there were more dead men than living, was still to come. Also still to come were the long, bloody months of trench warfare, as this miserable war dragged on far beyond the six weeks that both sides had so optimistically predicted. The war lasted for four years, and when it was finally over nearly two million Frenchmen had lost their lives.[88]

But even this systematic slaughter, horrible as it was, does not tell the story of life at the front. These ill-fated soldiers also had to endure the insufferable boredom, the dehumanization, and the emptiness of day-to-day existence which Jacques Vaché so vividly described in his letters. To cope with these hardships, they could either retreat, like Vaché, into their own private fantasies or, what was more likely, completely desensitize themselves. "Just as he tried to delouse himself as regularly as possible," wrote Jacques Rivière in his essay "French Letters and the War," "so the combatant took care to kill in himself, one by one, as soon as they appeared, before he was bitten, every one of his feelings. Now he clearly saw that feelings were vermin, and that there was nothing to do but to treat them as such."[89]

While these young men were serving their time in Hell, those at home were making the grim preparations that war dictates. Activating a jingoistic campaign, the French proved that they could rival the Germans in beating the drums of war. This systematic indoctrination incessantly hammered away at the idea of the civilized Frenchmen as opposed to the barbaric German. Promoted by the government, the military, and the press, this idea became omnipresent in France: it was the most popular image on posters, placards, designs, and even postcards, as well as the most common theme for the numerous patriotic stories that circulated during this period. Even the music hall picked it up. The celebrated Damia of Montmartre, for example, would serenade her audience of soldiers on leave, unescorted women, and cocaine addicts—most of whom were probably trying their best to forget the war—with a patriotic little ditty entitled "The Chase," which, among other things, called for her countrymen to stop "the wolves of Prussia."[90] It is interesting to note, in passing, that the fearless Damia continued her performances until the very night that Paris was attacked by German planes and "Big Bertha" screamed her defiance across the city.[91]

The exponents of popular culture were not the only ones to trumpet their praises of the brave French soldier while damning his German counterpart. Professional men, spiritual leaders, and intellectuals all jumped on the patriotic bandwagon. Even Henri Bergson who, ironically enough, was the President of the Academy of Moral Science added his voice to the fierce condemnation of the Germans and their culture.

Just as the Germans had tried to rewrite cultural history by banning Shakespeare from the stage and claiming that Dante had been Germanic, the French intelligentsia forbade the music of Mozart and Wagner and declared that Beethoven had been a Belgian. Their decrees against Wagner were so successful, incidentally, that Louis Aragon recalls that even those who tried to play Wagner's music in their own apartments would often be stopped by their neighbors. Established writers, like Edmond Rostand, Jean Richepin, Paul Bourget, and Anatole France, all of whom struggled to outdo each other in their patriotic zeal, spearheaded this movement. But towering above all of them was the singular figure of Maurice Barrès—"The President of the League of Patriots"—whose writings celebrated the heroism and self-sacrifice of the men at the front in drippingly sentimental terms.

The only major French writer to try to counter the superpatriots was Romain Rolland. Living in exile in Zurich, Rolland reminded his fellow intellectuals of the madness of their excessive nationalism. He pleaded with both sides to end this shameful war; this "sacrilegious mêlée," as he called it, "which offers the spectacle of a maddened Europe ascending its funeral pyre, and, like Hercules, tearing itself to pieces with its own hands!"[92]

The long war of attrition began to have its effects on the French as it did on the Germans. After three years of bitter fighting, the morale at the front and at home reached its lowest ebb. Widespread profiteering (even gas masks were sold on the black market), corruption, and the endless procession of wounded and battle-scarred men—those who, in the parlance of the day, were called the "gueules cassées"—eventually weakened the resolve of even the most enthusiastic warmonger. Some idea of what it was like in Paris comes from a passage in Céline's celebrated novel *Journey to the End of the Night:*

> Wounded men in increasing numbers hobbled along the streets, in rags as often as not. Collections were made on their behalf. There was a "Day" for these, a "Day" for those, Days above all for the people who organized them. Lie, copulate and die. One wasn't allowed to do anything else. . . . Lies in the papers, lies on the hoardings, lies on foot, on horseback and on wheels. . . .
>
> Everything you touched was faked in some way—the sugar, the aeroplanes, shoe leather, jam, photographs; everything you read, swallowed, sucked, admired, proclaimed, refuted or upheld—it was all an evil myth and masquerade.[93]

As D. H. Lawrence has said, "all the great words were cancelled out,"[94] for the generation that grew up during this war. This was especially true for young men like André Breton, Louis Aragon, and Philippe Soupault—"the three musketeers" of Paris Dada—who experienced its horrors most directly.

The war cut short the professional careers of these three typical members of the middle class (when it broke out, Breton and Aragon were medical students and Soupault was studying law). Although they did not yet know each other, both Breton and Aragon, trying perhaps to retain some continuity in their lives, joined the Medical Corps. They met in Paris, where both were stationed for a time. Breton remained in the Medical Corps and was later transferred to Nantes, but Aragon volunteered for the infantry and was sent to the front as a medic.

While Breton came in contact with Vaché in Nantes, Aragon's experiences were just as crucial, albeit for a different reason. On June 20, 1918, he was awarded the *Croix de guerre* for his heroic actions in evacuating the wounded under the most perilous conditions. Despite his heroism, or perhaps because of it, Aragon came away with a profound disgust for the war and few illusions about the nature of the society which had caused it. Writing about his experiences in an essay ironically titled "Beauties of War and its Reflections in Literature," he recalled that it was "a sad time to be young." And, in taking exception with those poets who, like his hero Apollinaire, wrote glowingly of "rockets, flares, and exploding shells,"[95] Aragon asked why they did not follow the trajectory of the shells they were so enthusiastic about into the human flesh where they imbedded themselves? And why, he asked, didn't they write about the blood and corpses?

Like Breton, Soupault never got to the front, but his experiences were no less traumatic. Called up in 1916, he and his company became the guinea pigs for a new typhoid fever vaccination which backfired and sent them all to the hospital. Even there, Soupault could not escape the nerve-shattering experiences of a country at war: the tension of constant bombing alerts, the corruption of the war profiteers, and the piercing hatred of the propagandists. Looking back on these things, Soupault wrote that it is difficult for someone living today to realize how devastating this war was for the youth of his generation. The hopelessness they must have felt was later captured in one of Soupault's most mordant poems:

> Philippe Soupault in his bed
> born a monday
> baptized a tuesday
> married a wednesday
> sick a thursday
> dying a friday
> dead a saturday
> buried a sunday
> that's the life of Philippe Soupault[96]

For those young men who put their trust in the arts, this was an especially difficult time. Most writers and artists either remained silent, tacitly accepting what was happening, or sang "the French song." But there were exceptions, like Romain Rolland, who, while his works were considered subversive by the French government, managed to retain the respect of the young. Feelings ran so high against Rolland that, according to Aragon, mothers would burst into tears if they caught their sons reading his novel *Jean Christophe.*

Writers like André Gide and Paul Valéry as well as painters like Picasso and Matisse had also succeeded in keeping their moral posture somewhat intact by retreating into their work. Expressing a revolutionary spirit akin to Rimbaud's in his *Evening with Mr. Testé,* Valéry temporarily became a particular favorite of

Breton, Aragon, and Soupault. They were disappointed in him, however, when in 1917 he published *The Young Fate* which moved away from his earlier, more subversive tone. Soupault summed up their feelings when he proposed that Valéry was "already thinking about his royalties and a seat in the Académie Française."[97]

The attitudes Breton, Aragon, and Soupault expressed toward Apollinaire were more ambivalent. They admired him for his openness to experience and his daring spirit, but were disturbed by his nationalism, and by his enthusiasm for the "beauties of war." Like Marinetti, Apollinaire had, while at the front, written poems which celebrated the aesthetics of battle.[98]

For anyone else this would have been unforgivable. But in Apollinaire's case, it had to be balanced against his other accomplishments. Although resentful of Apollinaire's false image of war, Aragon admitted that he was "the only man who still could . . . pour precious alcohols in France, dried-up in wartime."[99] Breton was even more enthusiastic: he proclaimed that Apollinaire had most clearly anticipated the "new spirit" and was "the greatest poet of this century."[100] "To have known him," Breton added, "will pass for a rare advantage."[101]

The "new spirit" to which Breton alluded, was a postwar rebirth in the arts ushered in by writers like Apollinaire, Max Jacob, and André Salmon, and painters like Kisling and Modigliani. An important aspect of this "new spirit" was the development of an avant-garde journal entitled *Sic*—short for "Sounds, Ideas, [Forms], Colors." Edited by Pierre Albert-Birot, *Sic*, as its title indicates, began as a forum for Futurism. Eventually, however, it became a vehicle for all types of artists and writers, including the Dadas. The magazine's circulation extended to Zurich, where Tzara lost no time in incorporating it into his grand design for an international Dada movement.

Pierre Reverdy began to publish his own magazine *Nord-Sud*, whose title was derived from the subway line connecting Montmartre and Montparnasse, in March of 1917. Reverdy's basic intention was to unify the diverse tendencies which had been expressed in modern art and literature. More sophisticated than *Sic*, *Nord-Sud* centered on contributions by three of the most important poets of the period: Apollinaire, Jacob, and Reverdy himself. Although Reverdy and his collaborators devoted much energy to trying to find the literary equivalents for pictorial Cubism, they never became doctrinaire about it, remaining open to influences from such essentially Dadaist writers as Paul Dermée and Vincent Huidobro. Soupault, Breton, Tzara, and Aragon also contributed poems to *Nord-Sud*.

The publication of *Sic* and *Nord-Sud* was but one aspect of the cultural rebirth which took place toward the end of the war in Paris. There was also a renewed interest in popular forms of culture—music-hall, jazz, and cinema. Perhaps the first real indication of this was the performance of *Parade* in May, 1917. *Parade* was the result of the collaboration of three of the most significant figures of modern art, Picasso, Cocteau, and Erik Satie; Picasso created the backdrop (a curious mélange from his harlequin and Cubist periods), Satie wrote the score (a kind of "musical collage" based on popular music and jazz), and Cocteau contributed the scenario (a "ballet-réaliste" complete with music-hall performers and clowns). The première performance of *Parade* on May 18, 1917 culminated in what had become the supreme compliment for avant-garde spectacles: a public scandal. Unable to understand *Parade's* spirit of absurdity, the shocked audience unleashed all of the emotions they had suppressed since the war. They whistled, clapped, shouted, and even threatened the performers. This raucous reception foreshadowed their reactions to the Dada demonstrations which were to rock postwar Paris.

During the following month, Apollinaire's play *The Breasts of Tiresias,* a disjointed and fanciful burlesque which made use of some of the same techniques as *Parade,* was also staged. The performance, which took place on June 24, 1917, also resulted in a scandal of sorts; one which, in this case, involved the legendary Jacques Vaché. According to Breton, Vaché became so excited by the tension in the audience that he drew his revolver on the crowd.[102]

Less than a year after the performances of *Parade* and *The Breasts of Tiresias,* the emphasis on popular culture reached its peak: jazz was introduced to Paris. Brought from the United States, where they had achieved an unparalleled success, the Negro jazz bands helped bring in the Jazz Era with all of its crazy antics and wild devil-may-care attitudes. After four years of wartime anxiety, restrictions, sufferings, and tensions, peace had come to Paris in the form of a great orgasmic release, and nothing symbolized this better than the advent of jazz. "A kind of musical alcohol," wrote William Gaunt, "it whipped a disillusioned generation into frenzy. Le 'Jazz hot' was taken up in Paris with fervour. The tom-tom beat, the sensual chuckle of the saxophone, made a derisive symphony pervading the city by night, where the sky was reddened with the lights and signs of a thousand haunts of pleasure."[103]

Another import from the United States—American movies—also fit nicely into this Paris scene. The flamboyant gestures of Douglas Fairbanks and the cavortings of Mack Sennet's favorites became as much a part of the Jazz Era in Paris as they were in New York. And the indomitable Pearl White and her *Perils of Pauline* came to symbolize the love of adventure for French as well as American youth. But, above all, it was Charlie Chaplin—the beloved Charlot—who conquered Paris with his "sublime" filmic poetry. Writing about this post war period when American films meant so much to him and his generation, Soupault remarked that "those darkened halls . . . became the living theater of our laughter, our anger, our pride. In those miraculous crimes and farewells our eyes read the poetry of our age. We were living with passion through a most beautiful period of which the U.S. cinema was the brightest ornament."[104]

These exotic American imports, however, were not the only films to make a strong impression upon this generation. Certain French films, most notably those of Louis Feuillade, also became a source of inspiration. During this period, Feuillade made three films that were bound to excite the imagination of the young: *Fantomas,* a film about the bizarre adventures of a master of crime who makes fools of the police; *Les Vampires,* a horror film which featured the mysterious actress Musidora; and *Judex,* a film about a Batman-like character who uses his powers to defend the weak and combat evil.

Against the background of all these activities—many of which had begun in the midst of the hostilities—the Dada movement, almost imperceptibly at first, began to take shape. As a result of Tzara's correspondence with Cocteau, Dermée, Albert-Birot, Reverdy, and Apollinaire, word of the activities of the Zurich Dadas had begun to reach Paris prior to 1917. Some, like the enterprising Cocteau, had even begun to make use of the term Dada. After the scandalous reception of *Parade,* he referred to the Parisian public as "Dadaists."[105] Nevertheless, judging by the sparseness of allusions to Dada in the avant-garde periodicals, very little was actually known about the movement in Paris at this time. Max Jacob, in alluding to Tzara in the Paris section of *391* during the spring of 1917, had even spelled his name wrong ("Tristan Tsara").

Like the rest of Paris, Breton, Aragon, and Soupault knew little

about the Dada movement at this time. The poems they published in *Sic* and *Nord-Sud,* marking their literary debut, eloquently testify to this: Breton's are reminiscent of the Symbolists,
who were his earliest mentors—Mallarmé, Valéry, Saint Pol-Roux,
Francis Vielé-Griffin, etc; Aragon's display the influence of Blaise
Cendrars and Paul Verlaine; and, Soupault's, which were more
daring and less derivative, were basically experiments in a kind of
"cinematic poetry."[106]

The three came in contact with Dada for the first time through
Apollinaire in 1917. Tzara had sent Apollinaire copies of the Zurich periodicals—*Cabaret Voltaire, Dada* I, and *Dada* II—and Marie
Laurencin, his ex-mistress, had forwarded some of the issues of
391 from Barcelona and New York as well. At first, like Apollinaire himself, they seem to have had certain reservations about
the Zurich movement. For example, when they were asked to
contribute to *Dada* III, they hesitated to do so.[107] But, in time,
they became more sympathetic to Zurich Dada in general and
Tzara in particular. What brought about this change of heart?
Three events seem to have been instrumental: one, Apollinaire's
death in November, 1918; two, the actual appearance of *Dada* III
in December, 1918; and, three, Jacques Vaché's death from an
overdose of drugs in January, 1919.

The successive deaths of Apollinaire and Vaché, two of the
men whom they had admired most, came as a stunning shock to
these young poets, and left a tremendous void in their lives.
Amidst this crushing sadness, the only ray of hope seems to have
been communicated by *Dada* III; for it was with this issue that, at
least in the mind of Breton, the Zurich movement "set the pow-
der on fire."[108] He and his companions were especially impressed
with Tzara's "Dada Manifesto of 1918" with its dramatic call for
"a great negative work of destruction" and its appeals to the idea
of spontaneity. The young French poets now began to recognize a
kinship between Tzara's movement and Vaché's attitude that
"Art is a silly thing."

Soon after their discovery of Tzara, Breton, Aragon, and Soupault decided to publish their own magazine, which at Valéry's
suggestion, they called *Littérature.* Apparently, this title was
meant to be an "antiphrase," but considering some of the things
that appeared in its first issue—an unedited fragment of Gide's
Nourritures Terrestres, a series of poems entitled *Le Cantique des
colonnés* by Valéry, *La Rue Ravignan* by Jacob, and *Carte Blanche*
by Reverdy—there is some question as to whether it was really
intended as a mockery of literature.

By this time, Breton had begun to correspond with Tzara, but his impact and that of his movement was negligible in this first issue; a critique by Aragon of Tzara's *Twenty-five Poems* was the only demonstrable evidence of the Rumanian's work in the magazine. Ironically enough, the closest thing to Dada was Gide's *Nourritures Terrestres,* in which its author called for a *tabula rasa.* Gide wrote: "I have swept everything away. It's all done! I stand nude upon the virgin earth with the heavens to replenish."[109]

The next issue of *Littérature* was hardly more concerned with Dada than the first. Among other things, it contained the first part of Lautréamont's *Poésies* which Breton had slavishly copied by hand at the Bibliothèque Nationale. The only trace of Dada was Tzara's brilliant poem "Maison Flake." But even this was a second choice; for the editors had originally searched for a text by Jarry. Unable to find it, they substituted the Tzara poem instead.

Beginning with the third issue, which featured Vaché's *Letters of War,* the editors of *Littérature*—having grown tired of what Breton has termed "the anthological side" of their magazine— began to express a more independent spirit. This culminated in the famous "inquiry" of November, 1919. Posing the question "why do you write?" to some of the most important modern writers of the time—men such as Henri Ghéon, Jean Giraudoux, Max Jacob, Cendrars, Reverdy, Francis Jammes,—they ranked their answers in order of preference. Just how sweeping their indictment of "traditional" literature was becoming is indicated by the nature of their choices. Although he found most of the replies "lamentable," Breton praised Knut Hamsun's answer ("I write to shorten the time") and added that writing to lengthen the time was equally satisfying.[110] Among the other answers that the editors appreciated was Valéry's humble "out of feebleness."[111]

During this period, when the editors of *Littérature* were beginning to discover their own voices, important new members, like Picabia, Paul Eluard, and Georges Ribemont-Dessaignes became part of the movement. Although the arrival of Eluard and Ribemont-Dessaignes helped set the stage for Paris Dada, it was the meeting between Picabia and the editors of *Littérature* which was most significant. Perhaps more than any other single individual, Picabia expressed the anti-art spirit of New York and Zurich, and when this was fused with the kind of amorphous but explosive youthful energy of the *Littérature* group, all the conditions necessary for the development of the Dada movement in Paris had been fulfilled. What was needed now was someone like Tzara to focus these energies and ignite the spark.

Given this atmosphere, it is not surprising that Tzara was awaited, in the words of Breton, "a little like the Messiah."[112] He finally arrived in Paris on January 17, 1920. At first, he seems to have had a little difficulty in living up to the fabulous legend that had preceded him. When Breton, Aragon, Soupault, and Eluard came to visit him at the apartment of Picabia and Germaine Everling, where he was staying, they were greeted by a small, shabbily dressed man who spoke broken French with a ridiculous Rumanian accent. Was this the man whose poetry they found so extraordinary and whose exploits they admired?

Within a week, however, at a demonstration organized by the *Littérature* group, Tzara proved that their admiration for him was not unfounded. When Aragon announced that the great Tzara would read from his poems, the Rumanian stunned the audience by reading a newspaper account of Leon Daudet's last speech. To add to the confusion, Tzara's words were drowned out by the loud ringing of bells from offstage. This exasperated the crowd, especially those patriotic souls who, during these trying times, would have been disturbed by Tzara's Rumanian accent with its subversive connotations, regardless of what he had read. They shouted obscenities and screamed for him to go back to Zurich. "All that I wanted to convey," Tzara later wrote in explanation of his actions, "was simply that my presence on the stage, the sight of my face and my movements, ought to satisfy people's curiosity and that anything I might have said really had no importance."[113]

Prior to Tzara's provocative debut, which came during the second part of the program, only one other truly Dadaist gesture had occurred; this had been the exhibition of Picabia's paintings. The first of these, entitled *The Double World,* came in a carton covered with strange inscriptions topped off by the obscene L.H.O.O.Q. The audience sensed the obscenity in the thing immediately and was outraged. Even before their outrage had died down, a second work done on a blackboard and titled *Rice in the Nose* was brought out. It was greeted with wild cries of rage by the spectators, who recognized that they were being made fools of. And, when Breton appeared to erase the writing on the blackboard, the audience virtually exploded.

Despite the fact that the revolutionary gestures of Picabia and Tzara were sandwiched in among all sorts of modern art, i.e., readings of the poetry of Apollinaire, Cendrars, Reverdy, Jacob, and Albert-Birot; exhibitions of the works of Léger, Gris, De Chirico, etc.; and music by "the Six"—all of which seem to have been vestiges of *Littérature's* earlier concerns—the Dada movement was launched at this "First Friday," which took place at the Palais des Fêtes on January 23, 1920.

Fresh from his triumphs in Zurich and flushed with the success of his sensational debut, Tzara naturally took command of the burgeoning Paris movement and became the impresario of its massive "provocation-demonstrations." He felt so much at home in Paris, amidst the steadily growing turmoil that he and Picabia were creating, that he quickly resumed publication of his periodical *Dada*, entitling this, the sixth issue of the magazine, *Dada Bulletin.*

Characterized by insulting statements, spoonerisms, and absurd notations rather than articles, this magazine was a radical departure from the periodicals—including *Littérature*—that were being published in Paris at this time. What distinguished it from these other magazines, aside from its absurd content, was its disjointed format and disorderly typography, which called to mind *391* and the Zurich periodicals. Tzara's Paris edition of *Dada* even featured the now-familiar false news section which, among other things, announced that Soupault had gone to Geneva to commit suicide.

Even before the Parisian public had completely recovered from the "First Friday," the Dadas organized a series of new "provocation-demonstrations" which explored the breach that had been opened up. The first of these took place at the Salon des Indépendants on February 5th. It attracted spectators under the pretense that Charlie Chaplin would appear to pledge his allegiance to the Dada movement. Chaplin never arrived, but the Dadas were there in full regalia, reading individual and collective manifestos (Picabia's was read by ten people, Ribemont-Dessaignes's by nine, etc.) and doing everything in their power to insult and vilify the audience. These manifestos ran the gamut from denunciations of "traditional" literature to out-and-out calls for anarchy, to vicious personal attacks against those in the hall. While Soupault affirmed that "literature exists only in the heart of imbeciles," Aragon went even further, denouncing "painters, writers, musicians, sculptors, religions, republicans, royalists,"[114] etc., and Ribemont-Dessaignes combined all of this with a terrifying threat:

TO THE PUBLIC:
Before going down among you to pull out your decaying teeth, your running ears, your tongues full of sores,

Before breaking your putrid bones,

Before opening your cholera-infested belly and taking out for use as fertilizer your too fatted liver, your ignoble spleen and your diabetic kidneys,

Before tearing out your ugly sexual organ, incontinent and slimy,

Before extinguishing your appetite for beauty, ecstasy, sugar, philosophy, mathematical and poetic metaphysical pepper and cucumbers,

Before disinfecting you with vitriol, cleansing you and shellacking you with passion,

Before all that,

We shall take a big antiseptic bath,

And we warn you:

we are murderers.[115]

The next major demonstration took place at the Théâtre de l'Oeuvre, where the performance of Jarry's *King Ubu*—the prototype of all the scandals in modern theater—had occurred in 1896. The program the Dadas presented to the public on March 27, 1920, was more elaborate and ambitious than anything that they had previously conceived. Among other things, it included a cacophonous piece for piano composed according to the laws of chance by Ribemont-Dessaignes and played in a nicely discordant style by Margueritte Buffet. Also featured were a series of Dadaist sketches and plays by Dermée *(The Out of Tune Ventriloquist)*, Ribemont-Dessaignes *(The Mute Canary)*, Breton and Soupault *(If You Please)*, and Tzara *(The First Celestial Adventure of Mr. Antipyrine)*.

Dermée's "play," which showed signs of having been thrown together especially for the occasion, featured a ventriloquist who enacted three other roles and a girl played by a male actor. In contrast to this, Ribemont-Dessaignes's *The Mute Canary*, which had been written about a year before, was a more ambitious effort. Performed by Breton, Soupault, and Louise Barclay, it brought together into a bizarre triangle a husband who pretends to be a prince and panther hunter (Riquet, played by Breton), a wife who thinks she is Messaline (Barate, played by Louise Barclay), and a black man who believes that he is the composer Gounod (Ocre, played by Soupault). While this play was not, in its author's words, "a circumstantial piece solely destined for dada propaganda,"[116] it had enough Dadaist elements to cause problems for an audience that was used to more traditional drama and a more conventional use of the stage.

An experiment in automatic writing comparable to *The Magnetic Fields*, Breton and Soupault's *If You Please*—carefully divided into acts and scenes and provided with minute scenic details and seemingly conventional characters—used the very rules of dramatic art to ridicule the idea of traditional theater. But it was Tzara's *The First Celestial Adventure of Mr. Antipyrine*, which had already created a public scandal when it was performed in Zurich, that undoubtedly made the strongest impression.

Unlike *If You Please*, which was staged in a rather straightforward manner, Tzara arranged to have his work, which he himself described as "a boxing match with words," performed in a way calculated to bring out its most absurd qualities. With Picabia's assistance, he had devised a series of costumes and a set which fit the text perfectly; the costumes called to mind the doodlings of the insane, and the set—a kind of transparent decor which was placed in front of rather than behind the performers—consisted of a bicycle wheel, a few pieces of rope hung across the stage, and some frames with certain mystifying inscriptions, i.e., "Paralysis is the beginning of wisdom," and "You hold out your arms, your friends will cut them off"[117] which bore the unmistakable mark of Picabia.

Tzara's own peculiar twists added still further to the absurd atmosphere of this production. He confined the performers in huge, brightly colored paper sacks which made it virtually impossible for them to move around, punctuated their most Dadaist remarks with the honking of "a diabolical machine composed of a klaxon and 3 successive invisible echoes" which he had invented specially for this performance, and arranged to have all of the action (or perhaps better, inaction) "bathed in an eerie greenish light."[118] And, as Tzara himself recalled, these devices achieved their desired ends upon an already overwrought audience: they made such an impact that "it was impossible to hear a single word of the play."[119]

In addition to these theatrical pieces, the usual anarchistic manifestos were on the program; Picabia let the audience know in no uncertain terms that their hopes, their paradise, their idols, their politicians, their artists, and their religions were all—like Dada—nothing. And Ribemont-Dessaignes turned his searchlight of doubt on everything, from the celebrated boxer Georges Charpentier to the renowned General Foch.

As Tzara has said, this demonstration "showed the vitality of Dada at its height."[120] The massive audience which had flocked to the theater for a taste of Dada's scandal, was not disappointed. Insulted, confused, mystified, and belabored in turn, the people fought back and did their best to give the Dadas some of their own medicine. Just how tumultuous these proceedings became is illustrated by an incident involving Miss Hania Routchine, a well-known singer who herself was the furthest thing from a Dada. She had been asked to sing "Clair de Lune" to calm the audience and end the demonstration on a soothing note. However, she had the misfortune of following the performance of Tzara's play—a riotous high point in the demonstration. Thus when, in the best tradition of the serious performer, she politely requested the crowd "to do her the honor of listening," she was greeted instead with raucous catcalls and jeers. Things had gone too far. Try as she might, she could not calm the now insane spectators; for the crazed public had, in the truest sense and to the everlasting glory of those who had masterminded the demonstration, become Dadas themselves.

Flushed with success, the Paris Dadas decided to stage a variation on this demonstration two months later at the Salle Gaveau, a much larger auditorium than the Théâtre de l'Oeuvre. Although there was no mention of Charlie Chaplin this time, the advance publicity for this demonstration, which was to take place on May 26, 1920, was just as ingenious: it promised "sodomistic music," the revelation of Dada's sex, and a chance to see the Dadas have their hair cut on stage. "Each of you," the publicity notice belligerently informed the public, "has an accountant, a watch, and a little package of shit in your heart."[121]

The actual proceedings of the Dada Festival were, for the most part, patterned closely upon what had become a successful formula: Breton and Soupault substituted another dramatic sketch, *You Will Forget Me*, for their earlier *If You Please*, and Tzara—not to be outdone—offered *The Second Celestial Adventure of Mr. Antipyrine*. One notable exception to this by now familiar format was the imaginative routine that Phillippe Soupault came up with. Calling himself "The Celebrated Illusionist," he appeared on stage in blackface wearing a huge white bathrobe and carrying a knife and a satchel. When he solemnly opened the satchel, he let loose five colored ballons, each of which was inscribed with a different name: Benoit XV, Rachilde, Clemenceau, Pétain, and Cocteau.[122] With a great flourish of his knife, Soupault ended his act by slicing the balloon with Cocteau's name on it in two.

As for the rest of the program, the sodomistic music was played by sixty musicians ceremoniously dressed, who included in their group six Dadas attired all in black with huge cylinders covering their heads, and Dada sex turned out to be a large white papier-mâché cylinder shaped like a phallus, resting on two balloons. But, alas, there was one thing missing: none of the Dadas had his hair cut.

On the whole, this long and often boring program indicated that the Dadas were running out of ideas and losing some of their enthusiasm for this kind of "provocation-demonstration." Despite this apparent loss of interest by the performers, the audience, which had come to the Salle Gaveau to get a taste of Dada, were as enthusiastic as ever. They were still in the process of throwing off the lethargy that had dogged their lives since the war. The Salle Gaveau, which, prior to the Dada Festival, had been the scene of piano and organ recitals of music by Bach and Mozart, was an ideal place for working out their remaining frustrations. Armed with all sorts of missiles—tomatoes, rotten eggs, oranges, coins, etc—they flocked to the great hall and, at any chance they got, shouted, screamed, hissed, booed, and fired volleys of fruit and vegetables at their antagonists. A few of the most enterprising ones even went so far as to heave chunks of beefsteak which they had conveniently purchased from a butcher next door. Filled with admiration for their resourcefulness, Tzara later boasted that "for the first time in the history of the world, people threw at us, not only eggs, salads and pennies, but beefsteaks as well."[123] Under the pressure of their confrontation with Tzara, Breton, and company, the public had thus once again proved that they too—deep down beneath the civilized veneer—were "extremely Dadaist."

But the only Dada who was able to match the public's enthusiasm was Tzara himself. With obvious relish, he had replaced his *First Adventure of Mr. Antipyrine* with a second exemplar. His erstwhile colleagues, however, were growing impatient with the monotony of the proceedings. Breton summed up the boredom they were beginning to feel when he noted that "each time a Dada demonstration is forecast—naturally by Tzara who doesn't tire of them—Picabia reassembles us in his dining-room and, one after another, we're supposed to have ideas for this demonstration. Finally, the harvest is not very abundant. The *pièce de résistance* will inevitably consist of the first, or the second, or the

umpteenth *Adventure of Mr. Anti-pyrine* by Tristan Tzara interpreted by his friends. . . ."[124]

During the period when all of these demonstrations were being
staged, the Parisian Dadas not only continued to publish their
favorite periodicals, but also put out a whole series of admittedly
short-lived new ones. Picabia's *391*, which after the first three
Paris issues was given the new name *Cannibal*, continued to express the spirit it had become notorious for in New York and Zurich. And two Paris issues of the periodical *Dada*, the first of
which, *Dada Bulletin*, has already been alluded to, and the second
of which was entitled *Dadaphone*, appeared. The May, 1920, issue of *Littérature* was also consecrated to Dada. It presented all
twenty-three of the manifestos which had been read at the demonstrations. In addition to these reviews, which had demonstrated
their staying power, a series of magazines and pamphlets—$D^d O^4 H^2$,
Lead Me There, Proverb, Z, Projector, etc.—popped to the surface,
then were seen no more.

Under the auspices of René Hilsum, an old friend of Breton's
who had set up a publishing house called Au Sans Pareil, the Parisian Dadas also published their writings in book form. Au Sans
Pareil put out two major series dealing with Dada: the first, "The
Littérature Collection," included *Rose of the Winds*, and *Bonfire*,
volumes of poetry by Soupault and Aragon respectively, *The
Magnetic Fields*, a collaboration between Breton and Soupault,
and *The Animals and Their Men the Men and Their Animals*, a
book of poetry by Eluard; the second series was called "The Dada
Collection" and featured Tzara's *Cinema Calendar of the Abstract
Heart* and the later works of Picabia *(Unique Eunuch, Jésus-Christ
Rastoquouère*, etc.).

The massive "provocation-demonstrations" and the steady
stream of magazines, pamphlets, and books made the year 1920
the climax of the Dada movement in Paris. Not surprisingly, this
was also the year in which the Paris group swelled its ranks with
new recruits. By this time, the Parisian Dadas had begun to fre-
quent the Café Certa, a curious bar located off the beaten path in
the Passage de l'Opéra, which became their official gathering
place. They not only hosted the visiting dignitaries from the international Dada movement—Duchamp, Ray, Ernst, Arp, and
Serner—at the Certa and its annex, Le Petit Grillon, but also
greeted the very young artists and writers who had come to Paris
to pay homage and join the movement. The first wave of these recruits included Jacques Rigaut, a sort of latter-day Vaché who was

obsessed with the idea of suicide,[125] and Drieu la Rochelle, a young friend of Aragon's who contributed to the Dada periodicals but remained on the periphery of the movement. A year or two later, a group of young writers who would span the period from Dada to Surrealism—Benjamin Péret, Pierre de Massot, René Crevel, Robert Desnos, Roger Vitrac, and Jacques Baron—also began to appear at the Café Certa.

After reaching its high point in Paris in 1920, the Dada movement began gradually to decline. The publicity the movement had received as a result of its notorious demonstrations and publications had made Dada what amounted to a household word. This had naturally taken much of the starch out of its scandalous connotations. Written about in the popular magazines, sung about in the music-halls, and talked about by the intelligentsia, Dada had quickly become the rage of Paris.[126] Moreover, a schism had begun to develop between Tzara, Picabia, and Breton. As the dominant personalities of the Paris group, these three men were charged with the responsibility of determining its future direction. But there was no agreement among them: Tzara favored continuing with more of the same ("provocation-demonstrations" which would keep the public in a constant state of exasperation); Picabia was against this program, but all he could offer in its place was the dictum that they must live for the moment; and Breton advocated abandoning the demonstrations because they had become too stereotyped, and opening the way for new ideas and activities.

This disagreement about means and ends, as well as the clash of temperaments of which it was a symptom, ushered in a period of internecine strife, which was aggravated by the fact that Breton and Aragon decided to take the initiative. The two editors of *Littérature* proposed a serious program of activity which—unlike the improvised events of old—would be carefully planned. According to Aragon, what they had in mind was an intellectual equivalent of the famous Reign of Terror of the French Revolution. Despite the fact that Dada had touched their lives, the *Littérature* group were thus still romantic enough to see their activities within the context of something as grandiose as the French Revolution.

Curiously enough, this great plan began with a series of guided tours of some of the famous monuments and places of interest which, in the words of the Dadas, "have no reason for existing."[127] The first excursion, which took place on April 14 at the Church of Saint Julien-le-Pauvre, was also the last: a driving rain, thick mud, and a series of monotonous speeches caused this event, which had been conceived for pleasant weather, to end in dismal failure. When it was finally over, the somewhat demoralized participants retired to their favorite haunt to plan their next move.

The new course of action that Breton and company decided upon was a mock trial of Maurice Barrès. Accusing the former "President of the League of Patriots" of "an offense against the security of the spirit," they decided to bring him before a mock tribunal to answer for his actions. Presumably, this trial, which took place on May 13, 1921, at the Salle des Sociétés Savantes with Barrès in absentia, was meant to be the first of a series of judgments against those writers who in the Dadas' opinion were traitors to their fellow men. They had chosen Barrès as their first victim not so much because of his past actions, but because he had retained his popularity and was still able to exercise a certain seductive power over the young. But Tzara, Picabia, and Ribemont-Dessaignes, who had never put their trust in Barrès and, therefore, had never felt betrayed by him could not share the abiding hatred of Breton and Aragon and could not fully grasp the rationale for these proceedings. When he realized that he could not talk Breton out of this scheme, Tzara—perhaps because he was still looking for a way to regain the initiative—decided to use this opportunity to reaffirm his conception of Dada.

Assuming the role of a witness, Tzara—sporting the monocle which he liked to wear on public occasions—appeared before Breton, who was the President of the Tribunal. The Rumanian began his testimony by stating that he had "no confidence in the process of justice even when administered by a Dada tribunal" and went on to say "that we are all nothing but a pack of fools, and that consequently the little differences—bigger fools or smaller fools—make no difference."[128] When Breton asked him if there was anyone whom he respected, Tzara answered with what had, by now, become his classic reply: "Well, I myself am really a charming fellow." This attitude so exasperated Breton that he charged the witness with being "an utter imbecile" and sternly asked him if he would like to be put away. Even this failed to dissuade Tzara, who continued to make jokes and obstruct the proceedings during the rest of his testimony.

Picabia, who had also scorned the idea of such a trial, went along with it initially, but this was only his way of registering his disapproval all the more dramatically: just before the high point in the proceedings—the appearance of Benjamin Péret as "the unknown soldier," a goose-stepping German officer wearing a gas mask over his face—Picabia stood up and walked out, never again to participate in a Dadaist demonstration.

About a month later, Picabia began the process of disassociating himself from Paris Dada. In an article written in June, 1921, he denounced Dada for having "a tribunal, and lawyers" and predicted that soon it would even have "police."[129] He went on to say: "I'm separating from certain Dadas because I'm being smothered by them, each day I'm becoming sadder, I'm terribly bored."[130] And he concluded that the true spirit of Dada had only existed for about three or four years when it was expressed by Duchamp and himself from 1912 on. Since 1918, it had, according to him, gradually been subverted by those who were Dada in name only. It was unmistakable who Picabia was referring to here: "I don't like illustrations," he noted bitterly, "and the directors of *Littérature* are only illustrators."[131]

Despite his turn against the *Littérature* group, Picabia, initially, remained on fairly good terms with Tzara, even going so far as to help him plan a large Dada exposition, Season 1921, which was designed to bring this turbulent year to an apt close. This exposition, which took place in June, 1921, at Jacques Hebertot's Montaigne Gallery in the Champs-Elysées, was of particular importance to Tzara, as a way of both regaining the initiative that he had lost to Breton and bringing at least the semblance of unity back to the movement. It was to consist of an exhibition of paintings, objects, and ready-mades, a Dadaist soirée, and a couple of afternoon lectures.

The exhibition, which began on June 6, was not restricted to artists alone; the poets also made contributions. Alongside of the creations of Arp, Ernst, and Ray were the "plastic works" of Tzara, Aragon, and Rigaut, among others. Preceded by the usual publicity and fanfare, the soirée took place on June 10, before a crowd of several hundred. The first part of the program featured another of Soupault's imaginative routines. This time he appeared as the dignified "President of the Republic of Liberia." Wearing a black jacket and red tie and followed by an entourage of Dadas, he passed inspection on the audience and the art works scattered all around him. Soupault's performance was followed by Aragon's Dadaist parody of Billy Sunday and his fire-and-brimstone sermons, Ribemont-Dessaignes's scatological poem "The Book of the Kings," and Péret's discordant reading of a manuscript by

Eluard. These routines were a prelude to Tzara's play, *The Gas Heart,* which was featured in the second part of the program. From its opening speech to its final lines, this performance (with Soupault playing "the Ear," Ribemont-Dessaignes, "the Mouth," Theodore Fraenkel, "the Nose," Aragon, "the Eye," Péret, "the Neck," and Tzara himself, "the Eyebrow,") caused a wild uproar.

Despite this response, which proved that the Dadas were still capable of provoking scandal, and which was instrumental in Hebertot's decision to cancel the two afternoon lectures, Tzara was unable to heal the growing rift in the movement. Breton gave a minimum of cooperation, but refused to actively participate in the exposition because of his resentment of Tzara and his essentially negative feelings about its anti-art tone. As far as Picabia' was concerned, he, too, helped organize the exposition, but also refused to take part on the grounds that it would have been inconsistent with his most recent attacks against Dada.

Relations between Picabia, Tzara, and Breton deteriorated still further after the exposition, as charges and countercharges flew back and forth. In July, 1921, Picabia published a supplement to *391,* bearing the exotic title "Pilhaou-Thibaou," in which, under the curious pseudonym of "Funny Guy," he continued to attack his former friends, even going so far as to belittle Tzara's role in the development of Zurich Dada. With all the sarcasm he could muster, Tzara replied that Picabia had "invented Dadaism in 1899, cubism in 1870, futurism in 1867 and impressionism in 1856."[132] Not to be outdone, Picabia later retorted that "the first mechanical work"[133] was created by Tzara's mother when she brought Tristan into the world.

These dissensions were further exacerbated in the early part of 1922 when Breton proposed an International Congress to determine the future direction of "the Modern Spirit." His rationale was that Cubism, Futurism, and Dada were not three distinct movements, but part of one great stream which needed to be charted and explored more deeply. To help him organize this Congress, Breton chose a group of established artists, writers, and musicians which included Robert Delaunay, Fernand Léger, Amédée Ozenfant, Jean Paulhan, Roger Vitrac, and Georges Auric.

When Breton first advanced the idea of his International Congress, Tzara's reply had been that "modernism doesn't interest me at all."[134] Assuming that this recalcitrance came from wounded pride, Breton offered to put him on one of the committees, but the Rumanian still refused to participate. As he explained to the future leader of Surrealism in a letter dated February 3, 1922, he was not doing this out of any personal pique, but because "I prefer to keep quiet rather than encourage an action that I consider detrimental to that *search for the new*, which I love so much, even when it takes the form of indifference."[135]

For some reason, Breton overreacted to Tzara's letter. On February 7, he sent a public communiqué to the magazine *Comoedia* in which, among other things, he referred to Tzara as "an impostor" interested only in publicity. Taken aback by what he rightly considered a slanderous attack upon him, Tzara answered this charge in an open letter to the same magazine, stating that a few days earlier, when he was invited to be on one of the committees of the Congress, he was not such an impostor.

Bitterly fought out in the press and in a public hearing at the Closerie des Lilas, the repercussions of this battle wrecked the Congress, shattered what was left of the friendship between Breton and Tzara, and split the Dadas into two hostile camps. The issue which ultimately created the most heat was the perennial question of whether Tzara was actually the inventor of the word Dada and the author of the manifesto of 1918.[136]

The events surrounding the Congress of Paris marked the climax of what Philippe Soupault has poignantly referred to as the "agony of friendships" and brought Paris Dada, at least as a coherent movement, to a close. By the spring of 1922, the participants in this seemingly endless infighting had reached a point where, drained of their energy, they could go no further. As Georges Ribemont-Dessaignes has said, Dada's death was not a pretty one. Now, except for a few scattered gestures and actions which took place under the banner of Dada, the great adventure that this movement had symbolized in Paris was finally over.

Tzara made what might be considered the last real attempt to revive Dada. In July, 1923, he organized the Evening of the Bearded Heart, a mixed bag of poems, dances, films, plays, etc., which included, among other things, "the Six" accompanied by Cocteau. The appearance of Cocteau, who remained the *bête noir* of the *Littérature* group, was enough to cause trouble.

Led by Breton—under whose direction they had slowly begun to reorganize—the members of the *Littérature* group arrived in the hall on July 6, the evening of the performance, determined to create some fireworks. Their chance came when Pierre de Massot stood up to recite a proclamation which contained some rather ambiguous remarks about Gide, Picasso, Picabia, and Duchamp. On the pretense of defending Picasso, Breton, Desnos, and Péret charged up onto the stage and demanded that De Massot leave. When he refused, Breton swung his cane at him, striking him on the left arm and breaking it. The stunned crowd, shaken by this gratuitous act of violence, started toward Breton. But before they could harm him, Tzara summoned the police, who were on hand to prevent just such an occurrence, and the three assailants were thrown out of the auditorium.

After the expulsion of Breton and his two companions, things returned pretty much to normal. Aside from some heckling by Eluard and Aragon, the program went along as scheduled, with a recital of Satie's "Pieces in the Form of a Pear," a reading of Apollinaire's "Hills," and the showing of some films by Man Ray and Hans Richter. But when it came time for Tzara's play, a repeat performance of *The Gas Heart,* there was more trouble. Eluard, who resented the fact that the play was being staged in a Cubist style and was on a program with so many "so-called modern" works, had sworn to sabotage it. Even before the curtain went up, he loudly demanded that Tzara come out and explain why he had expelled Breton. As Tzara made his appearance, Eluard leaped onto the stage and struck both Tzara and René Crevel, who was standing next to him—an action which brought the stage hands streaming out. In the ensuing mêlée, Eluard was roughed up and thrown into the scenery. To add insult to injury, he was later charged for damages.

But, taking all things into account, it was Tzara who was hurt the most. By summoning the authorities he had, ironically, made Picabia's earlier prediction—that Dada would some day have the police on its side—come true. This oversight, which Breton never let him forget, proved a tremendous blow to Tzara's prestige. Thus, instead of reviving Dada, he had given over the initiative to Breton and finally proved that Dada was dead.

Eighteen months after the Congress of Paris, Breton started upon the path that would ultimately lead him to Surrealism. Dada "like so many other things," he explained, "had been for some merely a way of sitting down"[137] and now he called for the young men of his generation to follow him beyond it:

> Leave everything. Leave Dada. Leave your wife. Leave your mistress. Leave your hopes and fears. Leave your children in the woods. Leave the substance for the shadow.

Leave your easy life, leave what you are given for the future. Set off on the roads.[138]

But some, who could not get over the death of Dada quite so easily, held back. Soupault, in particular, expressed the emptiness young men like himself, who had been faithful to Dada, now felt: "I was ready. I preferred calling myself Philippe Dada to Philippe Soupault. . . . It's all over now! I write novels, I publish books. I keep busy! And that's that!"[139] Others, such as Aragon and Eluard, followed Breton into the new world that was Surrealism, but that, as Tzara himself has said, "is the beginning of another story."[140]

Summary

By drawing some comparisons between its three most important phases in Zurich, Berlin, and Paris, we can retrace the basic lines of the Dada movement in Europe. Zurich Dada's greatest strength was its loosely organized structure, which at least in its early stages was flexible enough to allow for all types of individual creativity, but organized enough to make collective expression possible. With Paris Dada, this began to change. To a greater extent than in Zurich, the Dada movement in Paris developed along cohesive lines; its nihilism fit nicely with the postwar disillusionment of the general populace and, consequently, it achieved some of its greatest triumphs. But ultimately, Paris Dada seems to have lost that balance between the individual and the group which was so evident in Zurich, as well as much of its spontaneity. In Paris, the Dada movement often degenerated into a series of provocative but highly self-conscious actions and gestures.

One reason for this seems to have been the resounding popularity which the movement achieved. Once the initial shock wore off, the Parisians welcomed Dada with open arms; they talked about it, sang of it, and flocked to each new demonstration, eagerly in search of perpetual scandal. Under these conditions, it is not surprising that Dada soon became a kind of cult; for as Germaine Everling has wisely remarked, "a scandal which lasts is no longer a scandal."[141]

The one person who does not seem to have realized this, however, was the group's erstwhile leader, Tristan Tzara. Blinded perhaps by all the public attention he was getting, Tzara continued to advocate more of the same—bigger and better "provocation-demonstrations." It is interesting to note that even as late as the Dada Festival on May 26, 1920, Tzara was still obsessed with the idea of the massive demonstration. This becomes particularly clear if we compare Ribemont-Dessaignes's frank appraisal of the proceedings, where he admits that the Dadas were performing in a more and more self-conscious manner and losing interest in this type of demonstration, with Tzara's account, which seems to be oblivious that anything was wrong.[142]

Another essential difference between Zurich and Paris Dada centers on the idea of anti-art. As anarchistic as Zurich Dada became, it rarely approached the nihilistic paroxysm of Paris Dada. The preoccupations of the Zurich group were, for the most part, aesthetic; even their anarchy was expressed within the context of art and literature. Consider, for example, the following quote from Arp, which explains their actions:

> In Zurich in 1915, losing interest in the slaughter houses of the world war, we turned to the fine arts. While the thunder of the batteries rumbled in the distance, we pasted, we recited, we versified, we sang with all our soul. We searched for an elementary art that would, we thought, save mankind from the furious folly of these times. We aspired to a new order that might restore the balance between heaven and hell.[143]

Richter echoed this sentiment when he stated that, above all, "we wanted to stay human!"[144] It is hard to imagine one of the Paris Dadas explaining his actions either in such aesthetic or humanistic terms.

Neither their self-conscious activities nor their anti-art attitudes, however, can fully account for the spirit of the Paris Dadas. Without taking into account the *joi de vivre* which characterized so much of the communal life of these young men, it is virtually impossible to understand Paris Dada. Instead of leading to suicide, as one might have expected, their "cult of negative values" paradoxically resulted in a greater feeling for life. Addressing himself to this curious phenomenon, Noel Arnaud has noted that "the Dadaists had reversed Tolstoi's famous dictum: 'Art is not a joy, a pleasure, an amusement: art is a great thing' so that it read 'Art is not a great thing unless it is joy, pleasure, amusement.'"[145] Or, as Eluard put it:

For us, everything is an occasion to have a good time. When we laugh, we empty ourselves and the wind passes through us, rattling doors and windows, introducing into us the night of the wind. . . . We need distractions. We remain what we are or what we will be. We need a free, empty body, we need to laugh and nothing else.[146]

In attacking the traditional patterns of art and life, the Paris Dadas were, at the same time, able to express a wide range of new-found freedoms. Thus, they struck out not only against the horrors of war, but also against the boredom which was at its opposite pole. And, as Soupault has noted, they felt free for the first time:

. . . Those who in early youth were witnesses of nothing but death and destruction, those who survived that cataclysm of stupidity (which seemed as if it would never end) turned with a kind of fever toward life. My generation wanted to be *alive* at all costs. . . . We wanted to love life—with which we had good reason to be disgusted. And we did love it. The greatest evil was to be dead. We could always distinguish among persons we knew, by saying that so and so was 'alive,' but so and so was 'dead.'[147]

Eluard expressed this same sentiment in a poem:

I have had a useless face for a long time,
But now
I have a face to be loved
I have a face to be happy[148]

What made this *joi de vivre* all the more vital was that it was part of a genuine communal spirit. In a very real sense, these young men were able to banish the boredom which dogged their lives and find a reason for living in their communal existence. Perhaps it was an outsider, Matthew Josephson, who, in his book *Life Among the Surrealists*, best summed up the values of this kind of existence. Comparing them with the Franciscans or the Jesuits, Josephson contrasted the "warm spirit of comradship" of the Dadas with the feelings he had found among his fellow American artists:

Whereas, in contrast, a gathering of avant-garde American writers and painters would have found everyone talking at cross-purposes, these men were in full accord in opposing the same stupidities, assailing the arrivistes of the arts as with one voice, and expressing a common enthusiasm for the program of action and intrigue by which they would spread confusion and disorder.[149]

Although the Berlin Dadas were not as political as one might suppose, their involvement with social and political questions tends to set them apart from the Zurich and Paris Dadas. Thus, while these groups were preoccupied with artistic freedoms, the members of the Club Dada were trying to demonstrate their solidarity with the working classes who had been exploited by the ruling powers in Germany. But, being Dadas first and politicians second, the Berlin Group could never have expressed their ideas in a doctrinaire manner. As Grosz has pointed out, their definition of Dada left no room for doctrine. "Nothing was holy to us," he wrote. "Our movement was neither mystical, communistic nor anarchistic. All of these movements had some sort of program, but ours was completely nihilistic. We spat upon everything, including ourselves. Our symbol was nothingness, a vacuum, a void."[150] Echoing Grosz's words, Mehring has declared that in the Dadas' eyes there were only two types of people: "the Dadaist, who saw how funny the madhouse was" and "the solid mass of paranoid idiots who thought themselves normal."[151] Mehring concluded that "the Dadaist transposed everything he heard, whether in verse, in official prose, in stock-exchange quotations, in addresses from pulpits and platforms, into: 'Dada-dada-dada . . . blablablah.' "[152]

The Zurich Dadas were never faced with the kind of dire social and political conditions of their Berlin counterparts but it is surprising, considering the fact that they lived in a city thick with revolutionaries and spies, that they had so little actual involvement with politics. Lenin and his wife Kroupskaya were living right across from the Cabaret Voltaire, and Janco recalled that he often recognized Lenin's "impressive mongol features" looming up out of the thick smoke amid the incredible din of the Cabaret.[153] In addition, Richter noted that he saw Lenin several times in a nearby library and remembered that Radek and Zinoviev also lived in the vicinity of the Cabaret. He commented, in passing, that the Swiss authorities were more suspicious of the Dadas than they were of these quiet, studious, but authentic social revolutionaries.[154]

Ball also called attention to Lenin in an entry in his diary dated June 7, 1917. He commented that Lenin lived across from the Cabaret and mused that "while we opened our gallery in the Bahnhofstrasse, the Russians went off to St. Petersburg to get the revolution going."[155]

An important clue to the Zurich Dadas' lack of political involvement comes from Ball's discussion of Lenin and the Revolution. Commenting on this in his diary, he asked if Dada was not the counterpart of Bolshevism, expressed on a different level in a different way. This was an indication that, for Ball and his colleagues, Zurich Dada's moral, poetic, and spiritual revolution took the place of, and satisfied any need for, a social revolution. Thus, when Lenin was mysteriously traveling from Switzerland to Russia in a sealed train to ignite the spark that would set off the Revolution, the Dadas, intent upon giving the public all that it had bargained for and more, were involved in one of their notorious soirées, in this case devoted to "New Art" and featuring "Cold Light," a simultaneous poem by Tzara to be read by seven people.

What was true of the Zurich Dadas was even more true of their Paris colleagues. Despite their revulsion toward the war and their hatred for bourgeois society, the Paris Dadas took no part in the various attempts to bring the war to a halt or to overthrow the system which had brought it about. As Breton later explained, he and his compatriots had little, if any, social conscience, at this time.[156] And it was not until the advent of Surrealism that this posture began to change. Until that time, the Paris movement developed along the distinctly apolitical lines laid down by Tzara.

Here were new subjects waiting
to be described, machinery, mas-
sacre, skyscrapers, urinals, homo-
sexuality, revolution—for Dada
nothing could be too common-
place or novel, too cruel or shock-
ing, to be celebrated by the writer
in his own fashion.

MALCOLM COWLEY

Disgusted with the role that art and literature had played during the war, the Zurich Dadas began by wholeheartedly denouncing all the traditional forms of written poetry. "It seemed to us," Tzara later stated, "that the world was losing itself in idle babbling, that literature and art had become institutions located on the margin of life, that instead of serving man they had become instruments of an outmoded society. They served the war and, all the while expressing fine senti-ments, they lent their prestige to atrocious inequality, sentimental misery, injustice and degradation of the instincts."[1]

Hugo Ball

Guided by Hugo Ball, whose stated intention was "to re-nounce the language devastated and made impossible by journal-ism," [2] the members of the Cabaret Voltaire experimented with various techniques, some borrowed from the Cubists and Futurists (simultaneous poetry, bruitism, etc.), others more or less their own inventions (free association and polyglot poetry), inspired by the crazy-quilt of languages they spoke.

That the Zurich Dadas placed an especially high value on their simultaneous poetry is evidenced by Ball's comments. In an entry in his diary, dated November 30, 1916, Ball defined the simulta-neous poem as "a contrapuntal recitative in which three or more voices speak, sing, whistle, etc., simultaneously, in such a way that the resulting combinations account for the total effect of the work, elegiac, funny or bizarre." [3] He went on to say that it "car-ries the message that mankind is swallowed up in a mechanistic process. In a generalized and compressed form, it represents the battle of the human voice against a world which menaces, en-snares and finally destroys it, a world whose rhythm and whose din are inescapable." [4]

Expressing a desire for poems which would "discard language as painting had discarded the object," [5] Ball also inspired the Zu-rich Dadas to explore ways of going beyond the idea of words alto-gether. This resulted in the *Lautgedicht* or sound poem.

While Ball and his colleagues did not invent the idea of sound poetry,[6] they were the first ones to give it a public performance. Some idea of the nature of these performances can be gleaned from a discussion of Ball's famous "O Gadji Beri Bimba" recital, which took place at the Dada Gallery sometime in 1917. With Marcel Janco's assistance, Ball had fashioned himself a costume for the occasion which made him look like some kind of Cubist High Priest; he was decked out in a tall, cylindrical blue-and-white hat and a gigantic cardboard collar, which was scarlet on the inside and gold without, and which was attached to his body in such a way that when he flexed his elbows it flapped like wings. To complete this incongruous picture, his hips and torso were wrapped in shiny blue cylinders, which made him look more like an obelisk than a man. Tightly encased in these curious paraphernalia, Ball was hardly able to move a step. He even had to be carried on to the stage by his friends during a blackout. As the lights came back up, he began reciting his weird litany:

> gadji beri bimba
> glandridi lauli lonni cadori
> gadjama bim beri glassala
> glandridi glassala tuffm i zimbrabrim, . . .[7]

Imagine the shock and astonishment of an audience confronted by this strangely garbed, priestlike creature and his mysterious language. While the spectators' surprise soon gave way to hysterical laughter and wild applause, Ball—unable to move even if he had wanted to—somehow managed to retain his composure. Without pausing, he continued to recite his sound poems, punctuating their most rhythmic passages with the flapping of his collar.

Just as he began to realize that his poetry could not match the spectacle of his costume, an amazing thing happened. As Ball himself later described it in his diary, "I noticed that my voice, which had no other way out, was taking on the age-old cadence of priestly lamentation, the liturgical chanting that wails through all the Catholic churches of East and West."[8] Continuing with this lament until the end of the performance, Ball virtually hypnotized the audience with his incantatory verse.

This experience was a traumatic one for Ball even more than for his audience. In a very real sense, it was his epiphany: the culmination of a long-lasting desire to "return to the deepest alchemy of the Word."[9] Commenting on the poetic experiments of the Zurich Dadas, Ball wrote that "we have charged the word with forces and energies which made it possible for us to rediscover the evangelical concept of the 'word' (logos) as a magical complex of images."[10] The most vibrant expression of this was his own inspired performance at the Dada Gallery in which he was able, for a fleeting moment, to realize his exalted intentions.

As a result of his shattering ordeal, Ball suffered a nervous collapse and was forced to leave Zurich for the second and last time. His departure, which was a serious step for him as an individual, was also, it seems, a crucial one for the Dada movement. It brought an end to his sense of "constructive anarchy" which, despite the chaos prevailing in much of their activity, had kept the Zurich group moving in a "positive" direction. A dramatic sign of this was the unmistakable presence of the three most significant spokesmen of modern art—Kandinsky, Marinetti, and Apollinaire—whose aura presided over even the most derisive gestures of the group, and whose ideas and creations, given a prominent place in their demonstrations and journals, became the model for many of the Zurich experiments.

Underscoring this even further was the tone of religious mysticism which apparently held sway during this early period. The most turbulent experiments were carried out within this atmosphere, and even someone like Huelsenbeck, who claimed to be antireligious, found, in retrospect, that the poetry he wrote during this time had acquired religious overtones.[11]

Tristan Tzara

All of this began to change drastically, however, when Tzara—driven by the madness of the war into a frenzy of nihilism—took over the movement. His intentions were vividly expressed in his celebrated "Dada Manifesto of 1918." In addition to setting forth many of the ideas that were to preoccupy the Dadas for the next five years, this work beautifully illustrates Tzara's distinctive style.

Breaking with Cubism and Futurism, and declaring a desire to be liberated from all schools of modern art, Tzara lashed out at those artists who had sold their souls for material security. "Is the aim of art to make money," he sarcastically asked, "and cajole the nice nice bourgeois? Rhymes ring with the assonance of the currencies and the inflexion slips along the line of the belly in profile. All groups of artists have arrived at this trust company after riding their steeds on various comets. While the door remains open to the possibility of wallowing in cushions and good things to eat."[12]

"I am against systems, the most acceptable system is on principle to have none,"[13] Tzara went on to say; and, like some kind of avenging angel, he trumpeted a modern apocalypse:

> Let each man proclaim: there is a great negative work of destruction to be accomplished. We must sweep and clean. Affirm the cleanliness of the individual after the state of madness, aggressive complete madness of a world abandoned to the hands of bandits, who rend one another and destroy the centuries. Without aim or design, without organization: indomitable madness, decomposition. Those who are strong in words or force will survive, for they are

quick in defense, the agility of limbs and sentiments flames on their faceted flanks.[14]

In the name of an "absolute spontaneity," Tzara wildly challenged his followers to brush aside the very foundations of society—morality, art, religion, and the family—and destroy every last trace of history:

> Every product of disgust capable of becoming a negation of the family is Dada; a protest with the fists of its whole being engaged in destructive action: *Dada; knowledge of all the means rejected up until now by the shamefaced sex of comfortable compromise and good manners: Dada; abolition of logic, which is the dance of those impotent to create: Dada; of every social hierarchy and equation set up for the sake of values by our valets: Dada; every object, all objects, sentiments, obscurities, apparitions and the precise clash of parallel lines are weapons for the fight: Dada; abolition of memory: Dada; abolition of archaeology: Dada; abolition of prophets: Dada; abolition of the future: Dada; absolute and unquestionable faith in every god that is the immediate product of spontaneity.*[15]

Tzara's faith in the gratuitous and the spontaneous can, for the most part, be traced to his involvement with primitive art and poetry. Seeking a viable alternative to a civilization which had proved unworthy of his allegiance, Tzara, like so many of his Zurich companions, immersed himself in the primitive with its promises of new insights into the meaning of life. Not only was he one of the prime movers of their African Evenings, but he also wrote articles comparing primitive and Western art and published more than forty African poems between 1917 and 1918.

These articles and poems attest to Tzara's fascination with primitive spontaneity and provide an indication of how it would change his life. One article, "Note 6 on Negro Art"—the first written discussion of primitive art by a Zurich Dada—which appeared in the September-October issue of *Sic* in 1917, even contained the germ of Tzara's famous phrase: "Thought is made in the mouth."[16] Commenting on the mysterious, irrational power of primitive poetry, he noted that "the mouth contains obscure power, invisible substance, goodness, fear, wisdom, creation, fire." [17] And in a note that was published for the first time in

Dada II in 1917, he compared the Renaissance with certain more "primitive" periods, concluding "We want to continue the tradition of Negro, Egyptian, and Byzantine art and destroy the atavistic sensibility"[18] of Western civilization.

Aware that what he called its "atavistic sensibility" went deeper than its art and literature, Tzara attacked the basic concepts of his society—"language as the agent of communication between individuals, logic as the cement." "Everything collapses with logic," [19] he stated. Elaborating on this, he proclaimed in the manifesto of 1918:

> What we need is works that are strong straight precise and forever beyond understanding. Logic is a complication. Logic is always wrong. It draws the threads of notions, words, in their formal exterior, toward illusory ends and centers. Its chains kill, it is an enormous centipede stifling independence. Married to logic, art would live in incest, swallowing, engulfing its own tail, still part of its own body, fornicating within itself, and passion would become a nightmare tarred with protestantism, a monument, a heap of ponderous gray entrails.[20]

In place of the static rewards of logic, he offered, for those who were willing to follow him into the abyss, "continuous movement, perpetual change, a headlong flight of time."[21]

Having some idea of the underlying motivations behind his actions, we should now turn to one of the most important weapons in Tzara's all-out campaign against logic and rationality: his early poetry. Created perhaps as a practical demonstration of the "great negative work of destruction" he had proclaimed, these poems vividly illustrated Tzara's "Trojan horse theory": they were designed, like so many of Dada's written and plastic expressions, as a way of infiltrating behind the enemy's lines and destroying his most cherished conventions—the traditional structures of art and literature. "Dada opposed everything that was literature," Tzara later explained, "but in order to demolish its foundations we employed the most insidious weapons, the very elements of the literature and art we were attacking."[22]

Reacting against the idea of traditional poetry, Tzara wrote poems which blatantly disregarded syntax and pushed "the dislocation of language" almost to a point of no return. Consider, for example, the following excerpt from his "The Leprous White

Giant of the Landscape" which provides an indication of how far
he was prepared to go in eliminating the traditional elements of
poetry:

the salt gathers in constellation of birds on the tumor of
/ wadding
in its lungs the asteria and bugs swinging back and forth
the microbes crystallizing in palm-trees of muscles
/ see-saws
hello without cigarette tzantzantza ganga
bouzdouc zdouc nfounfa mabaath mbaah nfounfa[23]

The question is what, if anything, remains after Tzara has
stripped away all of the traditional poetic elements? There is a
structure in these early poems, albeit a loosely organized one,
closer to that of a highly abstract film, in which words and images pass before our eyes in a rapid, fleeting, discontinuous way,
than to that of traditional poetry. An excerpt from another of
Tzara's early poems "Cinema Calendar of the Abstract Heart,"
whose title even suggests its kinship with cinema, illustrates this
kaleidoscopic quality even more vividly:

wind desire cellar sonorous of insomnia tempest temple
the fall of the water
and the sudden leap of the vowels
in the looks which fix the points of the abysses
to come to surpass lived to conceive
call the human body light like matches
in all the fires of autumn vibrations and trees
petroleum sweat[24]

Extending the structural analogy between Tzara's poetry and
the cinema, we note a striking similarity between what Eisenstein
called "montage" and the dynamic clash of elements that derives
from Tzara's juxtapositions of unrelated words, verbal collages,
free associations, and "inane sonority." In his attempts to capture
the simultaneity of "inner speech" in his films and his theoretical
writings, Eisenstein explored an idea of montage which was based
upon the "collision" of images. His description of the way in
which this form of montage functions vividly calls to mind the
explosive atmosphere of Tzara's Dada poetry. "If montage must
be compared with something," Eisenstein proposed, "then a pha-
lanx of montage-pieces, 'shots,' should be compared to the series of

explosions of an internal combustion engine, multiplying themselves into montage dynamics and thereby serving as 'impulses' to drive along a tearing motor car or tractor."[25] Where Eisenstein and Tzara differ, of course, despite the similarity of their approaches, is in their intentions. While Tzara envisioned his dynamic method as part of a trojan horse to destroy traditional poetry, Eisenstein saw his as a way of "molding the feeling and intelligence of the masses." [26]

The analogy with cinema also holds true for the poetry of Clément Pansaers, the ill-fated Belgian poet,[27] whose poems are characterized by the same disjointed structure, drumlike rhythms, unexpected associations, and startling revelations as Tzara's. In a poem like Pansaers's "The Pan Pan on the Ass of the Nude Negro," for example, the elements seem to dissolve and recrystallize before our eyes like the images of a film. That Pansaers was himself aware of this analogy is evidenced by one section of this poem in particular, which is designed in the form of an early movie screen, complete with the kind of upper and lower case lettering that we associate with silent movie titles.[28]

Punctuated by a steady, incessant beat, "The Pan Pan on the Ass of the Nude Negro," as its title implies, illustrates that Pansaers, like Tzara, was fascinated with primitive experiences. Some idea of how he makes use of primitive rhythms in this poem can be derived from its concluding section:

> Zero is the smallpox.
> Burn an O in the flag:
> breathe the magnetism of rags,
> consummation in concentric circles
> bare cubical of the round table
> Pan-pan!
> Fin-fin
> Pan-pan
> Finale!
> Pan-pan
> o i u a
> pan pan
> Da capo
> Bê
> Pan-pan—Pan-pan
> Pan-pan
> FIN![29]

This primitive tone, characteristic of the poetry of both Pansaers and Tzara, seems to derive from their mutual attempts to
destroy traditional language, undermine its hierarchy of values,
and put an end to the resultant conventional forms of order. No
longer the center of the universe, man is forced, in these poems,
to compete with what Michel Leiris has called "the unlimited
bric-a-brac of things." [30] Like the primitives, these poets have
made a kind of magical pact with nature. Everything in their poetry, whether animal, vegetable, or mineral, speaks with its own
voice, and the words which pour forth from these strange voices
must be valued for their own particular resonance and color
rather than their ability to signify or symbolize.

Carrying the previous analogy with cinema one step further,
the words in these poems, delivered from the burden of denota-
tion and connotation, stand out in the same unexpected way as
inanimate objects do on film. Tzara himself commented on this
quality in an important article entitled "Note on Poetry," which
was published in *Dada* IV–V in 1919. Advocating that the poet
should "give each element its integrity and autonomy, a necessary
condition in the creation of new constellations," [31] he went on to
say, "I give the same importance to a crocodile, as to an active
mineral [*sic*], as to an herb. Eye, water, balance, sun, kilometer
and everything else that I can conceive together and that represents a value capable of becoming human: *the sensibility.* The
elements love to be so intimately pressed together, truly inter-
woven like the hemispheres of the brain and transatlantic com-
partments."[32]

From this pataphysical declaration of the equivalence of things
it was but a short step to Tzara's attempts to relinquish all conscious control in his poetry. While chance associations often account for the audacious imagery of a poem like "Cinema Calendar of the Abstract Heart," there is always the feeling that there
is a conscious mind somewhere in the background. But, beginning
with his notorious formula for making Dada poetry, Tzara did his
best to change this:

> To make a dadaist poem.
> Take a newspaper.
> Take a pair of scissors.
> Choose an article as long as you are planning to make
> your poem.
> Cut out the article.

Then cut out each of the words that make up this article
and put them in a bag.
Shake it gently.
Then take out the scraps one after the other in the order
in which they left the bag.
Copy conscientiously.
The poem will be like you.
And here you are a writer, infinitely original and endowed
with a sensibility that is charming though beyond the
understanding of the vulgar.[33]

With the "newspaper clipping" poems he created by this method, Tzara did away with conscious control and turned himself into a kind of medium for man's most irrational impulses. But, regardless of his intentions, he created some significant poetry before he reached this final impasse. As his old friend Richter has concluded, "despite the Biblical wrath of his denunciations of Art . . . he could not help furthering the cause of art. Poems as exquisite as freshly-picked flowers poured from lips dedicated to the cause of Dada."[34]

Tzara's amazing ability to distill poetry out of the Dada spirit is, above all, reflected in his poem "Maison Flake":

unlatch bugles the announcement vast and hyaline animals
    of the maritime service
aerostatic ranger all that is strides galloping clarity life
the angel with white hips umbrella virility
snow licks the road and the lily verifies virgin
3/25 altitude a new meridian passes here
stretched bow of my heart typewriter for the stars
who told you 'chopped foam of prodigious clock-blues'
offers you a word not found in Larousse
that wants its full growth

what steam from a lightning-tube pushes
ours against the eternal and multiform veil
here one does not murder men on terraces
that take the hue of an intimate succession of sluggishnesses
we try unheard-of-things
mirages quarto micrographies of chromatic souls and images
we carry around all jingle-bell tumults that we stir up
for the major holidays on the viaducts and for the animals

whirl of an octavo dance on meteor and violin
the play of glasses year that passes
drink a bumper I'm the crazy brother
skyey ink hydromel lake
of the opaque wine flake in hammock
practices the calm and fecund offertory
it scrapes the sky with its nails
and the skyscraper is but its shadow
in a bathrobe
the year shall be among the palm and the banana tree spurted
    from the halo in water cubes
simple productive vast music surging safely
and the crimson bread for the future and multiple season
of old engravings of kings at the hunt prettily colored
pipe and box in the vase under the ace of spades piddler with
the birds and the cool clouds a vigilant boat in the beak
of the rock motor with sparks of good news the eiffel tower
    is playing the rebeck
here each chair is soft and comfortable as an archbishop
ascetic enterprise guaranteed monks at all figures—this
    way, ladies—maison flake[35]

On first impression, this poem, like so many of Tzara's works, seems to be little more than a jumble of discordant words and images. But if one is willing to make the necessary connections, a new conception of life—like Plato's universe—gradually begins to emerge out of this seeming chaos. Out of the Futuristic trappings of modern civilization—the "typewriter," "skyscraper," and the "viaducts"—the image of a Dadaist paradise, where the imagination is as free as it should be, is born.

In this special kind of paradise, "one does not murder men on terraces/that take the hue of an intimate succession of sluggishnesses." This is a place where "we try unheard-of-things/mirages quarto micrographies of chromatic souls and images/we carry around all jingle-bell tumults that we stir up/for the major holidays on the viaducts and for the animals." And finally, in Maison Flake "each chair is soft and comfortable as an archbishop/ascetic enterprise guaranteed monks at all figures—this way, ladies—maison flake." Yes, ladies, here is Maison Flake: a phantasmagoric land in which, as in Jarry's "supplementary universe," the imagination reigns supreme and one is free to do what one wishes.

There are no rules here where any word can give birth to any other. What better symbol of the Dadas' unending search for absolute freedom can be found than Maison Flake? It is the perfect embodiment of Dada's dream kingdom; a realm where, in Arp's words, "every Dadaist can sing and say anything he likes without the risk of being hanged." [36]

Francis Picabia

Although Picabia's reputation is based upon the iconoclastic "object portraits," machine drawings, and "ready-mades" with which he confronted the fashionable art world, we must give some consideration to his decidedly antiliterary poetic experiments. Like those of Tzara, these experiments, which began as variations upon the "words in liberty" of Apollinaire and the Futurists, were designed to undermine the idea of logic and rationality. As we have seen, Picabia had begun writing this kind of poetry while he was living in New York and Barcelona and had even gone so far as to publish some of his poems, first in *391,* then in a volume entitled *Fifty-Two Mirrors.* But, until he moved to Switzerland, he continued to devote most of his energies to the plastic arts and wrote poems only in the intervals between paintings. In Switzerland this situation began to change. Forced to remain in the hospital while recuperating from a severe attack of neurasthenia, Picabia passed the time writing poetry. The fruit of his efforts was a book of poetry entitled *Poems and Designs of the Daughter Born without a Mother* (1918).

Either out of gratefulness for their efforts on his behalf or simply as an ironic gesture, Picabia dedicated this book to neurologists the world over, three of whom—Drs. Collins in New York, Dupré in Paris, and Brunnschweiller in Lausanne—had helped him find relief from his neurasthenia. This dedication for a book with such an unusual title was bound to cause no end of complications for the Swiss medical profession who might, at first, have thought that it was a treatise by a Spanish doctor named Picabia on what was indeed a controversial case: a conception without a mother. But, as these doctors would perhaps have realized from the book's mechanical illustrations, the "daughter born without a mother" in its title was merely an allusion to a machine, an almost obsessive preoccupation of Picabia's at this time.

Even though they were characterized by many of the same pessimistic sentiments, the poems in this volume are structurally very different from Picabia's earlier poetry. They demonstrate an almost desperate desire to break out of the traditional mold of language. In a poem such as "Void," for example, words and images are freed of almost every logical constraint:

> Two directions, contrary to all tongues,
> for the phantoms empty the abstractions
> and develop perfect forms
> in the wonder of an egg shell.
> As one sees it by the human word,
> under the influence of actual life,
> the internal exhaustion of the heart
> supervenes from without.
> It is the continual movement
> separating God, who hides,
> from the will of men.
> Three gray rays imply
> that the atmosphere of putrefaction
> reigns on the diseased Earth,
> suffering of a spiritual nature.[37]

This tendency grew even more marked in Picabia's later poetry, beginning with *Poetry Ron-Ron* (1919), the last of his books of poems published in Switzerland. In a note accompanying this volume, which is actually one long, meandering poem, Picabia underscores its discontinuous structure and, at the same time, warns the reader about what to expect when writing that "this poetry has neither beginning nor end, imagine that it has no cover and that it is bound with copper rings."[38]

Despite this ironic warning, *Poetry Ron-Ron*'s string of undivided, unsubordinated, and unstructured images, seemingly held together by the poet's voice alone, must have come as a shock even to the most advanced lover of poetry. The brittle, absurd tone of the poem was foreshadowed in the curious Picabian proverb which preceded the actual text: "Fashion is a dead leaf."[39]

Having prepared the reader for almost any kind of surprise, Picabia starts his poem off on a rather surprising note of intimacy:

> Love me I permit it
> That will be great happiness for you
> Love my poems that caress
> your delicious body

that perfume your brain
in singing the impure union
of useless works[40]

Thus dispensing with the amenities, Picabia embarks upon a miraculous journey in which the idea of "words in liberty" ultimately gives way to what might be called "thoughts in liberty." Consider, for example, a typical excerpt from the poem:

novio of the unheard vehicle of the mass
comic
nightmare visions of chocolate haciendas
in the rain
skirts hold back the night by pale clouds
it must not
Jesus
like the Spanish alcalde-like companion
all saddled
the earth is a box
whose bottom is rotten
all men are abominable coffins
whose odor
has neither action
nor thought[41]

With his poetry coming more and more to resemble Tzara's "words in a hat," Picabia moved to Paris in March, 1919. Soon after arriving in that city, the prolific Spaniard published another volume of poems, most appropriately entitled *Thoughts Without Language.* These poems, largely a continuation of the experimentation begun in *Poetry Ron-Ron,* have the distinction of being the first overt expression of the Dada spirit in Paris.[42] For those who remained unconvinced of the value of this exploration, Picabia gave the following bit of sober advice: "To all those who itch with the desire to say that this language is without thought I recommend a dangerous visit to the zoological garden." [43]

After devoting his energies primarily to painting for more than a year, Picabia published another book of poetry, *Unique Eunuch,* which was far and away his most radical experiment. In typical Dada fashion, he dedicated this work to his best friend, without bothering to say who it was. But this *blague* could not hide the essential seriousness with which Picabia viewed *Unique Eunuch,* a seriousness which was, above all, underscored by a quote from

Pascal that appeared in the preface. Actually, the book had two prefaces: one by Tzara, which praised Picabia for his ability "to live without pretension" and "dance on the teeth of telegraph wire,"[44] and a second one from Pascal, which called attention to the dangers inherent not only in what we say, but how we say it.[45]

Picabia went on to underscore the spirit of *Unique Eunuch* still further by including three epigrams in this preface: the first was Oscar Wilde's statement that "authority is as destructive for those who exercise it as for those upon whom it is exercised";[46] the second was Nietzsche's question as to how, if man makes an action precious, an action can make man precious; and, the third and final epigram was Picabia's own synthesis of the first two— "all conviction is a sickness.[47]

The passage from Pascal and the three epigrams, taken together, function as a kind of apology for Picabia's experiments with absolute spontaneity. An important aspect of his refusal to be committed was a desire—like Tzara's—to relinquish all conscious control in his poetry. *Unique Eunuch* is perhaps the most clearcut example of this urge; it is a poem in which every trace of conscious creation—including the poet's voice—has been eliminated. What remains is a seemingly endless succession of images which meet each other only by chance encounter. One can illustrate this by quoting at random from anywhere in the poem. The first few lines are as representative as any other:

> Try the actual hour
> In the alphabet chase guarded
> Of the shadow slowly
> Truly books sterling
> Under virginal louis cou cou[48]

Thus, Picabia had arrived at a point similar to Tzara's in his "press clipping" poems. He had succeeded in completely undermining the basic conventions of traditional poetry and, in the process, had removed all possibility of conscious choice on the part of the poet, leaving in its place a cluster of images whose meaning and value had to be determined by the individual reader.

What, we might now ask—having reached the same impasse as with Tzara—is the value of Picabia's poetic experiments? Should his poems be dismissed as merely the perverse, negative, and,

above all, destructive outpourings of an antiliterary sensibility? Or
is there, in retrospect, more to them than that? We have noted that
Tzara, despite his avowedly antiliterary stance, created real poetry. The same may be said, albeit for a different reason, of Picabia.

Picabia's poetry illustrates one of the most important Dada
tendencies: what Tzara later referred to as "the confusion of
genres."[49] Elaborating upon this, Tzara wrote that this confusion
of genres developed out of the Dadas' desire to give "some play to
Art, to this rigid edifice, taken also as play, to this mongrel notion
used to cover, behind a sham disinterestedness, the lies and hypoc-
risy of society."[50]

By introducing his painter's sensibility into his poems, Picabia
was able to give a new plasticity to language. Alluding to the
ever-changing ebb and flow of this language, his former wife
Gabrielle has said that "words have none of that closed, absolute
sense of the dictionary for Picabia."[51] "His poems," she continued, "are a succession of very simple images that one must 'look
at,' as, on a trip, one looks at the scenery file past, without
searching for an innuendo or an interpretation. . . ."[52] As Gabrielle Buffet-Picabia implies, these poems are neither hermetic nor
complex in any real sense, but, as a result of their haunting,
indefinable plasticity, they leave us with the feeling that Picabia
has somehow managed to transcend the realm of thought altogether.

Francis Picabia was a man who could not stay in one place
—either geographically or aesthetically—for very long. Thus
it is not surprising that, once he had perfected his technique of
"automatic writing" in *Unique Eunuch*, he was ready to move on
to new challenges. This ultimately meant disassociating himself
from the Dada movement; but before we conclude this discussion
of his work there is one other of his writings—*Jésus-Christ
Rastaquouère*—we must comment upon.

Published in July, 1920, *Jésus-Christ Rastaquouère*, which, like
Jarry's *Exploits and Opinions of Dr. Faustroll Pataphysician*, is a
summary of its author's most significant thoughts and ideas, is
considered by many to be Picabia's most important literary work.
Ironically enough for someone like Picabia, who is reputed to
have read little or no philosophy, it is a kind of philosophical
treatise, albeit one with a distinctly Dadaist tone.

The title, which apparently was chosen both for its shock value
and its ability to evoke an image of absolute freedom, provides a

clue to the unusual nature of the book, as well as to its author's intentions. "The Rastaquouère," Gabrielle Buffet-Picabia informs the reader in the introduction, "is possessed with the desire to eat diamonds. He is the owner of several motley costumes and naïve sentiments; he is simple and tender; he juggles with all the objects which come into his hands; he does not know how to help himself; he only wants to juggle—he has learned nothing but he invents."[53]

Combining this with the dictionary description—"foreign nobleman of doubtful antecedent"[54]—we get a picture of a man who embodies Picabia's nomad philosophy perfectly: "One must pass through life, red or blue, completely nude, with the subtle music of a fisher, ever ready for the celebration."

So many diverse and remarkable things are woven into the texture of *Jésus-Christ Rastaquouère* that it is virtually impossible to do it justice. This is especially true since Picabia has provided the book with no single line of development or logical structure. With little or no transition, seemingly serious philosophical questionings trail off into pithy, absurd little sayings which, in turn, are followed by soaring lyrical passages; and these are transformed into the wildest, most pataphysical speculations.

There are, for example, sections in the book where Picabia mercilessly attacks everything his readers hold dear and tries to entice them into exploring those dangerous freedoms which they have hitherto shied away from. "Don't work," he writes, "don't love, don't read, think of me; I found the new laughter which sets men free. There is nothing to understand, live for your pleasure; there is nothing to understand[sic] nothing, nothing, nothing but the value that you yourself give to everything."[55]

But there are other parts of the book in which Picabia expresses his nomad philosophy in a far more lyrical manner. In the most striking of these, he symbolizes the futility of trying to stop the ever-constant flow of life with the tale of a fabulous, imaginary species of birds:

> There is a species of birds which are extremely rare and very difficult to recognize because they never perch; the female lays her eggs in the air at a great height and the hatching of the little ones takes place before they have had time to fall to earth; the flapping of their wings, flying without a stop, ignoring repose, is like the throbbing of our heart; stopping means death.[56]

And, finally, there are passages where Picabia, speaking from a perspective very much like Jarry's "supplementary universe," ridicules man's puny behavior. Consider, for example, the section entitled "The Cold Eye," in which, making use of what might best be called a pataphysical style, he brilliantly mocks man's elaborate funeral preparations and petty desires for immortality:

> After our death, somebody should put us in a colored, wooden ball. They would roll it to lead us to the cemetery and the undertaker's men, charged with this care, would wear transparent gloves to recall the memory of caresses for the lovers.
>
> For those who would wish to adorn their furniture with the objective pleasure of the dearly departed, there would be crystal balls, through which one would perceive the ultimate nudity of his grandfather or twin brother!
>
> Passageway of the intelligence, steeplechase lamp; humans resemble crows with fixed gaze, who take their flight above corpses—and all the redskins are stationmasters![57]

Pointing up the earlier comparsion with Dr. Faustroll, this pataphysical style seems to offer the possibility that *Jésus-Christ Rastaquouère* was influenced by Jarry, a possibility that is even further reinforced by indications that Jarry was one of the few writers, apart from Nietzsche, whose works Picabia had read and admired.[58] In particular, it is Jarry's "Speculations," a series of brief pataphysical ruminations on a variety of subjects, which he wrote for *La Revue Blanche* between 1901 and 1903, that may have provided a model for Picabia. "It is one of our human superstitions," Jarry proposed in one of the most extraordinary of these "Speculations," "that when we wish to speak with friends temporarily absent, we throw the written expression of our kind feelings into apertures especially made for that purpose, which resemble sewer vents; this after encouraging the tobacco trade, insidious as it is, with a small gift, and receiving in return little images, no doubt sacred, which we devoutly kiss on their backsides. This is not the place to criticize the incoherence of these gestures."[59]

Perhaps even more revealing, one of the specific motifs of Jarry's "Speculations" is echoed in *Jésus-Christ Rastaquouère;* this is the motif from Jarry's "The Passion Considered as an Uphill Bicycle Race" in which it is concluded that "the deplorable accident familiar to us all took place at the twelfth turn. Jesus was in a dead heat at the time with the thieves. We know that he continued the race airborne—but that is another story."[60] In Picabia's book, Jesus is also seen as an unsuccessful racer, only in this case he is a jockey:

> Jesus-Christ jockey!
> Yes, he became the curiosity of the crowds, he made the race, everyone bet on him, result for the betters: nothing.[61]

The various Picabian sayings, proverbs, and homilies with which the book is studded, also call Jarry to mind. Thus Picabia's "THE MOST BEAUTIFUL DISCOVERY OF MAN IS BICARBONATE OF SODA"[62] seems to echo Jarry's "The Work of Art is a Stuffed Crocodile" or "Clichés are the Armature of the Absolute."[63] But, in this instance, as in the previous ones, while Picabia may have absorbed certain of Jarry's ideas, he must be given credit for having taken off in new directions, substituting a more direct style and an overt form of sarcasm for Jarry's deadpan humor and esoteric subtleties.

More than anything else, *Jésus-Christ Rastaquouère* reveals Picabia's amazing ability to strip away the dross of literary conventions and get down to the fundamental questions of life and death. As his friend Pierre de Massot has so aptly put it, Picabia preaches a "Gospel of skepticism" which mercilessly tears the mask from the basic truths of human existence: that man is and knows nothing.[64] And nowhere is this more apparent then in *Jésus-Christ Rastaquouère*, where he ultimately reduces man's finest sentiments to "automatic chemical reactions."[65]

Jean Arp

Although Arp's critique of modern man was often expressed in more jocular terms than those of Tzara and Picabia, it was just as unsparing. Singling out man's naïve faith in material progress as a special target for his scorn, Arp wrote that man "fails to suspect that the robot who now holds the reins is driving him to the meaningless. In the midst of all the horn-blowing, howling, screeching, thundering, crashing, whistling, gnashing and chirping, he feels confident. His anxiety is calmed. His inhuman emptiness grows like a monstrous gray plant."[66]

According to Arp, traditional forms of art, which since the Renaissance had "taught men the haughty exaltation of their reason,"[67] had helped bring this desperate situation about. Calling for a new form of art which would help man to rediscover his true humanity, Arp began to experiment with certain techniques that were to carry him far beyond the realm of traditional aesthetics. "I became more and more removed from aesthetics," he later recalled, "I wanted to find another order, another value for man in nature. He was no longer to be the measure of all things, no longer to reduce everything to his own measure, but on the contrary, all things and man were to be like nature, without measure. I wanted to create new appearances, extract new forms from man."[68]

Possessed with this desire to return man to his humble origins in nature, Arp, like so many of his fellow Dadas, became increasingly preoccupied with the laws of chance. Even before he had begun to explore the expressive value of chance elements in his painting (a discovery which was prompted by his realization that the pieces of an unsuccessful drawing, which had been torn up and thrown onto his studio floor, formed an exciting pattern of their own), Arp—influenced perhaps by Tzara—experimented with chance effects in his poetry. As he himself recalled, he was writing poems that were inspired by chance as early as 1917:

> Words, sayings, sentences which I selected from newspapers and especially from their advertisements were in 1917 the foundations of my poems. Often I shut my eyes and chose words and sentences in newspapers by underlining them with a pencil. I called these poems *Arpaden.* It was the beautiful Dada time when we hated and reviled the chiselling of work, the distracted look of the spiritual wrestlers, the titans, from the depths of our hearts. I twisted and turned easily, improvising words and sentences from words and sentences chosen from the newspapers.[69]

That Arp seems to have emphasized chance effects in his poetry prior to doing so in his plastic work is significant; it provides some indication of how important a role poetry has always played in his life. In contrast to someone like Picabia who only wrote poems when he could not paint, plastic and written expressions seem to have been so inextricably fused in Arp's life that it is difficult to say where drawings and sculptures leave off and poems begin. Some indication of how closely these and other artistic activities were linked in his mind comes from his comment that "the soul of music and of poetry, painting and sculpture mingle and come together like dreams."[70] Thus, those critics who have excluded Arp's poetry from their considerations of his work seem to have done him a serious disservice. Whatever spur might be needed to help correct this oversight was provided by Arp himself when he made the surprising confession that "if by the impossible I was obliged to choose between plastic work and written poetry, if I was forced to abandon either the sculpture or the poems, I would choose to write poems."[71]

Although he had been writing poetry since 1902, it was not until the period between 1915 and 1920 that Arp began to explore what he later described as "automatic poetry." This kind of poetry, he explained, "issues straight from the entrails of the poet or from any other organ that has stored up reserves. Neither the Postillion de Longjumeau nor the Alexandrine, nor grammar, nor aesthetics, nor Buddha, nor the Sixth Commandment can interfere with it in the least. It crows, curses, sighs, stammers, yodels, just as it pleases. Its poems are like nature: they stink, laugh, rhyme, like nature."[72]

Inspired by Tzara's *Twenty-Five Poems,* which he later ranked with the best in French poetry, and Huelsenbeck's *Fantastic Prayers,* which also evoked his greatest admiration, Arp began a series of far-reaching experiments with this technique, beginning with a cycle of poems aptly titled *Hyperbole of the Crocodile-Barber and the Walking Cane.* This cycle, which was largely the result of a collaboration between Arp, Tzara, and Serner, was soon followed by more of Arp's poems, many of which were first recited at the Cabaret Voltaire, and subsequently published in two volumes *Die Wolkenpumpe* and *Der Vogel selbdritt,* both of which appeared in 1920.

Filled with a violence and an aggressiveness which Arp was gradually to soften as time went on, these poems seem to represent the poet's powerful struggles to free himself totally from all traces of traditional poetry. Arp's own description of this struggle reveals his state of mind perfectly:

> In these poems I tore apart sentences, words, syllables. I tried to break down the language into atoms, in order to approach the creative. At length I rejected art, because it distracts us from the depths and disturbs the pure dream.

Out of the billowy breast of height and depth, I awaited
the figures upon whose brows gleam tiaras of diamond
kisses. Chance opened up perceptions to me, immediate
spiritual insights. Intuition led me to revere the law of
chance as the highest and deepest of laws, the law that
rises from the fundament. An insignificant word might
become a deadly thunderbolt. One little sound might destroy the earth. One little sound might create a new universe.[73]

Perhaps the best illustration of what resulted from his daring
approach is the poem "kaspar is dead" which first appeared in
Der Vogel Selbdritt:

alas our good kaspar is dead.
who will now carry the burning banner hidden in the pigtail of
    clouds to play the daily black joke
who will now turn the coffee-mill in the primaeval barrel
who will now entice the idyllic deer out of the petrified paper
    box.
who will now confound on the high seas the ships by addressing
    them as parapluie and the winds by calling them keeper of the
    bees ozone spindle your highness.
alas alas alas our good kaspar is dead. holy ding dong kaspar is
    dead.
the cattle fish in the bellbarns clatter with heartrending grief
    when his christian name is uttered. that is why I keep on
    moaning his family name kaspar kaspar kaspar.
why have you left us. into what shape has your beautiful great
    soul migrated. have you become a star or a watery chain at-
    tached to a hot whirlwind or an udder of black light or a trans-
    parent brick on the groaning drum of a jagged being.
now the part in our hair the soles of our feet are parched and the
    fairies lie half-charred on the pyre.
now the black bowling alley thunders behind the sun and there's
    no one to wind up the compasses and the wheels of the
    hand-barrows any more.
who will now eat with the phosphorescent rat at the lonely bare-
    footed table.
who will now chase away the siroccoco devil when he wants to
    beguile the horses.

who will now explain to us the monograms in the stars.
his bust will adorn the mantelpieces of all truly noble men but
    that's no comfort that's snuff to a skull.[74]

Like all of Arp's earlier poetry, this poem was written in German. Nevertheless, a fairly strong case can be made for his being a French poet. If we keep in mind his divided loyalties as an Alsatian, it is not surprising that Arp saw fit to adapt most of these early poems from German into French. Perhaps even more revealing, is Arp's comment, when asked about the difference between the two languages by Marcel Jean, that "the word is 'fresher' for me in French. I have known German rather well since school. But the French that I have always spoken gives me the feeling of a discovery."[75]

"The feeling of a discovery" comes across beautifully in a poem entitled the "onions dance" which forms part of *The Siege of the Air,* the first French edition of his collected poetry. In this poem, language loses most of its traditional restrictions as things become personified and objects interchangeable:

the onions get up from their chairs
and dance as red as if one had giantized the juice of dwarfs.
the lunar machine blows plumed diamonds
around the mouth of the fruit.
the onions have forgotten to hold on to their chairs with
watchful teeth and already the chairs are held by the tables
who take themselves for continents.
Are the continents excepted or forbidden fruit
in the hour when night comes to an end like a shoe of charcoal
a mandoline eyeletted like a rose.
the tables get up from their chairs
and dance as red as if the sky were falling from the sky.
the tables have forgotten to hold on to their chairs with watchful
teeth
and there's why the chairs are again held by the onions.[76]

In his attempts to disrupt the denotative and connotative value of words and create what he later called "concrete poetry," Arp went even further afield than the kind of "word magic" represented here. Basing his poetry on the syllable, the most fundamental element of meaning, Arp—like some kind of demonic child—was able literally to pulverize traditional meanings and create a poetic world which is peopled by the strangest creatures imaginable. Can we, for example, recognize the owl in his untranslatable new guise?

> un hibou chante si longtemps hi
> qu'il ne lui reste plus qu'un tout petit bou du hi.[77]

Or even more of a test, the butterfly?

> le papillon empaillé devient un papapillon empapaillé
> le papapillon empapapaillé devient un grandpapapillon
> grandempapaillé[78]

Like most forms of "nonsense," Arp's wordplay was a great source of humor as well as a path into the unknown. With characteristic whimsy, he himself defined humor as "the water of the beyond mixed in the wine of the here-below."[79] Beneath the mystification, Arp seems to be suggesting that humor derives from the unexpected impinging upon everyday events. According to Marcel Duchamp, himself a famous exponent of this kind of humor, Arp must be given much of the credit for introducing it into the Dada movement. His trademark, as Duchamp has noted, "was 'humor' in its subtlest form; the kind of whimsical conceptions that gave to the Dada movement such an exuberant liveliness, as opposed to the purely intellectual tendencies of Cubism and Expressionism. Arp showed the importance of a smile to combat the sophist theories of the moment."[80]

Although Arp's concept of humor emphasized the workings of chance ("the water of the beyond") within the context of the conscious world ("the wine of the here-below"), he never abandoned himself completely to chance, even in his early poetry. Or, as Carola Giedion-Welcker has put it, his art "obeys the laws of chance, but never chance itself."[81] Having opened himself up to the mysteries of the unknown and the unexpected, Arp—in apparent contrast to Tzara and Picabia—reserved the right to orchestrate whatever "spiritual insights" chance had brought to him. Even in those poems where he has done away with the last trace of punctuation and reduced the word to a sonorous syllable, the feeling remains that the poet is still somehow in control.

Any consideration of Arp's early poetry must ultimately return to the poems themselves. Perhaps the best way of concluding this discussion is with a poem entitled "Age, Lightning, Hand, and

Leaf" which brilliantly illustrates Arp's subtle humor, complex simplicity, and mystical feeling for nature:

> age has hands of arrows.
> age is a plant
> which speaks like a nude leaf
> and sets traps of white light.
>
> the lightning strikes on a nude hand.
> the lightning speaks of age without bell
> and salutes the nude space
> which comes from the silent light.
>
> the hand is white like a plant-plume.
> the hand is white like an arrow-leaf.
> the hand carries a sleeping bell
> by the silent space
> and sets it up on a sleeping lightning.
>
> the leaf is a silent hand
> the leaf forgets that it sleeps.
> it speaks like a nude bell
> and awakens the white space
> which falls in a silent trap
> the leaves change sleeping spaces.[82]

The Littérature Group

The inspiration provided by Arp, Picabia, and Tzara was an important factor in drawing the editors of *Littérature* to Dada. This was especially true of Tzara, whose "admirable spirit of revolt" completely captivated them. Some idea of how they felt about Tzara comes from a letter that Breton wrote him in March, 1919. "Your poems are marvelous," Breton exclaimed, "of all the living poets, you are the one who moves me the most."[83]

Gradually, the spirit represented by Tzara, Picabia, and Arp found its way into the poetry of Breton and his companions as well. In Breton's case, this new spirit was heralded by a poem entitled "The Mysterious Corset," which was first published in *Littérature* in June, 1919, then inserted as the last poem in his initial volume of poetry, *Mountain of Piety*. Echoing Tzara's own disjointed style, "The Mysterious Corset" was composed of a seemingly random series of newspaper captions and advertising blurbs which not only demonstrated that Breton had begun to take to heart the Rumanian's contention that "advertising and business are also elements of poetry,"[84] but, in addition, furnished evidence that he had begun to turn away from the prior influences of Mallarmé and the Cubists.

By March, 1920, Breton had apparently become so caught up in Dada that he was writing poems that seem completely out of character for him. Consider, for example, an excerpt from "False Pièce," a poem which he contributed to Tzara's periodical *Dadaphone:*

> Du vase en cristal de Bohème
> Du vase en cris
> Du vase en cris
> Du vase en
> En cristal
> Du vase en cristal de Bohème
> Bohème
> Bohème[85]

The mocking, playful tone of this poem, which has been compared to "a couplet for chorus-singers in an opera," seems to belie the sober, almost pontifical style so many observers have associated with Breton.

During this period, Soupault and Aragon also engaged in various verbal experiments that seem to have been inspired by Dada. Thus, in April, 1920, Soupault contributed a doggerel poem entitled "Litanies" to Picabia's magazine *Cannibal.* As the following excerpt illustrates, this poem was based on the gratuitous use of the names of his fellow Dadas:

> Breton sees better without spectacles
> Francis Picabia doesn't have syphilis
> Fraenkel doesn't wear glasses
> Soupault doesn't wear glasses
> Aragon [Louis] doesn't wear glasses
> Fraenkel doesn't wear glasses
> Fraenkel doesn't wear glasses
> Fraenkel doesn't wear glasses
> Tristan [Tzara] needs a doctor
> Breton forgets his purse
> and then
> and then
> Shit[86]

Not to be outdone, Aragon published, in this same issue of
Cannibal, a poem entitled "Suicide" in which, as he later put
it, he "signed the alphabet":

A b c d e f
g h i j k l
m n o p q r
s t u v w
x y z [87]

Despite the impact of Dada upon Breton, Soupault, and Aragon, it never succeeded in completely erasing the mark of an earlier, more literary strain in their writings. Consistent with the
editorial policy they had adopted for their magazine, in which
they reserved the right to publish all forms of literature, the editors of *Littérature* explored the possibilities of Dada in their poetry, but left themselves open to other experiences as well. This
was especially true during the transition from Dada to Surrealism
when Dadaist and non-Dadaist writings were found in the same
issues of *Littérature,* and Dadaist and pre-Surrealist elements often coexisted in the same piece of writing. This latter tendency is
illustrated by one of the most fascinating works of this period—
The Magnetic Fields. The result of a series of far-reaching experiments by Breton and Soupault begun as early as 1919, this work
brings the question of the relationship between Dada and Surrealism sharply into focus.

In an interview with André Parinaud, Breton himself proposed
that *The Magnetic Fields* was "the first surrealist work (and not
at all Dada) as far as it is the fruit of the first systematic applications of automatic writing."[88] But critics of this view have asked:
how can this be the first Surrealist work when Surrealism did not
officially come into existence until five years later? Moreover, both
Tzara and Picabia, as we have seen, engaged in a form of automatic writing prior to the creation of *The Magnetic Fields.* And
there is evidence that, like Breton and Soupault, they even collaborated on these experiments.[89] What seems to be the key to Breton's statement, however, is the phrase "systematic applications of
automatic writing." While Tzara and Picabia and even, to a certain extent, Arp experimented with various types of automatic
expression, they did so in the same unsystematic manner in
which they had done everything else. But, as Breton said, beginning with *The Magnetic Fields,* a new and more systematic spirit,

which was the prelude to Surrealism's almost scientific explorations of the unconscious, came into being. Thus, *The Magnetic Fields* contained the seeds for a new approach, seeds which, when carefully nurtured by Breton and others, would eventually sprout into the new plant, Surrealism.

The nature of its automatic writing can perhaps be questioned,[90] but it is difficult to deny the significance of *The Magnetic Fields* both from a historical and a literary standpoint. As a kind of a bridge between Dada and Surrealism, this work brings together the pre-Surrealist influences of Lautréamont and the Dadaist influences of Tzara and Picabia, both of which have been filtered through the poetic sensibilities of Breton and Soupault. In this sense, it is a fascinating common ground where what might be termed the Surrealist-literary strain meets the Dadaist-antiliterary one.

These opposing tendencies can be seen even more clearly if, as Sanouillet suggests, we compare the antipoetry published by Tzara and Picabia in 1920 *(Cinema Calendar of the Abstract Heart, Thoughts without Language, Unique Eunuch*, etc.) with the more traditional works brought out by Breton, Soupault, and Aragon *(The Magnetic Fields, Rose of the Winds, Bonfire*, etc.). All of these works were published by Au Sans Pareil, but the publisher, recognizing the obvious, placed them into two different collections, the former entitled "Dada" and the latter "Littérature."

This continued preoccupation with literature on the part of Breton, Aragon, and Soupault was even more pronounced with Paul Eluard, who carefully balanced his involvement in Dada with his desire to write more traditional poetry. Although Eluard took part in the Dada demonstrations and wrote manifestos celebrating the movement, he lived more or less on its fringes. Thus, when the editors of *Littérature* chose to express their scorn for the idea of traditional literature by remaining silent from about 1920 to 1921, bringing out only those works which they had written or even published previously, Eluard continued to write his poetry and engage in research into the nature of language.

That Dada had begun to have an impact upon Eluard's work, however, is evidenced by the preface that he wrote for a volume of his poetry entitled *The Animals and Their Men the Men and Their Animals*, which was published in 1920. Speaking for his generation of poets, Eluard stated in this preface that modern poetry must transcend the traditional concepts of beauty and ugliness which man, in his vanity, had made so restrictive. But he went on to say—unlike Tzara and Picabia—that he was interested in reviving poetic language rather than sabotaging the very idea of literature.

The poems in this volume provide further evidence that Eluard's intention was to create "a charming language" rather than to destroy the idea of written poetry altogether. Stripped of all excess verbiage, these poems—the perfect embodiments of his famous desire "to remain absolutely pure"—make one feel that words are being used for the very first time. Consider, for example, the poem entitled "Paw," in which Eluard, like the exponents of the Japanese haiku, is able, with a few essential images, to evoke the wistful presence of that most mysterious creature:

> ʹThe cat sets himself up in the night to cry,
> In the free air, in the night, the cat cries.
> And sad with human shame, man hears his cry.[91]

In the same year in which he published *The Animals and Their Men*, Eluard also founded *Proverb*, a periodical devoted to the exploration of language which lasted for only five issues. Judging from two letters he wrote to Tzara, Eluard's decision to publish *Proverb* was influenced by Dada's antiliterary spirit. In the first of these, dated December, 1919, he proposed that "it is going to be a question . . . of showing that the French language (and the expression of thought, naturally) is no longer a literary instrument."[92] And, in the second, which was sent to Tzara in January, 1920, he went even further, proclaiming that "we will humiliate the word in fine fashion."[93]

Without abandoning the childlike simplicity which was to become the hallmark of his mature style, Eluard moved closer to Dada in his next volume of poetry, *The Necessities of Life and the Consequences of Dreams*, which was published in 1921. But even as disjointed a poem as "The Great Day," which Eluard dedicated to his wife Gala, still retains something of his earlier, more literary tone:

> Come, ascend. Soon the lightest feathers, sky-divers, will hold you by the neck.
> The earth only endures the necessary and your beautiful space-birds, smile. In place of your sadness, like a shadow behind love, the landscape covers everything.

Come quickly, run. And your body goes faster than your thoughts, but nothing, do you hear? nothing, can surpass you.[94]

The literary tendencies that existed alongside the antiliterary ones in the poetry of Eluard, Breton, Soupault, and Aragon must not be underestimated; in a very real sense, they were the symptoms of Surrealism. When these young poets became disheartened with Dada, they were able to pick up these threads and fashion them into a new philosophy. This is not to say, as some critics have done, that the Surrealist movement was already formed by the time Tzara arrived in Paris. But the *Littérature* group's continual preoccupation with a form of poetry which, in the words of Breton, "leads somewhere" made Surrealism a potentially more positive movement for them than Dada.

Before concluding this discussion of the writings of the *Littérature* group, we must examine Aragon's *Anicet*, an unusual experiment which, among other things, seems to have anticipated the efforts of the so-called New Novelists. This work, which Aragon published in 1921, flew directly in the face of the Dadas' sanctions against the novel. While they could rationalize the use of poetry and painting as trojan horses for destroying traditional art and literature, the leaders of the Dada movement felt nothing but contempt for the novel, which they labeled "railroad literature" and which could not be condoned under any circumstances.

Aragon had begun writing *Anicet* earlier, but his decision to publish it in 1921 could only be interpreted as an act of provocation by his fellow Dadas. This was particularly true since, as he later recalled, he made no attempt to disguise that it was intended as a novel.

Looking at the work today, however, we would be hard-pressed to call it a novel. Admittedly, *Anicet* is divided into paragraphs and chapters and makes use of orthodox grammar and syntax, but these things serve only to create the impression, reinforced by a letter Aragon sent to Jacques Doucet, that it was meant to be some kind of antinovel. Writing to Doucet, a propos *Anicet*, Aragon expressed his disdain for the psychologically oriented, formularized novel which was so much in vogue during this period.

In telling the story of *Anicet*, a rootless young poet who becomes embroiled in a series of unlikely intrigues involving the mysterious Mirabelle and her secret society of desperate admirers, Aragon has reacted against the basic ingredients of these novels:

three-dimensional characters and carefully planned events. Signaling his intentions in the very first line of the book, he informs us that "from his secondary school studies, Anicet has retained only the rule of the three unities and the relativity of time and space which circumscribes his knowledge of art and life."[95] True to its protagonists' contradictory beliefs, this work, which is governed by a strict sense of time, place, and action, seems to take place in another dimension altogether, outside of conventional time and space.

This other-dimensional aspect of *Anicet*, as well as the paradoxical situation from which it emerges, in many ways calls to mind Jarry's pataphysics, a philosophy which, as we have seen, allowed its author to say the most absurd things in the most logical manner. Piling gratuitous incident upon incident and causing his cast of characters to appear and disappear mysteriously, Aragon has created the kind of arbitrary, dislocated atmosphere which is the perfect metaphor of Jarry's "supplementary universe." As if to complete the picture, he has also—by his own testimony—modeled Omne, one of the seven desperadoes who have pledged themselves to the heroine, Mirabelle, upon Dr. Faustroll.[96] Throughout the book, Omne is enveloped in that aura of mystification which Jarry invariably shared with his characters.

Jarry was not the only one of Aragon's heroes to play a role in *Anicet*. In a document purported to be a "key" to the work, Aragon informed Doucet that the character of Anicet was, in large part, based upon that of his friend Pierre Maison, who had been killed in the war, and there were also figures who represented Rimbaud (Arthur), Cocteau (Ange Miracle), Breton (Baptise Ajamais), Charlie Chaplin (Pol), and Vaché (Harry James), among others. Later, in an interview with Francis Crémieux, Aragon repudiated this "key" and warned that he had not intended to provide a description of these men, but only to make use of their external characteristics. The nature of his characterizations lends weight to his contention; the figures are little more than stock types who undergo no inner development and whose sole *raison d'être* seems to be to function as mouthpieces for the author.

The most important of these silhouettes was Anicet himself who, in giving expression to the nihilistic feelings of sensitive young poets like Aragon, vividly embodied the Dada spirit both in word and deed. Dazzled by Mirabelle's beauty, Anicet swears to carry out any activity that pleases her regardless of its peril. The first of these—a daring art robbery—is symbolic of Dada's anti-art attitudes. Instead of trying to sell the paintings, Anicet and his cohorts place them in an immense brazier at the top of the Arc de Triomphe and burn them to ashes. Anicet's explanation for this seemingly gratuitous action is even more reflective of his Dadaist philosophy. Commenting that all of the bastions of civilization— God, the nation, the family—have been swept away, he notes that the only thing that remains to be destroyed is art.

The Dadas' fascination with the romantic world of popular culture also finds its expression in *Anicet*. Aragon himself provided a rationale for this when he wrote that "everything which did not impose a morality attracted us; extravagance, celebrations, the great orchestra of vices, as well as the image of the heroic, sacred adventuress."[97] He went on to say that he and his companions idealized the "splendid bandits" and, while "the newspapers denounced the cinema as a school for crime," they discovered "the single sun which was not tarnished"[98] in what their society called crime.

In the light of these comments, it is not surprising that the atmosphere of *Anicet* is steeped in those things which Aragon found so intriguing: Nick Carter detective stories, American and French movie serials, and, of course, Charlie Chaplin. While the band of assassins and anarchists who become Anicet's henchmen seems to have stepped straight out of an early detective story or movie serial, its leader—the exquisitely beautiful Mirabelle—evokes the presence of the legendary Musidora and is the perfect embodiment of Aragon's image of the "heroic, sacred adventuress." Even the illustrious Nick Carter, sent from America to combat the gang, takes part in the strange goings-on. And another of Aragon's favorites, the inimitable Charlie Chaplin, in the character of Pol, adds an element of comic relief with his immortal sight gags.

Aragon was indebted to early cinema not only for much of the content of *Anicet*, but also for its basic structure. Instead of making use of the traditional forms of transition, he shifts from event to event in a way which corresponds to the rapid cutting of film, a technique which helps account for the dislocated atmosphere of the work and, at the same time, illustrates Anicet's belief in the relativity of time and space. Paralleling the slow and fast motion as well as the fade and the dissolve of film, time is alternately speeded up and slowed down, and space expands and contracts.

Underscoring this parallel still further, Aragon even went so far as to incorporate actual scenes from films into his work. One of these scenes, which centers on the exploits of the fabulous Pearl White, illustrates his technique while providing an idea of the overall significance of the cinema for him and his colleagues.

Just how personalized Aragon intended this scene to be is shown from the fact that, in addition to Anicet, its participants include Baptise Ajamais, the character who stands for Breton, and Harry James, a figure who represents his now legendary friend Vaché, who is credited with having introduced the *Littérature* group to the beauties of the popular film.[99] Opening on a simulated meeting between Breton and Vaché, which fittingly takes place in Nantes in 1916, the scene suddenly changes (an illustration of Aragon's use of a kind of jump cut instead of a more traditional transition) to the Electric Palace, where Baptise and Anicet have gone to watch a Pearl White extravaganza.

After describing the sheer pleasure these young men felt in just being in this movie theater, where, among other things, they could provide their own running commentary on what was happening on the screen, Aragon went on, using Anicet as his spokesman, to contrast the philosophical values of the cinema with those of the theater.

> What makes the theater so dead for us, said Anicet, is without doubt, that its unique subject matter is morality, the rule of all action: Our period hardly interests itself in morality. In the cinema, speed appears in life and Pearl White doesn't act to obey her conscience, but for sport, for her health: She acts for action's sake.[100]

To illustrate this point most vividly, he provided a detailed account of Pearl White's adventures, as they were taking place on the screen of the Electric Palace.

Drawing upon yet another aspect of the film art, which had fascinated him since as early as 1918, Aragon in *Anicet* transformed the most banal objects into mysterious presences. By de-emphasizing his individual characters and dislocating their world, he has managed at the same time to push certain objects from the background into the foreground, where, in approximation of the seemingly magical quality of film, they now stand out as in relief. Consider, for example, the gift-giving ceremony of Mirabelle's devotees in which seemingly everyday objects—"a silver glass bowl, a tangerine wrapped in transparent red paper," etc.—take on a mystery all their own. Some of the flavor of this ceremony, which takes up more than fifteen pages in the book, can be gained by quoting Aragon's description of the first gift:

> One of the seven men moves forward, bows, and holds out a silver glass ball, the kind one sees in gardens, to the lady and says: "Dear Mirabelle, behold the globe in which astronomers contemplate the universe, so that they see it completely round, circular, spherical, which is very convenient in order to set up systems or carry out calculations. When you look at the world in it, you will perceive it simplified, easy to grasp, nicely theoretical and enhanced with several pleasing reflections. In it, your image will appear the center of all things, not without undergoing the deformations owing to the particular aesthetic of the mirror's sphericals. Thus you will always have at your disposal, for sad days, an easy and consoling way of considering life which will enable you to completely revive yourself and, without difficulty, to introduce order and reason into your conceptions and phenomena. When you are tired of searching for general ideas in it, this glass will still be able, without hidden motive, to serve as a way of playing with the sun's rays. I picked it up in a park in the vicinity of Paris."[101]

Aragon's attacks against the idea of the conventional novel in general, and his attempts to undermine its traditional plot and psychology of character development in particular, seems to make him an important precursor of the New Novelists. Judging by the comments of two of their most vocal spokesmen, Alain Robbe-Grillet and Nathalie Sarraute, these novelists not only share Aragon's intention of destroying the conventional novel with its outworn conception of life, but, they also have a similar desire to replace its well-defined characters with types who are more expressive of the author's point of view than they are reflective of the individual in society.

Stemming perhaps from this common intention, there are some interesting structural similarities between Aragon's *Anicet* and some of the new novels. In reacting against what he considered to be the contrived atmosphere and formularized intrigues of the conventional novel, Aragon created a kind of circular structure for *Anicet,* in which there is no clearly defined beginning, middle, or ending, and where time and space are completely relative. In consequence of its formal structure, *Anicet* can thus be seen as an interesting link between past and present: on the one hand, it seems to look back to the eighteenth-century philosophical fables from which, according to some authorities, Aragon got his original conception for the work; and, on the other, it looks ahead to the form of the New Novel where, as Laurent Lesage has noted in his book *The French New Novel,* "the notions of chronology, of causality, and all the other props of the common-sense universe"[102] are consistently undermined.

This conception of the universe, which Aragon holds in common with the New Novelists, can, in large part, be traced to their mutual involvement with visual experiences in general and the cinema in particular.[103] What might be called Aragon's cinematic tendencies have become even more pronounced in many of the New Novels in which, in Lesage's words, "the novelist's notion of himself as chiefly a recording consciousness reduces him to a sort of seeing eye roving about the surface of things."[104] Elaborating upon this point, Lesage has noted that "one could well say a camera, as far as physical description goes; for, just as the organization of the new novel reminds one of films, most of the descriptions, presented objectively, that is to say, in tableaux where conceptual knowledge is not permitted to modify the data presented by the eye, resembles what one sees at the movies. Hence descriptions are partial, selective, with proportions dictated by the limitations of the camera, the eye, or the preoccupation of the consciousness behind the eye."[105]

Summary

Despite their divergent styles, there was one thing on which the Dada poets and antipoets, regardless of whether they were most inspired by Ball's "constructive anarchy," Tzara's uncompromising nihilism, or Breton's idea of automatic writing, seemed to agree: that poetry must be more than a way of communicating thoughts and emotions; it must be, in Tzara's words, "an activity of the mind," a way of life that reflects the very existence of its creator.

Interpreting poetry in this way, it is not surprising that the Dadas chose the path of such modern revolutionaries as Rimbaud, Lautréamont, and Jarry. What is more important, however, as far as the significance of their own revolt is concerned, was that they sought to widen the paths. As Tzara himself later remarked, "our impertinence went perhaps a little further. We proclaimed our disgust, we made spontaneity our rule of life, we repudidated all distinctions between life and poetry, our poetry was a manner of living."[106]

Jacques Rivière, the French critic who witnessed the birth of Dada in Paris, provided the best description of this intention—in its purest form—when he wrote that the Dada experiments were designed "to grasp our being before it has yielded to consistency; to seize it in its incoherence, or better, in its primitive coherence, before the idea of contradiction has appeared and compelled it to reduce and construct itself; to replace its logical unity, which can only be acquired, by its absurd unity, which alone is innate."[107] On the basis of his own analysis and Breton's contention that "it would be absurd, *a priori,* to expect a DADA masterpiece in the fields of literature and painting,"[108] Rivière concluded that the Dada experiment, "an experiment as mad and logical as those that take place every day in laboratories: the experiment of absolute psychological reality" could only end in "psychological and linguistic nothingness."[109]

Granting the validity of Breton's statement that it would be foolish to look for a literary masterpiece in Dada, can we dismiss the Dadas writings quite so lightly as Rivière, who seems to have concentrated almost exclusively on what has been termed the "absolute Dadaist poem," i.e., Tzara's press-clipping poetry or Picabia's *Unique Eunuch?* What about the many instances in which the Dada poets and antipoets either could not or would not surrender themselves to Rivière's "psychological and linguistic nothingness?" As we have seen, these poems, which stand somewhere between the conscious and the unconscious, were often charged with meaning.

One of the first to try to explain this phenomenon was Tzara himself who, in looking back upon his own poems, as well as those of his Dada colleagues, suggested that they often functioned in terms of a form of "non-directed thought." Calling attention to the amazing paradox of a distinctly negative movement which speaks so positively to our time, Moholy-Nagy has also alluded to this idea. In these poems, he noted, "without one's having been able to register its exact meaning, a mutation occurred: clearly, a fabric became comprehensible to the reader—in a very suggestive unconscious way, through the magic of the words, their affinities and modulations. This was the result of a new lyric expression, like an x-ray revelation, making transparent that which was previously opaque; a new structure and topography of the psychological existence, the rendering of psychological space-time."[110]

This reference to "psychological space-time" once again brings us to the art of cinema, where, as we have seen, the Dada poets and antipoets derived much of their inspiration. From Erwin Panofsky on, various film theoreticians have spoken of the cinema's remarkable ability to translate time into space and vice versa. Writing about this in an essay titled "The Nature of the Cinema," the French critic André Levinson commented that this "is the greatest philosophical surprise since Kant—a prodigious and paradoxical mechanism which interlaces and substitutes, one for the other, the two categories in terms of which we consider the universe."[111] Levinson's description of our response to cinema might just as easily be applied to the Dadas' poetic experiments. "The association of images in our brain is irrational," he concluded, "they flock to the threshold of our consciousness, whirl among the shadows behind the door, strike upon that door and finally enter the zone of light. The cinema treats images with that same ductility."[112]

In concluding this discussion of the Dada poets and antipoets, we must take up the complex question of their influence upon later writers. Despite the differences that existed between Dada and Surrealism—differences that will be explored more fully in the final chapter of this book—the Surrealists, at first, bore the brunt of this influence. This is not surprising if we take into account that there were bound to be essential similarities in two movements like these, which had developed out of the same climate of artistic protest and revolt.

According to Ribemont-Dessaignes, one of the few members of Paris Dada who never became a Surrealist, "everything in Surrealism which belonged to the domain of liberty, revolt, and non-conformism was contained in Dada."[113] Although he tried to minimize its importance, even Breton could not help but admit the debt he and his fellow Surrealists owed to Dada. In an essay in which he explained why he was abandoning the Dada movement, Breton wrote that "it should not be said that dadaism would have served other than to keep us in that perfect state of non-attachment that we are at."[114]

Breton tried to play down the significance of this "perfect state," but there are indications that, if not for him, then for his colleagues Soupault and Aragon, it was a crucial experience. Soupault, in particular, had found it so necessary that it was virtually impossible for him to break with Dada, even though he had no illusions about its future. Breton himself noted this in a lecture he gave in Barcelona in 1922, when, with a mixture of sadness and irony, he informed his audience that "at the present time only Philippe Soupault has not lost hope in Dada, and it is rather moving to think that until his death he will perhaps live as Dada's toy as we have seen Jarry live as Ubu's."[115]

Aragon also experienced a sense of loss over Dada. But he found it easier than Soupault to embrace Surrealism. Even though he became Breton's greatest ally and was an important figure in the Surrealist movement in his own right, however, Aragon continued at times to express himself in what can only be called a Dadaist style. Thus, as late as 1927, he was still writing poems like the following wry account of Dada's impact:

> Old Combatant
> I did the Dada Movement
> said the dadaist
> I did the Dada Movement
>
> and in effect
> it did me[116]

As Aragon's case illustrates, the influence of Dada was so all-pervading in the early days of Surrealism that it is often impossible to distinguish what was Surrealist from what was Dadaist. Gradually, however, as the Surrealists began to move in the direction of politics and became involved in their doctrine of love, the Dada influence vanished.

Although not as directly affected as the Surrealists, other writers, such as the expatriate American novelist Henry Miller, who lived on the fringes of both the Dada and Surrealist movements, also felt the impact of Dada. In "An Open Letter to Surrealists Everywhere," which was part of his *The Cosmological Eye,* Miller testified to the influence of both movements on his work. But he went on to say that he preferred the Dadas because "the Surrealists are too conscious of what they are doing."[117]

Miller made the kinship which existed between himself and the Dadas even clearer in the concluding passage of *The Cosmological Eye.* "I have no interest," he declared, "in the intentions of the existing governments of the world. I hope and believe that the whole civilized world will be wiped out in the next hundred years or so. I believe that man can exist, and in an infinitely better, larger way, without civilization."[118]

While they were not as outspoken in acknowledging its influence as Miller, writers like James Joyce and E. E. Cummings may also have absorbed something of the Dada spirit from the literary climate in Europe. Joyce was living in Zurich when Dada first emerged, and although there was never any question of his joining the movement, he frequented the same cafés as the Zurich Dadas and shared their fascination with the turbulent world of the irrational.

According to A. W. Litz in *The Art of James Joyce*, it was during this period that Joyce began to perfect his "stream of consciousness approach" which, interestingly enough, closely parallels the Dadas' free-association techniques.[119] Since there is no evidence that the Dadas' revolt against language and rationality had a direct influence upon Joyce's approach, this similarity may be coincidental, but this does not preclude the possibility of some form of indirect influence. Certainly Joyce's work was affected by both the literary and psychological climate of Zurich, a city which, in addition to being the place of exile of the Dadas, was also the center of the International Psychoanalytic Movement led by Carl Jung.

The manner in which Joyce's technique developed lends further credence to this idea. In moving from *Ulysses* to *Finnegans Wake,* he followed a path similar to that of the Dadas. As David Grossvogel has pointed out, "the evolution that leads him from *Ulysses* to *Finnegans Wake* indicates a change in the author's concerns, from the inner representation of character through analysis of consciousness to a freer enjoyment of words and their revelatory possibilities."[120] And with this last stage in his evolution, Grossvogel concluded, "Joyce ends close to the unstructured fun of the Dadaists and relatively free of the formal concerns that normally limit the author through an awareness of his audience."[121]

Cummings came in contact with the Dada movement in Paris during the early twenties. Like Joyce, he was too much of an individualist to join the movement, but he did become friends with the Paris Dadas, whose boisterous antics made a lasting impression upon him. Looking back nostalgically to this period, just after the demise of the Dada movement, Cummings asked:

What's become of (if you please)
all the glory that or which was Greece
all the grandja
that was dada[122]

Further evidence of the impression which Dada made upon Cummings comes from his poetry in general and his play *Him* in particular. By devising his own system of punctuation and grammar and making use of popular expressions and slang in his poems, Cummings served notice that he, like the Dadas, was intent upon capturing life's essential spontaneity before it could be frozen into rational form.

The Dada influence underlying this preoccupation with the immediate and the spontaneous is also marked in *Him*, Cummings's most ambitious attempt at playwriting. Making use of a nonlinear plot and nondiscursive symbolism to express the ambiguities of the modern artist's life, this play anticipated many of the innovations of the theater of the absurd; its juxtapositions of serious love scenes and raucous circus acts and bawdy burlesque routines looks ahead to the attempts of Beckett and Ionesco to create a new form of experience based upon the spontaneities of popular theater.

The dialogue in *Him*, if that term can be used to categorize speeches which often border on the unintelligible, is characterized by the kind of word play which is most often associated with Dada. Moreover, there is even a scene (one of the scenes in the play-within-a-play, in which the curtain rises, stays up for about a minute, then falls again with no other action taking place) in which Cummings makes use of an empty stage in a manner that one astute critic has termed "pure Dada."

That Cummings' kinship with the Dadas goes even deeper than this, however, is illustrated by his view of the tenuousness of communication. In the second scene of the play, Him, the poet, describes his art as a perilous acrobatic act, balancing three chairs in the sky. When asked by his mistress, Me, what will happen to the chairs (the completed work), the poet answers:

The chairs will all fall by themselves down
from the wire and be caught by anybody, by
nobody; by somebody whom I don't see and who
doesn't see me; perhaps by everybody.[123]

By the 1930s and 40s, Dada had become so submerged that it is virtually impossible to trace its influence, except as a kind of underground force. But toward the end of World War II, seemingly as the result of two new phenomena on the literary scene, this situation began to change. The first of these was the development of Lettrism, a movement led by Isidore Isou, a young writer who, like Tzara, was a Rumanian exile living in Paris. Taking off from where the poetic experiments of Ball, Schwitters, and Tzara had ended, Isou systematically began to explore the possibility of creating poetry out of letters rather than words. While the originality of Isou's experiments has been questioned, it is difficult to deny that he and his followers helped provide the impetus that was necessary to bring Dada back to the surface.

The second phenomenon which contributed to this postwar Dada renaissance was the emergence of Existentialism. Declaring that "I am the new Dada,"[124] Jean-Paul Sartre called attention to the fact that some of the basic ideas of his philosophy had already been expressed, in a rudimentary form, by the Dadas. Richard Huelsenbeck has elaborated on this in his essay "Dada and Existentialism," in which he proposed, among other things, that the atmosphere of Berlin Dada was very close to that of Existentialism. Moreover, Huelsenbeck concluded that "the new man" whom he and his colleagues had envisioned was similar to Sartre's image of Existential man. In exploring this new image of man, the Dadas touched upon the concept of absurdity, which is a basic tenet of the Existential philosophy, and anticipated the Existentialists' tendency to elevate action above systems of thought.

We must be careful not to overextend the analogy between Existentialism and Dada—the one a serious, philosophical movement, and the other an elusive, more or less spontaneous outcry in the arts—but we can perhaps now see why the development of the former helped bring the latter back into prominence. The same postwar atmosphere, which was conducive to a philosophy of despair, like Existentialism, also brought about a reconsideration of Dada. That this atmosphere is still very much with us was made clear by a reviewer for a Düsseldorf newspaper who commented upon a Dada exhibit which was held in West Germany in 1958. "In its origin," this reviewer wrote, "Dada is the radical protest of artists with a prophetic vision against the suicide of Europe in the First World War, something which, in the middle of the twentieth century, one can see to have been only the overture to that senseless suicide of the world which has in the meantime become possible."[125]

The Dada rebirth was first heralded in the plastic arts with its quick succession of Dada-inspired phenomena—Abstract Expressionism, Pop Art, Assemblage, and the various other forms of "Neo-Dada." Paralleling these developments, certain new literary forms, such as the New Novel and Beat poetry, have appeared, raising the possibility that just as viable a Dada tradition exists in literature as in painting and sculpture. Having already discussed the ways in which Aragon's *Anicet* anticipated the experiments of the New Novelists, we might add that, in general, when the Dadas and Surrealists stripped the word of its denotative and connotative function, they were paving the way for the phenomenological approach of writers like Alain Robbe-Grillet and Michel Butor.

For the main thrust of Dada's influence on recent literature, however, we must look beyond the New Novelists, with their spirit of scientific detachment, to another group of writers who have adopted the techniques, if not the spirit, of the Dadas. Numbered among this group are Samuel Beckett, whose manner of expressing metaphysical anguish both in his novels and his plays sometimes calls Dada to mind; William Burroughs, whose novels are often constructed according to those principles of chance which were so dear to the Dadas; and John Barth, whose most recent work is an attempt to translate certain Dadaist concepts into the novel form.[126]

But, above all, it is the free-wheeling poets of the Beat generation who have not only inherited the Dadas' taste for absolute freedom, but also their radical ways of expressing it. For the Beats, Dada was a multifaceted symbol of modern nihilism: to LeRoi Jones, it was "Black Dada Nihilismus"; to Allen Ginsberg, it was the memory of heaving "potato salad at CCNY lecturers on Dadaism";[127] and to Lawrence Ferlinghetti, it was an intimation of life's everyday absurdities.

CHAPTER FIVE

.. CONCLUSION

Men with their reason seek the key that will open the gate of mystery, the gate of life. Never in this way will they penetrate to the infinite, peacock-colored halls, in which the golden flames dance and embrace one another.

MARCEL JANCO

HAVING EXAMINED the Dada movement's most important manifestations in literature, we must pose two essential questions in this concluding chapter: one, how is Dada related to the various other movements in the arts which either preceded or followed it? and two, what was the impact of the First World War on its development? In attempting to answer these questions, we will try to place the Dada movement within its artistic and cultural context and provide a better understanding of its overall significance.

Perhaps the most crucial aspect of Dada's relationship to such movements as Expressionism, Cubism, and Futurism was the vehemently anti-artistic attitudes of its principal spokesmen. More than a mere reaction against the "isms" of modern art, these attitudes were part of a bold attempt to destroy the "cult of art" completely and crush its would-be worshippers. Comparing Dada with Cubism and Futurism, Breton pointedly expressed this aspect of the movement when he wrote in the first of his two Dada manifestos:

> Cubism was a school of painting, futurism a political movement: DADA is a state of mind. To oppose one to the other reveals ignorance or bad faith.
> Free-thinking in religion has no resemblance to a church. DADA is artistic free-thinking.
> As long as the schools go in for prayers in the form of explanation of texts and walks in museums, we shall cry depotism and try to disrupt the ceremony.[1]

But this completely uncompromising position vis-á-vis modern art, an ideal few of the Dadas would or could live up to in practice, does not tell the full story. As Breton himself so eloquently put it, the Dadas were a group of artistic freethinkers who made up their own minds about everything, especially about their attitudes toward modern art. And it is this extreme individualism which seems to make the Dadas' relationship with earlier art movements more complex than it appears to be on the surface.

The ambivalent attitudes of the Zurich Dadas are a case in point. Developing during a climate when Expressionism, Cubism, and Futurism were dominant, the Zurich group could not help but be influenced by these movements, particularly since it remained in close contact with them. Thus, as we have seen, in the period when Hugo Ball was in command, the contributions of artists such as Kandinsky, Apollinaire, and Marinetti played such a prominent role in the performances at the Cabaret Voltaire and in the various Dada periodicals that it was often difficult to distinguish what was Dadaist from what was not.

Keeping in mind that even Tzara used at least the trappings of modern art to cloak the subversive nature of his Trojan horse, and taking into account that, while Tzara and Picabia were espousing their anti-artistic philosophy, men like Arp, Janco, and Richter were engaged in experiments with abstract art, we can perhaps get some idea of how ambiguous the Dada movement's relationship with modern art really was.

In recognizing the complexity of this relationship, however, we should not overlook certain essential differences between Dada and these other movements. The most important of these—that Dada was neither a cohesive group of artists nor a school of art—has already been suggested by the phrase "artistic free-thinkers." Rather than being joined by a common program, the Dadas were a group of independent-minded individuals who came together for a brief period, and then drifted apart. Once again, it was Breton who seems to have captured the true nature of their movement when he wrote that "our collective resistance to artistic or moral laws gives us only momentary satisfaction. We are very well aware that beyond and above this, a distinctive individual imagination is at work in each of us—and that this is more 'Dada' than the movement itself."[2]

Elevating individual freedom above everything else, the Dada movement broke with all the formal principles of modern art and concentrated, instead, upon providing the artist with a new climate within which to exercise his imaginative powers. In contrast to the Expressionists, Cubists, and Futurists, who conscientiously traced their development back to earlier movements and had their own program for the future, there was, for the Dadas, no immutable past or future: there was only the present. Having thus cut themselves completely off from history, these brave young men went on to affirm the transcendent nature of the artists' state of mind as opposed to art's finished product.

Distrustful of everything which, in Tzara's words, was "congealed, immutable, and definitive," the Dadas put more faith in their own revolutionary state of mind than in the once revolutionary tenets of Expressionism, Cubism, and Futurism which, again to quote Tzara, had become the "new academism."

In criticizing the modern artist for having lost sight of his revolutionary intentions, the Dadas were at the same time expressing their discontent with modern society. Modern art, in their view, had come to symbolize the rigid forms and corrupt practices of the very society which it had once opposed. As Tzara put it, they could feel nothing but disgust for all of this:

> Disgust with all the catalogued categories, with the false prophets who are nothing but a front for the interests of money, pride, disease, disgust with the lieutenants of a

mercantile art made to order according to a few infantile laws . . . Disgust finally with the Jesuitical dialectic which can explain everything and fill people's minds with oblique and obtuse ideas without any physiological basis or ethnic roots, all this by means of blinding artifice and ignoble charlatan's promises.[3]

This overwhelming disgust was crystallized by the First World War, which not only revealed to already disillusioned young men like Tzara just how spiritually bankrupt their society really was, but also helped determine the form their protest would take. Against the background of modern warfare, they saw institutions crumble and once noble concepts, like morality, the family, and religion, irremediably transformed into what Tzara has called "a skeleton of conventions." Faced with the fact of war, these young men quickly realized that art and literature either were powerless before its onslaughts or, what was worse, became a vehicle for its propaganda.

More than any other single phenomenon, it was the war which seems to have pushed the Dadas into open confrontation with their society and acted as the catalyst to spark their revolt; the bitter war-time experiences which so many of these young men underwent helped make them susceptible to Dada in the first place, and the complete collapse of values in the war's aftermath provided the perfect atmosphere for Dada to flourish.

Despite this fact, however, it would be a mistake to try to explain Dada strictly in terms of the war, without taking into account the revolutionary tradition of European art and literature of which the Dadas were part. As we have seen, they were not only influenced by anarchistic poets like Rimbaud and Jarry, but also by some of the same artists—Kandinsky, Apollinaire, and Marinetti —who provided the foundations for Expressionism, Cubism, and Futurism.

Perhaps the most important thing about the First World War, as far as its impact upon the Dada movement is concerned, is that it offered a model for the Dadas' spiritual revolt. The same analogy which Hugo Ball drew between the Russian revolution and the activities of Zurich Dada might be drawn between the Dada movement in general and the war itself: that Dada was the artistic equivalent of the war. As early as 1920, André Gide called attention to this possibility in an article which was published in the *Nouvelle Revue Française*. With curious glee, he compared the physical ravages of the war with the attempts by the Dadas to destroy language:

> What! While our fields, our villages, our cathedrals suffered so much, our style alone should remain untouched! It is essential that the spirit should not lag behind matter; it has a right to ruin. Dada will see to this.[4]

Like their reactions to modern art, the Dadas' response to war was rather ambivalent. On the one hand, they expressed a common hatred for the hostilities which had become so much a part of their lives, but on the other, they seem to have patterned their own war against reason and its conventions upon them. Using all of the weapons of artistic terrorism at their command, the Dadas carried their spiritual battles into the very streets where the war had been fought. And perhaps it was the uncompromising nature of war which helps account for their uncompromising stand. Thus, at least in theory, the Dadas refused to make those minimum compromises with rationality which previous revolutionaries in the arts had made.

Although certain of the Dadas swore their allegiance solely to the forces of the irrational, while others wavered on its brink, there was one idea which all of the members of the Dada movement more or less held in common: this was what the German art historian Werner Haftmann has called "the autonomy of the self."

> Every spontaneous impulse, every message from within, was . . . greeted as an expression of pure reality. Every possible artistic technique suited his [the individual Dada's] purpose of provoking these impulses. Absolute spontaneity, chance regarded as the intervention of mysterious and wonderful forces, pure automatism as a revelation of that store of hidden reality within the individual over which consciousness has no control—these were the techniques that opened the way to a more comprehensive view of the relationship between Self and world."[5]

Viewed within the context of this kind of experimentation and exploration, the Dadas' basic intent was to capture the elusive experience of spontaneity. "What we want now," Tzara explained, "is spontaneity. Not because it is better or more beautiful than anything else. But because everything that issues freely from ourselves, without the intervention of speculative ideas, represents us."[6] Not all of the Dadas were willing to go as far as Tzara and Picabia, whose daring experiments brought them to the verge of automatic writing, but, to a greater or lesser extent, they were all preoccupied with the idea of spontaneity and the "autonomy of the self." And it is in terms of these preoccupations that their fascination with "significant nonsense," popular culture, and primitive art can perhaps be best understood.

As J. C. Middleton has pointed out, the paradoxical, nonsensical gestures of the Dadas were "a means of defying the devil by capping his nonsense,"[7] but, perhaps even more important, they were also a way of asserting their absolute freedom from reason and logic. This last point helps to account for the Dadas' interest in popular culture—particularly film—where the immediacy of the experience often undercut traditional morality at the same time that it was undermining traditional logic. But above all, it was primitive art which provided the Dadas with their most vivid images of spontaneity. Turning to African art, as so many of their fellow artists had done before them, the Dadas found their greatest source of inspiration. Unlike the Cubists, who had used African sculpture as a model for their own works, the Dadas studied African dance, music, and poetry not so much in an attempt to imitate the finished product as to gain an insight into the primeval spontaneity of the primitive life style. That this insight became an essential aspect of Dada can be seen in the improvised rhythms of their African Evenings and the primitive nature of so much of their poetry.

Out of the Dadas' often desperate quest for spontaneity, a new approach to literature began to emerge. But perhaps because in the minds of many critics and historians, it has been overshadowed by Surrealism, the Dada movement has never been given the credit it seems to deserve for having fostered these new developments. This is especially true in the area of literature where most observers continue to see the Dada movement as a purely destructive phenomenon whose only virtue was that it paved the way for the more constructive movement of Surrealism.

While this interpretation allows for a neat division between Dada, the "negative" movement, and Surrealism, the "positive" one, it is an oversimplification of history which overlooks the Dada movement's contributions to literature and to the arts in general. Breton himself has called attention to its historical inaccuracies. Recalling that Surrealist and Dadaist texts had often appeared side by side in such magazines as *Littérature*, he stated that it is "inexact and chronologically abusive" to say that Surrealism grew out of Dada or that it corrected Dada's negative tendencies.[8] Elaborating upon Breton's remarks, Sanouillet has pointed out that "there is a Surrealist aspect of Dada and a Dadaist aspect of Surrealism."[9]

Because of this grey area, it is often difficult to distinguish Dada from Surrealism. But it is possible to divide the two movements along broad, philosophical lines. Some idea of how widely the Surrealist ideal differed from that of Dada can be gained from Breton's first definition of Surrealism: "Pure psychic automatism by means of which we propose to express either verbally, in writing, or in some other fashion what really goes on in the mind. Dictation by the mind, unhampered by conscious control and having no aesthetic or moral goals."[10]

Guided by this definition and influenced by the findings of Freud, the Surrealists began to explore the subconscious mind, in the process evolving a systematic, almost scientific doctrine. Based upon such techniques as automatic writing and experiments with the occult, this Surrealist doctrine was a far cry from the Dadas' more or less spontaneous activities.

An indication of the new spirit of scientific inquiry which had taken possession of the early Surrealists comes from the first issue of their periodical *The Surrealist Revolution*. The inside cover of this magazine contained the kind of cautionary statement usually associated with the tentative findings of scientists (" . . . no result of the research, experience, or work is as yet recorded: we must all await the future."), and the format itself, which was largely devoted to the automatic texts and elaborate descriptions of the dreams of the Surrealists, was arranged and presented in the systematic manner of a scientific journal.[11]

Just how far the Surrealists were willing to go in the systematic application of their discoveries is evidenced by the fact that they later founded an Office of Surrealist Research, an agency which, among other things, was responsible for amassing and analyzing data concerning the subconscious mind and its various manifestations. Like any serious research organization, this office was not above soliciting information from the public at large.

Comparing the systematic approach of Surrealism, at least in its purest state, with what has been termed "the gay blasphemy" of Dada, we can perhaps now understand why the former has eclipsed the latter in the minds of so many critics and historians.

With its clearly expressed methods and goals and its relatively systematic doctrine, Surrealism, has proved easier for them to grasp than Dada, with its elusive, enigmatic qualities and its virtual absence of theory. It is not surprising that, in the light of the seemingly obvious chronological sequence, they would be inclined to conclude that the Dada movement was merely a brief, but intensive, period of nihilism in the arts, a destructive interlude which prepared the way for the more lucid and positive advances of Surrealism.

The various pronouncements and manifestos of the Dadas which, if nothing else, attest that this movement was designed to be nihilistic, seem to bear out this conclusion. But if we look beyond the Dadas' rhetoric to their poems and performances, as we have tried to do in this book, we get a very different picture of the movement. These works pose yet another of the many Dada paradoxes: that these artists and writers, ostensibly sworn to out-and-out destruction, should have created so much that, in retrospect, is positive and constructive.

Setting aside for a moment the creations of someone like Arp, who never seems to have been as dedicated to the idea of anti-art as some of the other Dadas, how do we explain, for example, that Tzara, starting out to create his "great negative work of destruction" could "pulverize" words into poetry? Or, for that matter, the poetry which Picabia was able to write despite his insistence that "art is useless and impossible to justify?"[12] In short, how do we explain the paradox underlying the idea of destruction and construction in the Dada movement? Comparing the actions of the Dadas to those of a destructive child, Hans Kreitler has provided an important clue to this enigma: "A child breaking a toy does not merely destroy it; it also perceives something and with this perception it is later enabled to reconstruct. The Dadaists' process was similar."[13] Having pushed the idea of destruction as far as it would go, the Dadas thus discovered—or, perhaps better, allowed us to discover—that true nihilism can never really exist in the arts. For, as Sanouillet, taking Kreitler's point about the duality of destruction and construction in the creative act one step further, noted, "all negation is accompanied by a simultaneous affirmation, all destruction entails a construction. In all of the activity of the human spirit, the 'positive' and 'negative' poles are as inseparable as in an electric current: one cannot exist with the other. . . ."[14]

What prevented the Dadas' revolt from becoming nihilist in

the fullest sense of the word, then, was the fact that with few exceptions, most notably that of Duchamp, they refused to give up their creative activity. They were prepared to abandon all the values embraced by their society, especially its artistic ones, but, whether willingly or not, they remained artists and writers through it all, and the subversive poetry they wrote and the provocative demonstrations and other scandalous proceedings in which they engaged proved it.

Judged in these terms, the destructive activities of the Dada movement are not so much a manifestation of nihilism in the arts as they are an expression of moral outrage by a group of disillusioned young artists and writers who realized, above all, that they must arrive at the *reductio ad absurdum* of life and art so that they might begin anew. "We took Descartes' phrase: 'I don't even want to know that there were men before me,' as a motto for one of our publications," Tzara later recalled. "This meant that we wished to regard the world with new eyes, to reconsider the very fundamentals and test the truth of the notions handed down to us by our elders."[15]

The return to essentials which Tzara and his fellow Dadas advocated, could not and did not destroy the artistic impulse. What it did do, however, was to help put an end to traditional forms of art and liberate the modern artist from all prior philosophical, moral, or formal restraints. Moreover—and this is perhaps the most fascinating aspect of this Dada paradox—in freeing the artist from art's own tyranny, the Dadas helped to set the stage for future developments. Once again, if we were to judge by the Dadas' rhetoric, which rages against the very idea of a future, let alone those who believe in its mystique, this is the last movement which one would expect to have had an impact on the future of modern art. But this was exactly what did happen, not only in the plastic arts, but also in literature.

How do we account for this curious turnabout whereby a movement that was apparently meant to be negative and destructive becomes positive and constructive? In order to explore this ultimate paradox of Dada, we must elaborate upon two concepts which have been touched upon previously; discursive and non discursive symbolism. Using the language of discourse as her model, Susanne K. Langer has provided the following precise definition of discursive symbolism in her book *Philosophy in a New Key:*

All language has a form which requires us to string out our ideas even though their objects rest one within the other; as pieces of clothing that are actually worn one over the other have to be strung side by side on the clothesline. This property of verbal symbolism is known as discursiveness; by reason of it, only thoughts which can be arranged in this peculiar order can be spoken at all; any idea which does not lend itself to this "projection" is ineffable, incommunicable by means of words. That is why the laws of reasoning, our clearest formulation of exact expression, are sometimes known as "the laws of discursive thought."[16]

According to Langer, the concept of nondiscursive symbolism, which stands in marked contrast to the property of discursiveness, can best be understood in terms of the visual experience:

Visual forms—lines, colors, proportions, etc.—are just as capable of *articulation*, i.e. of complex combination, as words. But the laws that govern this sort of articulation are altogether different from the laws of syntax that govern language. The most radical difference is that *visual forms are not discursive*. They do not present their constituents successively, but simultaneously, so the relations determining a visual structure are grasped in one act of vision.

Langer goes on to say that "the symbolism furnished by our purely sensory appreciation of forms is a *nondiscursive symbolism*, peculiarly well suited to the expression of ideas that defy linguistic 'projection.' Its primary function, that of conceptualizing the flux of sensations, and giving us concrete *things* in place of kaleidoscopic colors or noises, is itself an office that no language-born thought can replace."[17]

In their attempts to capture what Langer has called "the inexpressible realm of feeling, of formless desires and satisfactions, immediate experience, forever incognito and incommunicado," modern artists in general, and modern poets in particular, have sought to move further and further away from discursiveness toward a more pristine form of nondiscursive symbolism. And, when seen in terms of this phenomenon, the Dadas' attacks against literature, which were actually part of an attempt to strip

167

away the last traces of discursive symbolism in the arts, take on a startling new dimension. As a result of their seemingly negative attempts to destroy the discursive elements of literature, the Dadas revealed the nondiscursive properties of these art forms perhaps more clearly than ever before. In a very real sense they proved that literature could, like the plastic arts, exist solely on the level of nondiscursive symbolism.

That this attempt to eliminate what Moholy-Nagy has called "the one dimensional linear form" of literature places the Dadas squarely within the revolutionary tradition of modern art was recognized by no less an authority than Tzara himself. Looking back upon the Dadas' revolt against poetry, Tzara wrote that "Dada, which had broken not only with the traditional succession of schools, but also with those values which were ostensibly most unassailable, actually prolonged the unbroken line of schools and poets; by this marvelous chain it was connected with Mallarmé, Rimbaud, Lautréamont, and going still further, with Baudelaire and Victor Hugo, thus marking the continuity of the spirit of revolt in French poetry."[18]

By refusing to abide by even the most basic ground rules of literature or to strike even the most rudimentary compromise with rationality, the Dadas were able to open themselves up completely to the vicissitudes of chance and free association and thereby arrive at a radically new form of nondiscursive symbolism. This was especially true in the case of Dada poetry. Whereas poets like Apollinaire and Cendrars had reserved the right to choose carefully among the elements to be emphasized in their expressions of simultaneism, the Dadas often went one step further in an effort to record only the rawest, most unfiltered emotions. Noting that "the dadaists proved that emotional traits are never describable, only recordable in the making, like functions of the organism, metabolism, or breathing," Moholy-Nagy has commented that "they came to a new device of the literary expression—to a crisscrossing, zigzagging thought-pulsation of as many currents and messages as could be transmitted at the same time."[19]

The ultimate significance of Dada's extraordinary turnabout seems to reside in its "cult of negative values." At the root of these "negative values" was the Dadas' constant preoccupation with the idea of doubt. In his "manifesto on feeble and bitter love," Tzara proposed that "a priori, that is with eyes closed, Dada places before action and above all: *Doubt*. Dada doubts all."[20] Underscoring this point, Breton wrote in the conclusion of his second Dada manifesto that "DADA attacks you with your own idea. If we reduce you to maintaining that it is more advantageous to believe than not to believe what is taught by all religions of beauty, love, truth, and justice, it is because you are not afraid to put yourself at the mercy of DADA by accepting an encounter with us on the terrain that we have chosen, which is doubt."[21]

Out of these feelings of doubt, a new "negative" aesthetic has begun to emerge. Recalling Ribemont-Dessaignes' bitterly skeptical declaration ("What is beautiful? What is ugly? What is great, strong, weak? . . . What is I . . . Don't know! Don't know, don't know, don't know!"), as well as Tzara's intentional blurring of opposites ("Order = disorder; ego = non-ego; affirmation = negation"), William Seitz, in *The Art of Assemblage,* has pointed out some of the most far-reaching implications of this new aesthetic:

> Finally and with authority—and for the first time in Western thought—dada substituted a nonrational metaphysic of oppositions for a rationalized hierarchy of values. As a consequence it accorded to unsureness, accident, confusion, disunity, and discontinuity a share of the attention formerly reserved for what had been commonly regarded as their moral opposites, and released a constellation of physical and intellectual energies through which an artist could (and still can) operate in a way that, at least in the West, was previously impossible. By a dynamism inherent in human experience, moreover, the recognition of live reciprocity turns the mind toward an indefinable central principle as transparent and vital as the Tao in Chinese thought and art. It was the knowledge of dada, in part, which led certain modern artists, after 1945, toward Zen Buddhism.[22]

What this new aesthetic meant for those artists who would follow Dada was perhaps best summed up by Marsden Hartley, the American painter who remained on the fringes of the Dada movement. "It is thrilling," Hartley wrote, "to realize that there is a healthy way out of all this dilemma of habit for the artist. One of these ways is to reduce the size of the 'A' in art, to meet the size of the rest of the letters in one's speech. Another way is to deliver art from the clutches of its worshippers, and by worshippers I mean the idolaters and the commercialists of art."[23] Now, he continued, "I have a hobby-horse . . . to ride away with, out into the world of intricate common experience; out into the arena with those who know what the element of life itself is, and that I have become an expression of the one issue in the mind worth the consideration of the artist, namely fluidic change."[24]

Placing their emphasis upon the state of mind which makes art possible, rather than on the work of art itself, the Dadas arrived at the very nature of the creative process. Given the proper state of mind and a public willing to be artistic partners rather than spectators, they proved that it was virtually impossible for the artist *not* to create art. That this was true regardless of the means employed was pointed up by Tzara himself when he articulated the liberating principle underlying Dada's "new image of the artist." Noting that he and his fellow Dadas had deliberately sought to confuse the genres of painting and writing in order to give "some play to art," Tzara went on to say that from now on, because of the legacy of Dada, art could "employ incongruous elements—materials noble or looked down upon, verbal clichés or clichés of old magazines, bromides, publicity slogans, refuse, etc.—these incongruous elements are transformed into unexpected, homogeneous cohesion as soon as they take place in a newly created ensemble."[25]

We have come a long way on Dada's so-called path of destruction. And, having watched the scenery change and new buildings emerge out of the ruins, we can only conclude, with Michel Seuphor, that "Dada, which has only been a liberator, destroyed nothing at all. It is on the other side of its wave that we live and it is on its foundation of vociferations and arrogant stammerings that the new art is being built and continues its conquests."[26]

NOTES

Notes for Introduction

1. Michel Sanouillet, *Dada à Paris* (Paris: Pauvert, 1965), p. 432; and Jacob Korg, "The Literary Aesthetics of Dada," *Works*, I:3 (Spring, 1968), p. 43.

2. Korg, p. 43.

3. John Richardson, "The Dada Movement," *The Times Literary Supplement*, Oct. 23, 1953, p. 669.

4. Quoted by Arturo Schwarz, *Cinquant' anni a Dada* (Milano: Galleria Schwarz, 1966), p. 38.

5. Quoted by Hans Richter, *Dada Art and Anti-Art* (New York: McGraw-Hill, n.d.), p. 32.

6. *The Dada Painters and Poets: An Anthology*, ed. Robert Motherwell (New York: Wittenborn and Schultz, 1951), p. 216.

7. *The Dada Painters and Poets*, p. 77.

8. *The Dada Painters and Poets*, p. 92.

9. See William C. Seitz, *The Art of Assemblage* (New York: Museum of Modern Art, 1961); and William S. Rubin, *Dada, Surrealism, and Their Heritage* (New York: Museum of Modern Art, 1968).

10. See Sanouillet, p. 420.

Notes for Chapter One

1. Quoted by Georges Lemaitre, *From Cubism to Surrealism in French Literature* (Cambridge, Mass.: Harvard University Press, 1941), pp. 53–54.

2. See *The Dada Painters and Poets*, p. 129.

3. *The Dada Painters and Poets*, p. 78.

4. Quoted by Maurice Nadeau, *History of Surrealism*, tr. R. Howard (New York: Macmillan, 1965), p. 69.

5. Tristan Tzara, *Le Surréalisme et l'Après-Guerre* (Paris: Les Editions Nagel, 1948), p. 14.

6. Quoted by Roger Shattuck, *The Banquet Years* (Garden City, N.Y.: Doubleday, 1961), p. 226.

7. André Breton, *Anthologie de l'Humour noir* (Paris: Pauvert, 1966), p. 359.

8. *Selected Works of Alfred Jarry*, ed. R. Shattuck and S. W. Taylor (New York: Grove Press, 1965), p. 76.

9. *Selected Works of Alfred Jarry*, p. 80. Interestingly enough, Jarry compared Ubu's actions to those of an anarchist in that "he carries out his own orders, ripping people up because he enjoys the idea, and imploring the Russian soldiers not to shoot in his direction because he does not enjoy the idea."

10. This technique, which Jarry made use of in *Ubu's Almanach*, a strange collection of witty notations, sketches, short essays, and dramatic pieces, was adopted by the other Dadas as well. For example, see the Soupault poem quoted in "Memoirs of Dadaism," in *Axel's Castle* (New York: Scribner's, 1931), p. 306.

11. Quoted by Shattuck, p. 214.

12. See Shattuck, p. 243.

13. *Selected Works of Alfred Jarry*, pp. 182–183.

14. *Selected Works of Alfred Jarry*, p. 190.

15. *Selected Works of Alfred Jarry*, p. 193.

16. *Selected Works of Alfred Jarry*, p. 192–193.

17. Quoted by Shattuck, p. 221.

18. See Georges Ribemont-Dessaignes, *Déjà Jadis ou du mouvement Dada à l'Espace abstrait* (Paris: Juilliard, 1958), p. 22.

19. Quoted by Georges Hugnet, *L'Aventure Dada* (Paris: Galérie de L'Institut, 1957), p. 63.

20. According to André Salmon,

(*Souvenir Sans Fin*, Deuxième Epoque, 1908–1920, [Paris: Gallimard, 1956], p. 218), Cravan may have patterned this lecture, including the firing of the pistol, upon Jarry's notorious introduction of *King Ubu*.

21. Quoted by Hugnet, p. 63.

22. Arthur Cravan, *Maintenant* (Paris: Losfeld, 1956), p. 28. Regarding the stylistic similarity of Cendrars and Cravan, see especially Cendrars's poem "Prose of the Transsiberian and of Little Jeanne of France."

23. Cravan, p. 45.

24. Cravan, p. 54.

25. ′Cravan, p. 52.

26. André Breton, *Les Pas perdus* (Paris: Gallimard, 1924), p. 258.

27. *The Dada Painters and Poets*, p. 4.

28. *The Dada Painters and Poets*, pp. 11–12. This libelous attack earned Cravan eight days in jail.

29. *The Dada Painters and Poets*, pp. 11–12. The outcome of this second attack was much more humorous. To avenge his own and his mistress's honor (Cravan had referred to him as "Apollinaire the Jew"), Apollinaire challenged him to a duel, but Cravan refused to take up the challenge and instead published the following tongue-in-cheek recantation in *Now*: "Not that I'm afraid of Apollinaire's great sabre, but because I have so little pride, I'm prepared to make all the rectification in the world and to declare that . . . Mr. Guillaume Apollinaire is not a Jew at all, but a Roman Catholic. To avoid any possible future misunderstandings, I should add that Mr. Apollinaire, who has a big belly, resembles a rhinoceros more than a giraffe, his head is more like a tapir's than a lion's, and that he draws more upon the vulture than the long-billed stork." (Cravan, p. 106).

30. *The Dada Painters and Poets*, p. 7.

31. *The Dada Painters and Poets*, p. 7.

32. *The Dada Painters and Poets*, p. 7.

33. *The Dada Painters and Poets*, p. 12.

34. *The Dada Painters and Poets*, p. 12.

35. *The Dada Painters and Poets*, p. 12–13.

36. Cravan, p. 14.

37. *The Dada Painters and Poets*, p. 15.

38. Cravan, p. 11.

39. Cravan, p. 25.

40. Quoted by Emile Bouvier, "Jacques Vaché," tr. S. Putnam, *The European Caravan* (New York: Brewer, Warren, and Putnam, 1931), p. 87. An indication of Vaché's indebtedness to Jarry comes from the orthographic similarity between his "Umour" and Jarry's "Merdre." And, a propos of Vaché's use of the term "theatric futility," one of Jarry's most important essays was entitled "Of the Futility of the 'Theatrical' in the Theater." See *Selected Works of Alfred Jarry*, pp. 69–76.

41. *Les Pas perdus*, pp. 17–19.

42. Letter dated July 5, 1916, in *Les Lettres de Guerre de Jacques Vaché* (Paris: K, 1949), pages not numbered.

43. Letter dated August 18, 1917.

44. Letter dated July 9, 1918.

45. Letter dated April 29, 1917.

46. Undated letter to Theodore Fraenkel.

47. *Anthologie de l'Humour noir*, p. 495.

48. *Les Pas perdus*, p. 9.

49. *The Dada Painters and Poets*, p. 200.

50. Sanouillet, p. 79.

51. Letter dated August 18, 1917.

52. Letter dated August 18, 1917.

Notes For Chapter Two

1. Quoted by William A. Camfield, "Francis Picabia (1879–1953) A Study of His Career from 1895 to 1918," Unpublished dissertation, Yale University, 1964, p. 174.

2. Quoted by John I. Baur, *Revolution and Tradition in Modern American*

Art (Cambridge, Mass.; Harvard University Press, 1951), p. 26.

3. Baur, p. 26.

4. Quoted by Camfield, p. 176.

5. The letters L.H.O.O.Q. stand for the French equivalent of the phrase "She has hot pants."

6. *The Dada Painters and Poets*, p. 259.

7. Marcel Duchamp, *Marchand du Sel*, ed. M. Sanouillet (Paris: Le Terrain Vague, 1958), p. 12.

8. *The Dada Painters and Poets*, p. 262.

9. Francis Picabia, "Magic City" in *391*, ed. M. Sanouillet (Paris: Le Terrain Vague, 1960), p. 40.

10. Picabia, p. 48.

11. Picabia, p. 48.

12. Picabia, p. 42.

13. Duchamp, p. 102.

14. Duchamp, p. 104.

15. Duchamp, p. 194.

16. *The Dada Painters and Poets*, p. 185.

17. *The Dada Painters and Poets*, p. 186.

18. *The Dada Painters and Poets*, p. 217.

19. Jean Arp, "Looking," in *Arp*, ed. J. T. Soby, (New York: Museum of Modern Art, 1958), p. 13.

20. *The Dada Painters and Poets*, p. 263.

Notes For Chapter Three

1. Marcel Janco, "Creative Dada," *Dada: Monograph of a Movement* (New York: Hastings House, 1957), p. 28.

2. *Dada: Art and Anti-Art*, p. 12.

3. Stefan Zweig, *The World of Yesterday* (New York: Viking Press, 1943), p. 261.

4. Quoted by Benjamin Goriély, "Hugo Ball, Prophète Rebelle," *Cahiers Dada-Surréalisme*, No. 1, 1967, p. 13.

5. Quoted in *Dada: Art and Anti-Art*, p. 35.

6. Quoted in *Dada: Art and Anti-Art*, p. 13.

7. *The Dada Painters and Poets*, p. 279.

8. Jean Arp, *On My Way*, tr. R. Manheim (New York: Wittenborn and Schultz, 1948), p. 45.

9. *Dada: Monograph of a Movement*, p. 30.

10. *The Dada Painters and Poets*, p. 287.

11. *The Dada Painters and Poets*, p. 287.

12. *Dada: Monograph of a Movement*, p. 32.

13. Quoted in *Dada: Art and Anti-Art*, p. 23.

14. Quoted in *Dada: Art and Anti-Art*, p. 23.

15. Quoted in *Dada: Art and Anti-Art*, p. 23.

16. *Dada: Monograph of a Movement*, p. 28.

17. *The Dada Painters and Poets*, p. 235.

18. *The Dada Painters and Poets*, p. 23.

19. Quoted in *Dada: Art and Anti-Art*, p. 20.

20. *The Dada Painters and Poets*, p. 23.

21. *The Dada Painters and Poets*, p. 23.

22. The poems by Apollinaire ("Tree") and Cendrars ("Cracklings") were published without authorization (Hugnet, p. 18.). This, in part, accounts for Apollinaire's coolness toward the Zurich movement. He was also, of course, suspicious of what he felt was its "ententist" tone (Sanouillet, p. 97).

23. *The Cabaret Voltaire*, ed. Hugo Ball, Zurich, 1916. According to Hugnet, this disclaimer did not prevent certain French journalists from attacking Dada on this very point (Hugnet, p. 19).

24. *Dada: Monograph of a Movement*, p. 32.

25. *The Dada Painters and Poets*, p. 23.

26. *The Dada Painters and Poets*, p. 236.

27. Quoted in *Dada: Monograph of a*

Movement, p. 88. As further evidence of this, Ball asked "from where should calm and simplicity come, if no undermining, no clearance, and no spring-cleaning of the warped base preceded it?" (Quoted in *Dada: Monograph of a Movement*, p. 78).

28. *The Dada Painters and Poets*, p. 34.

29. Gerhardt E. Steinke, "The Anarchistic, Expressionistic, and Dadaistic Phases in the Life and Work of Hugo Ball," Unpublished dissertation, Stanford University, 1954, p. 262.

30. Quoted in *Dada: Art and Anti-Art*, p. 42.

31. *The Dada Painters and Poets*, p. 236.

32. *The Dada Painters and Poets*, p. 239.

33. *Dada* III, Dec. 1918, no page numbers.

34. Picabia, p. 64.

35. *Dada: Art and Anti-Art*, p. 36.

36. *The Dada Painters and Poets*, p. 240.

37. *Dada: Art and Anti-Art*, pp. 78-79.

38. *The Dada Painters and Poets*, p. 242.

39. *The Dada Painters and Poets*, p. 39.

40. Zweig, p. 228.

41. Quoted by Walter Mehring, *The Lost Library*, trans. R. and C. Winston (New York: Bobbs-Merrill, 1951), p. 148.

42. Quoted in *Dada: Monograph of a Movement*, p. 8.

43. Quoted in George Grosz, "The Saddest Man in the World," *New Yorker* Profile II, Dec. 4, 1943, p. 40.

44. *Dada: Art and Anti-Art*, p. 102.

45. *The Dada Painters and Poets*, p. 33.

46. *The Dada Painters and Poets*, p. 39.

47. *The Dada Painters and Poets*, p. 28.

48. Quoted by Mehring, p. 145.

49. In 1916, Hausmann, Jung, and Richard Oehring founded a journal called *Freie Strasse* which they most appropriately distributed gratis to all interested parties. Primarily, this was a vehicle for their antisocial attitudes and their psychoanalytic experiments.

50. Hugnet, p. 44.

51. Joseph C. Bradley, "George Grosz: A Study of his Life, Art and Philosophy," Unpublished dissertation, University of Wisconsin, 1954, p. XII.

52. According to Sanouillet, however, he was not made Commissar of the Fine Arts, as earlier historians, like Hugnet, had claimed. (Sanouillet, p. 37.)

53. Quoted in *Dada: Art and Anti-Art*, p. 110-111.

54. Quoted by J. C. Middleton, "Bolshevism in Art: Dada and Politics," *Texas Studies in Literature and Language*, IV (1962), 417.

55. "The Saddest Man in the World," p. 46.

56. *The Dada Painters and Poets*, p. 152.

57. Middleton, p. 416.

58. George Grosz, *A Little Yes and a Big No*, trans. L. Dorin (New York: Dial Press, 1946), p. 145.

59. Grosz, p. 146.

60. Grosz, p. 162.

61. Quoted by Bradley, p. 23.

62. Mehring, p. 147.

63. "The Saddest Man in the World," p. 35.

64. Grosz, p. 185.

65. *The Dada Painters and Poets*, p. 42.

66. *The Dada Painters and Poets*, p. 44.

67. Quoted in *Dada: Art and Anti-Art*, p. 125.

68. Quoted in *Dada: Art and Anti-Art*, *op.cit.*, p. 126.

69. Quoted by Middleton, p. 423.

70. *Cinquant' anni a Dada*, p. 76.

71. Middleton, p. 423.

72. *Cinquant' anni a Dada*, p. 76.

73. *The Dada Painters and Poets*, p. 60.

74. *The Dada Painters and Poets*, p. 60.

75. *The Dada Painters and Poets*, p. 60.

76. *Dada: Monograph of a Movement*, p. 58.

77. Quoted in *Dada: Art and Anti-Art*, p. 145.

78. *Dada: Art and Anti-Art*, p. 139.

79. *The Dada Painters and Poets*, p. 59.

80. Quoted in *Dada: Art and Anti-Art*, p. 141.

81. Laszlo Moholy-Nagy, *Vision in Motion* (Chicago: Paul Theobald, 1961), p. 325.

82. *Dada: Art and Anti-Art*, p. 142.

83. *Dada: Art and Anti-Art*, p. 142.

84. *Dada: Art and Anti-Art*, p. 143.

85. Raoul Hausmann, *Courrier Dada* (Paris: Le Terrain Vague, 1958), p. 114.

86. Sanouillet, p. 43.

87. Pierre Paraf, "Visite à une Ombre bleu," *Europe*, May–June, 1964, p. 6.

88. Sanouillet, p. 58.

89. Jacques Rivière, "French Letters and the War," *The Ideal Reader* (New York: Meridian, 1960), p. 271.

90. Quoted by Jacques Damase, *A History of the Music-Hall in Paris*, trans. T. White (Paris: Editions "Spectacles," 1960), p. 8.

91. Damase, p. 8.

92. Romain Rolland, *Au-Dessus de la Mêlée* (Paris: Albin Michel, 1915), p. 42.

93. Louis Céline, *Journey to the End of the Night*, trans. J. Marks (New York: New Directions, 1960), p. 50.

94. Quoted by Barbara Tuchman, *The Guns of August* (New York: Dell, 1962), p. 489.

95. Louis Aragon, "Beautés de la Guerre et leurs reflets dans la Littérature," *Europe*, Dec. 1935, pp. 474-475.

96. Philippe Soupault, *Poésies Complètes 1917-1937* (Paris: GLM, 1937), p. 139.

97. Philippe Soupault, "Dada's Daddies," *Realitiés*, No. 112, March, 1960, p. 16.

98. See his poems in *The European Caravan*, pp. 64-73.

99. Aragon, p. 475.

100. André Breton, "The Situation of Surrealism between the Two Wars," trans. R.G.C., *Yale French Studies*, No. 2 (1948), p. 70.

101. Quoted by Maurice Nadeau, *History of Surrealism*, tr. R. Howard (New York: Macmillan, 1965), p. 53.

102. According to Sanouillet, this incident, which did not appear in the newspaper and magazine accounts of the production, was much exaggerated by Breton and his friends. (Sanouillet, p. 81).

103. William Gaunt, *The March of the Moderns* (London: Jonathan Cape, 1949), p. 253.

104. Quoted by Matthew Josephson, *Life Among the Surrealists* (New York: Holt, Rinehart, and Winston, 1962), p. 123.

105. Quoted by Pierre de Massot, *De Mallarmé à 391* (Saint-Raphael: Au Bel Exemplaire, 1922), p. 75.

106. Sanouillet, pp. 92-95.

107. The single exception to this was Soupault who contributed a short poem entitled "Flame" to *Dada* III (*The Dada Painters and Poets*, p. 108).

108. André Breton, *Entretiens 1913-1952* (Paris: Gallimard, 1952), p. 52.

109. Quoted by Noel Arnaud, "Les Metamorphoses historiques de Dada," *Critique*, no. 134, July, 1958, p. 582.

110. *Les Pas perdus*, p. 13.

111. Quoted by Sanouillet, p. 121.

112. *Les Pas perdus*, p. 207.

113. *Axel's Castle*, p. 304.

114. Quoted by Sanouillet, pp. 154-155.

115. *The Dada Painters and Poets*, p. 109.

116. Georges Ribemont-Dessaignes, *Déjà Jadis, ou du mouvement Dada à l'espace abstrait* (Paris: Juillard, 1958), p. 71.

117. Quoted by Sanouillet, p. 167.

118. *Axel's Castle*, p. 307.

119. *Axel's Castle*, p. 307.

120. *Axel's Castle*, p. 306.

121. Quoted by Sanouillet, p. 174.

122. By accusing the Dadas of being German sympathizers, Rachilde had joined the ranks of Cocteau, who, because of his "arrivism," was a perennial target, as a butt for their jokes. The other three names speak for themselves. For a discussion of the complicated relationships between Cocteau and the Dadas, see Sanouillet, especially p. 105.

123. *Axel's Castle*, p. 308.

124. *Entretiens 1913–1952*, p. 58.

125. Rigaut, who had already tried to kill himself prior to joining the movement, was one of the few Dadas who actually went from thought to action in regard to suicide. He shot himself to death on Nov. 6, 1929, in a sanitarium in Châtenay.

126. Things reached such a state that many journalists wrote columns declaring that Dada should no longer be discussed. This prompted the following quip from Jean Paulhan: "If you must speak of Dada you must speak of Dada. If you must not speak of Dada you must still speak of Dada." (Quoted in *Axel's Castle*, p. 308).

127. *The Dada Painters and Poets*, p. 115.

128. Quoted by Nadeau, p. 66.

129. Quoted by Sanouillet, p. 267. I am indebted to Sanouillet for most of the material on the internal strife in Paris Dada.

130. Quoted by Sanouillet, p. 267.

131. Quoted by Sanouillet, p. 268.

132. Quoted by Sanouillet, p. 290.

133. Quoted by Sanouillet, p. 291.

134. Quoted by Sanouillet, p. 323.

135. Quoted by Sanouillet, p. 329.

136. On this point, Breton sided with Christian Schad and Huelsenbeck to the effect that Tzara had nothing to do with the invention of Dada and that Walter Serner had actually written the 1918 manifesto.

137. Quoted by Nadeau, p. 67.

138. Quoted by Nadeau, p. 67.

139. *The European Caravan*, p. 109.

140. Fold-out supplement to *The Dada Painters and Poets*, pages not numbered.

141. Germaine Everling Picabia, "C'Etait Hier: Dada . . ." in *Les Oeuvres Libres*, Paris, No. 109, Juin, 1955, p. 168.

142. *The Dada Painters and Poets*, pp. 113–115 and *Axel's Castle*, p. 308.

143. Arp, p. 39.

144. *Dada: Art and Anti-Art*, p. 60.

145. Arnaud, p. 601.

146. Paul Eluard, "Développement Dada," *Littérature*, No. 3, Mai, 1920, p. 7.

147. Quoted by Josephson, pp. 122–123. Interestingly enough, E. E. Cummings was also fond of this designation. See his classification of art and artists as alive or dead in *E. E. Cummings, A Miscellany Revised*, George J. Firmage, ed. (New York: October House, 1958). For a discussion of the relationship between Cummings and Dada, see Chapter Four of the present study.

148. Paul Eluard, *Choix de Poèmes* (Paris: Gallimard, 1951) p. 23.

149. Josephson, p. 119.

150. Grosz, p. 182.

151. Mehring, p. 152.

152. Mehring, p. 152.

153. *Dada: Monograph of a Movement*, p. 28. In response perhaps to the kinds of things he witnessed at the Cabaret Voltaire, Lenin wrote: "I will not admit that the creations of expressionism, futurism, cubism, and all the other kinds of 'ism,' are the highest revelation of artistic genius. I do not understand them, and they do not give me pleasure." (Quoted in *Dada: Monograph of a Movement*, p. 12.)

154. *Dada: Art and Anti-Art*, p. 16.

155. Quoted in *Dada: Monograph of a Movement*, p. 109.

156. *Entretiens 1913–1952*, p.40.

Notes For Chapter Four

1. Fold-out Supplement to *The Dada Painters and Poets*, no page numbers.

2. Quoted in *The Dada Painters and Poets*, p. XX

3. Quoted in *Dada: Art and Anti-Art*, p. 30.

4. Quoted in *Dada: Art and Anti-Art*, p. 31.

5. Quoted in *Dada: Art and Anti-Art*, p.41.

6. The origin of the sound poem can be traced at least as far back as the Medieval period. In more recent times, Christian Morgenstern, a turn-of-the-century writer of "metaphysical nonsense," whose verse was recited at the Cabaret Voltaire, invented his own form of "nonsense language" based on the idea of phonetic poetry. For a discussion of Morgenstern and other precursors of sound poetry, see Leonard Forster, *Poetry of Significant Nonsense* (London: Cambridge University Press, 1962).

7. Quoted in *The Dada Painters and Poets*, p. XIX.

8. Quoted in *Dada: Art and Anti-Art*, p. 43.

9. Quoted in *Dada: Art and Anti-Art*, p. 42.

10. *The Dada Painters and Poets*, p. 52.

11. Forster, p. 31. Forster has even gone so far as to compare the poetic recitations of the Zurich Dadas with the idea of "speaking with tongues." (Forster, p. 36.)

12. *The Dada Painters and Poets*, p. 77.

13. *The Dada Painters and Poets*, p. 79.

14. *The Dada Painters and Poets*, p. 81.

15. *The Dada Painters and Poets*, p. 81.

16. *The Dada Painters and Poets*, p. 87.

17. Quoted by Elmer R. Peterson, "The Critical Vision of Tristan Tzara," Unpublished dissertation, University of Colorado, 1962, p. 59.

18. *Dada* II, December 1917, pages not numbered.

19. Tristan Tzara, "Pamphlet for Dada Exhibition Sidney Janis Gallery, 1953," trans. M. Duchamp, in Museum of Modern Art Scrapbook, vol. 1, pages not numbered.

20. *The Dada Painters and Poets*, p. 80.

21. Fold-out Supplement to *The Dada Painters and Poets*.

22. Fold-out Supplement to *The Dada Painters and Poets*.

23. Tristan Tzara, "Le Géant blanc lepreux du Paysage," in *Tristan Tzara*, ed. René Lacôte (Paris: Seghers, 1952), p.101.

24. Tristan Tzara, *Cinéma calendrier du coeur abstrait* (Paris: Au Sans Pareil, 1920), pages not numbered.

25. Quoted by Dwight MacDonald, "Eisenstein, Pudovkin, and Others," in *The Emergence of Film Art*, ed. L. Jacobs, (New York: Hopkinson and Blake, 1969), p. 130. Eisenstein made it clear that the principle of montage need not apply exclusively to cinema. This "is a phenomenon invariably met with," he wrote, "in all cases where we have to deal with juxtaposition of two facts, two phenomena, two objects." (quoted by William Seitz, *The Art of Assemblage* (New York: Museum of Modern Art, 1961), p. 151.

26. Quoted in *The Emergence of Film Art*, p. 122.

27. Pansaers died in a Belgian hospital on Oct. 31, 1922, less than two years after he first made contact with the Dada movement.

28. Clément Pansaers, *Le Pan Pan au Cul du nu Nègre* (Brussels: Alde, 1920), pages not numbered.

29. Pansaers, pages not numbered.

30. Michel Leiris, "Présentation de La Fuite," *Labyrinthe*, XV/7 (Feb., 1946), p. 9.

31. Tristan Tzara, *Lampisteries* (Paris: Jean-Jacques Pauvert, 1963), p. 104.

32. *Lampisteries*, p. 104.

33. *The Dada Painters and Poets*, p. 92.

34. *Dada: Art and Anti-Art*, p. 54.

35. Tristan Tzara, *13 Poems*, trans. F. Rosemont (New York: Black Swan Press, 1969), pages not numbered.

36. *Museum of Modern Art Scrapbook*, vol. 1, pages not numbered.

37. Francis Picabia, "Vide," *Choix de Poèmes* (Paris: GLM, 1947), p. 16.

38. *Choix de Poèmes*, p. 44.

39. *Choix de Poèmes*, p. 37.

40. *Choix de Poèmes*, p. 37.

41. *Choix de Poèmes*, p. 39.

42. See Sanouillet, p. 111.

43. *Choix de Poèmes*, p. 51.

44. Francis Picabia, *Unique Eunuque* (Paris: Au Sans Pareil, 1920), p. 13.

45. *Unique Eunuque*, p. 15.

46. *Unique Eunuque*, p. 16.

47. *Unique Eunuque*, p. 16.

48. *Unique Eunuque*, p. 19.

49. *Museum of Modern Art Scrapbook*, vol. 1.

50. *Museum of Modern Art Scrapbook*, vol. 1.

51. Quoted by P. A. Benoit, *A Propos des "Poèmes de la Fille Née Sans Mère"* (Alès, France: P.A.B., 1958), pages not numbered.

52. Quoted by Benoit.

53. Gabrielle Buffet-Picabia, "Introduction," *Jésus-Christ Rastaquouère* (Paris: Au Sans Pareil, 1920), p. 9.

54. *Cassell's New French Dictionary*, E. Baker, ed. (New York: Funk and Wagnall's Co., 1951), p. 588.

55. *Jésus-Christ Rastaquouère*, p. 18. According to Sanouillet, the first "there is nothing to understand" should be eliminated to conform to the original manuscript. (Sanouillet, p. 220.)

56. *Jésus-Christ Rastaquouère*, p. 33.

57. *Jésus-Christ Rastaquouère*, p. 39.

58. William C. Camfield, "Francis Picabia (1879–1953) A Study of his Career from 1895 to 1918," Unpublished dissertation, Yale University, 1964, p. 176.

59. Quoted by Marcel Raymond, *From Baudelaire to Surrealism* (New York: Wittenborn and Schultz, 1950), p. 224.

60. *Selected Works of Alfred Jarry*, p. 124.

61. *Jésus-Christ Rastaquouère*, p. 20.

62. *Jésus-Christ Rastaquouère*, p. 34.

63. *Selected Works of Alfred Jarry*, page not numbered.

64. Pierre de Massot, *De Mallarmé à 391* (Saint Raphael: Au Bel Exemplaire, 1922), p. 119.

65. *Jésus-Christ Rastaquouère*, pp. 16–17.

66. Jean Arp, *On My Way*, tr. R. Manheim (New York: Wittenborn and Schultz, 1948), p. 37.

67. *On My Way*, p. 40.

68. *On My Way*, p. 47.

69. Quoted by Herbert Read, *The Art of Jean Arp* (New York: Abrams, 1968), p. 142.

70. Quoted by Jacques Bersani, "Arp et la Poésie," *Cahiers Dada-Surréalisme*, No. 2. 1968, p. 16.

71. Quoted by Marcel Jean, *Jours effeuillés* (Paris: Gallimard, 1966), p. 25.

72. *On My Way*, p. 46.

73. *The Dada Painters and Poets*, p. 294.

74. *On My Way*, p. 10.

75. Quoted by Jean, p. 13.

76. Jean Arp, *Le Siège de l'Air* (Paris: Vrille, 1946), p. 46.

77. Quoted by Jean, p. 12.

78. Quoted by Jean, p. 13.

79. Quoted by Jean, p. 12.

80. Quoted by Forster, p. 38.

81. Carola Giedion-Welcker, "Arp: An Appreciation," in *Arp* (New York: The Museum of Modern Art, 1958), p. 26.

82. Jean Arp, *Le Siège de l'Air* (Paris: Vrille, 1946), p. 33.

83. See Sanouillet, p. 443.

84. *The Dada Painters and Poets*, p. 78.

85. Quoted by Hugnet, p. 75.

86. Quoted by Hugnet, pp. 71–72.

87. Quoted by Hugnet, pp. 71–72.

88. *Entretiens 1913–1952*, p. 56.

89. See Francis Picabia, *391*, ed. M. Sanouillet (Paris: Le Terrain Vague, 1960), p. 62.

90. See Sanouillet, pp. 123–130, and Herbert S. Gershman, *The Surrealist Revolution in France* (Ann Arbor, Mich.: University of Michigan Press, 1969), p. 39.

91. Paul Eluard, "Patte," *Les Animaux et leurs Hommes les Hommes et leurs Animaux* (Paris: Gallimard, 1936), pages not numbered.

92. Quoted by Sanouillet, p. 211.

93. Quoted by Sanouillet, p. 211.

94. Quoted by Sanouillet, p. 317.

95. Louis Aragon, *Anicet ou le Panorama* (Paris: Editions de la Nouvelle Revue Française, 1921), p. 7.

96. Yvette Gindine, *Aragon Prosateur Surréaliste* (Genève: Droz, 1966), p. 5.

97. Quoted by Roger Garaudy, *L'Itineraire d'Aragon* (Paris: Gallimard, 1961), p. 25.

98. Quoted by Garaudy, p. 26.

99. An indication of this comes from Breton's allusion to Musidora's film *The Vampires* in the section of *Les Pas perdus* which is devoted to Jacques Vaché (see Sanouillet, p. 72). Even more revealing, in one of the last letters that Vaché sent to Breton, dated December 14, 1918, he looked ahead to the end of the war with a certain trepidation that he would not come out of it intact. Vaché consoled himself with the idea that at least it would make a good film. He went on to envision himself, first as Charlie Chaplin, then as a figure from the Old West who hung around at the "Arizona Bar."

100. *Anicet ou le Panorama*, p. 92.

101. *Anicet ou le Panorama*, p. 45.

102. Laurent Lesage, *The French New Novel* (University Park, Penn.: Pennsylvania State University Press, 1962), p. 32.

103. Aragon not only made a study of the approach of such painters as Duchamp, Picabia, Ernst, and Schwitters (*Le Peinture au défi*, Paris: Galérie Goemans, 1930), but also published numerous articles on the art of film. (For a description of these, see Gindine, pp. 1–22.)

104. Lesage, p. 32.

105. Lesage, pp. 32–33.

106. Fold-out Supplement to *The Dada Painters and Poets*, pages not numbered.

107. Quoted by Raymond, p. 275.

108. *The Dada Painters and Poets*, p. 204.

109. Jacques Rivière, "Gratitude to Dada," tr. B. Price, *The Ideal Reader* (New York: Meridian, 1960), p. 231.

110. Laszlo Moholy-Nagy, *Vision in Motion*, p. 315.

111. André Levinson, "The Nature of the Cinema," in *Introduction to the Art of the Movies*, ed. L. Jacobs (New York: Noonday Press, 1960), p. 149.

112. *Introduction to the Art of the Movies*, p. 150.

113. Georges Ribemont-Dessaignes, *Déjà Jadis ou du Mouvement Dada à l'Espace abstrait* (Paris: Juilliard, 1958), p. 81.

114. André Breton, *Les Pas perdus* (Paris: Gallimard, 1924) p. 136.

115. *Les Pas perdus*, p. 209.

116. Quoted by Hubert Juin, *Aragon* (Paris: Gallimard, 1960), p. 59.

117. Henry Miller, *The Cosmological Eye* (Norfolk, Conn.: New Directions, 1939), p. 163.

118. Miller, p. 363.

119. David I. Grossvogel, *Limits of the Novel* (Ithaca, N.Y.: Cornell University Press, 1968), p. 62. For a discussion of the similarity between Joyce's technique and that of the Dadas, see Renato Poggioli, *The Theory of the Avant-Garde*, tr. G. Fitzgerald (Cambridge, Mass: Harvard University Press, 1968), p. 192.

120. Grossvogel, p. 274.

121. Grossvogel, p. 274.

122. Quoted by Matthew Josephson, *Life Among the Surrealists* (New York:

Notes

Holt, Rinehart, and Winston, 1962), p. 161.

123. Quoted by Manuel L. Grossman, "*Him* and the Modern Theater," *The Quarterly Journal of Speech*, LIV (1968), p. 218.

124. Quoted in *Dada: Monograph of a Movement*, p. 50.

125. Quoted by John A. Thwaites, "Dada Hits West Germany," *Arts*, Feb. 1959, p. 32.

126. See Richard Kostelanetz, "Dada and the Future of Fiction," *Works*, I:3 (Spring, 1968), pp. 58-66. For evidences of Dada's continuing impact upon modern writing, see the same issue of *Works*, especially such poems as "R. Mutt," "Neon Digestion of the Lilacs," "Bal de Tête," and "Hymn to 20th Century Anarchy."

127. Allen Ginsberg, "Howl," in *A Casebook on the Beat* (New York: Thomas E. Crowell, 1961), p. 8.

Notes For Chapter Five

1. *The Dada Painters and Poets*, p. 203.

2. Quoted in *Dada: Art and Anti-Art*, p. 216.

3. *The Dada Painters and Poets*, p. 250-251.

4. André Gide, "Dada," tr. J. O'-Brien, in *From the N.R.F.* (New York: Farrar, Strauss, and Cudahy, 1958), p. 14. For a more recent discussion of this analogy, see Marc Le Bot, "Dada et la Guerre," *Europe*, No. 421-422 (June, 1964), pp. 166-173, and Jacques Bersani, "Dada ou la Joie de Vivre," *Critique*, No. 225 (Feb., 1966), pp. 99-117.

5. *Dada: Art and Anti-Art*, p. 219.

6. *The Dada Painters and Poets*, p. 248.

7. J. C. Middleton, "Bolshevism in Art: Dada and Politics," *Texas Studies in Literature and Language*, IV (1962), p. 420.

8. *Entretiens 1913-1952*, p. 56.

9. Sanouillet, p. 423.

10. Quoted by Gershman, p. 35.

11. Quoted by Clifford H. Browder, "André Breton: Arbiter of Surrealism," Unpublished dissertation, Columbia University, 1959, pp. 158-159.

12. Quoted in *Dada: Art and Anti-Art*, p. 215.

13. *Dada: Monograph of a Movement*, p. 78.

14. Sanouillet, p. 428.

15. Fold-out Supplement to *The Dada Painters and Poets*.

16. Susanne K. Langer, *Philosophy in a New Key* (New York: Mentor Books, 1964), p. 77.

17. Langer, p. 86.

18. Fold-out Supplement to *The Dada Painters and Poets*.

19. Laszlo Moholy-Nagy, *Vision in Motion*, p. 314.

20. *The Dada Painters and Poets*, p. 92.

21. *The Dada Painters and Poets*, p. 204.

22. William Seitz, *The Art of Assemblage* (New York: The Museum of Modern Art, 1961), p. 37.

23. Marsden Hartley, *Adventures in the Arts* (New York: Boni and Liveright, 1921), p. 249.

24. Hartley, p. 250.

25. *Museum of Modern Art's Scrapbook*, vol. 1, pages not numbered.

26. Michel Seuphor, "L'Internationale Dada," *L'Oeil*, No. 24 (1956), p. 75.

Adams, Charles L. "The Search for Form; An Examination of the Literary Theory and Technique of Cubism, Futurism, Dada and Surrealism." Unpublished dissertation, University of Oregon, 1959-60.

Aragon, Louis, *Anicet ou le Panorama*, Paris: N.R.F., 1921.

_____, *Entretiens avec Francis Crémieux*, Paris: N.R.F., 1964.

_____, *Feu de Joie*, Paris: Au Sans Pareil, 1920.

_____, "Les Beautés de la Guerre et leurs Reflets dans la Littérature," *Europe* (Dec., 1935), pp. 474-480.

_____, *La Peinture au Défi*, Paris: Corti, 1930.

Arnaud, Noel, "Les Métamorphoses historiques de Dada," *Critique*, No. 134 (July, 1958), pp. 579-604.

Arp, Jean, *Jours effeuillés*, Paris: Gallimard, 1966.

_____, *On My Way*, New York: Wittenborn and Schultz, 1948.

_____, *Le Siège de l'Air*, Paris: Vrille, 1946.

Balakian, Anna, *Literary Origins of Surrealism*, New York: N.Y.U. Press, 1947.

_____, *Surrealism: The Road to the Absolute*, New York: Noonday Press, 1959.

Barr, Alfred, ed., *Fantastic Art, Dada, Surrealism*, New York: Museum of Modern Art, 1947.

Baur, John I., *George Grosz*, New York: Macmillan, 1954.

_____, *Revolution and Tradition in Modern American Art*, Cambridge, Mass.: Harvard University Press, 1951.

Benoit, P. A., *A Propos des "Poèmes de la Fille Née sans Mère,"* Alès, France: P.A.B., 1958.

Bentley, Gilbert and Paul Bernard, "The French Army Mutinies of 1917," *The Historian*, II, 1 (Nov., 1959), pp. 24-41.

Bernard, Suzanne, *Le Poème en Prose depuis Baudelaire jusqu'à nos Jours*, Paris: Nizet, 1959.

Bersani, Jacques, "Arp et la Poésie," *Cahiers Dada-Surréalisme*, 2 (1968), p. 15-24.

_____, "Dada ou la Joie de Vivre," *Critique*, No. 225 (Feb., 1966), pp. 99-117.

Bouvier, Emile, *Initiation à la Littérature d'Aujourd'hui*, Paris: Renaissance du Livre, 1927.

Selected Bibliography

Bradley, Joseph C., "George Grosz: A Study of his Life, Art, and Philosophy," Unpublished dissertation, University of Wisconsin, 1954.

Breton, André, *Anthologie de l'Humour noir,* Paris: Pauvert, 1966.

———, *Entretiens 1913-1952,* Paris: N.R.F., 1952.

———, *Mont de Piété, 1913-1919,* Paris: Au Sans Pareil, 1919.

———, *Les Pas perdus,* Paris: Gallimard, 1924.

———, "The Situation of Surrealism between the Two Wars," *Yale French Studies,* No. 2 (Fall-Winter, 1948), pp. 67-78.

Browder, Clifford, "André Breton: Arbiter of Surrealism," Unpublished dissertation, Columbia University, 1959.

Buffet-Picabia, Gabrielle, *Aires abstraites,* Genève: Cailler, 1957.

Cabaret Voltaire: Receuil Littéraire et Artistique, Hugo Ball, ed., Zurich 1916.

Camfield, William E., "Francis Picabia (1879-1953): A Study of His Career from 1895-1918," Unpublished dissertation, Yale University, 1964.

Cassou, Jean, "Tristan Tzara et l'Humanisme poètique," *Labyrinthe,* No. 14 (Nov. 15, 1945), p. 1.

Céline, Louis, *Journey to the End of the Night,* New York: New Directions, 1960.

Cheney, Sheldon, "Why Dada?", *Century Magazine,* CIV (May, 1922), pp. 22-29.

Clancier, Georges-Emmanuel, *De Rimbaud au Surréalism,* Paris: Seghers, 1959.

Connolly, Cyril, "Surrealism," *Art News Annual,* XXI (1952), pp. 131-170.

Cowley, Malcolm, "The Religion of Art; the Death of a Religion," *The New Republic* (Jan. 17, 1934), pp. 272-275.

———, "The Religion of Art; A Discourse over the Grave of Dada," *The New Republic* (Jan. 10, 1934), pp. 246-249.

Cravan, Arthur, *Maintenant,* Paris: Losfeld, 1956.

Dada I, Zurich, July 1917.

Dada II, Zurich, Dec., 1917.

Dada III, Zurich, Dec., 1918.

Dada IV-V, "Anthologie Dada," Zurich, May 15, 1919.

Damase, Jacques, *A History of the Music-Hall in Paris,* Paris: Editions "Spectacles," 1960.

Eluard, Paul, *Les Animaux et leurs Hommes. les Hommes et leurs Animaux,* Paris: Au Sans Pareil, 1920.

———, *Choix de Poèmes,* Paris: Gallimard, 1951.

———, "Développement Dada," *Littérature,* No. 3 (May, 1920), p. 7.

———, *Misfortunes of the Immortals,* New York: Black Sun Press, 1943.

Engstrom, Alfred, "Poe, Lecomte de Lisle, and Tzara's Formula for Poetry," *Modern Language Notes,* LXXIII (1958), pp. 434-436.

Ernst, Max, *Beyond Painting,* New York: Wittenborn and Schultz, 1948.

Everling-Picabia, Germaine, "C'était hier: Dada . . ." (in: *Les Oeuvres libres,* No. 109, Paris, June, 1955, pp. 119-178).

Faye, Paul-Louis, "Dada and the Temper of 1917," *University of Colorado, Studies, series B, Studies in the Humanities*, I, 4 (Oct., 1941), pp. 309-314.

Firmage, George J., *E. E. Cummings: A Miscellany Revised*, New York: October House, 1958.

Forster, Leonard, *Poetry of Significant Nonsense*, Cambridge, Eng. Cambridge University Press, 1962.

_____, "Unser Gut Kaspar Ist Tot," *Cahiers Dada-Surréalisme*, No. 2 (1968), pp. 25-29.

Fowlie, Wallace, *Age of Surrealism*, Bloomington, Ind.: Indiana University Press, 1960.

Garaudy, Roger, *L'Itineraire d'Aragon*, Paris: Gallimard, 1961.

Gascoyne, David, *A Short Survey of Surrealism*, London: Cobdon-Sanderson, 1936.

Gaunt, William, *The March of the Moderns*, London: Cape, 1949.

Gavillet, André, *La Littérature au défi, Aragon Surréaliste*, Neuchâtel: A la Baconnière, 1957.

Gershman, Herbert, *The Surrealist Revolution in France*, Ann Arbor, Mich.: University of Michigan Press, 1969.

Gide, André, *Les Caves du Vatican*, Paris: Gallimard, 1922.

_____, "Dada," in *From the N.R.F.*, ed. J. O'Brien, New York: Farrar, Straus and Cudahy, 1958.

Giedion-Welcker, Carola, "Hommage à Kurt Schwitters," *K, Revue de la Poésie*, No. 3 (May, 1949), pp. 35-37.

_____, *Poètes à Ecart*, Bern-Bümplitz, Switzerland: Benteli, 1946.

_____, "Le Retour aux Elements dans le Poésie et la Peinture," *XX Siècle*, Nouvelle série, No. 3 (June, 1952), pp. 41-48.

_____ "Schwitters: or the Allusions of the Imagination," *Magazine of Art*, No. 41 (Oct., 1948), pp. 218-221.

Gindine, Yvette, *Aragon, Prosateur Surréaliste*, Genève: Droz, 1966.

Ginsberg, Allen, "Howl," in *Casebook of the Beat*, New York: Crowell, 1961.

Goriély, Benjamin, "Hugo Ball, Prophète Rebelle," *Cahiers Dada-Surréalisme*, No. 1 (1967), pp. 11-18.

Grossman, Manuel L. *"Him* and the Modern Theater," *The Quarterly Journal of Speech*, LIX (1968), pp. 212-219.

_____, "The Language of Dada," *The Journal of Communication*, XVIII, 1 (March, 1968), pp. 4-10.

Grossvogel, David I., *Limits of the Novel*, Ithaca, N.Y.: Cornell University Press, 1968.

Grosz, George, "Demons in the Suburbs," *The New Yorker*, Profile I (Nov. 27, 1943), p. 32.

_____, *A Little Yes and a Big No*, New York: Dial Press, 1946.

_____, "The Saddest Man in all the World," *The New Yorker*, Profile II (Dec. 4, 1943), p. 39.

_____, "The Yankee from Berlin," *The New Yorker*, Profile III (Dec. 11,

1943), p. 37.

Hartley, Marsden, *Adventures in the Arts*, New York: Boni and Liveright, 1921.

Hausmann, Raoul, *Courrier Dada*, Paris: Le Terrain Vague, 1958.

———, "Dadaism and Today's Avant-Garde," *Times Literary Supplement* (Sept. 3, 1964), pp. 800-801.

———, and Kurt Schwitters, *Pin*. London: Gaberbocchus Press, 1962.

Hire, Marie de la, *Francis Picabia*, Paris: Galérie La Cible, 1920.

Hoffman, Frederick, *The Little Magazine, A History and a Bibliography*, Princeton, N.J.: Princeton University Press, 1946.

Hugnet, Georges, *L'Aventure Dada (1916-1922)*, Paris: Galérie de l'Institut, 1957.

Hughes, H. Stuart, *Consciousness and Society*, New York: Knopf, 1958.

Jarry, Alfred, *Oeuvres complètes*, Lausanne: Editions du Livre, 1948.

———, *Ubu Roi*, in *Tout Ubu*, Paris: Librarie Générale Française, 1962.

Jolas, Eugene, "From Jabberwocky to 'lettrism,' " *Transition Forty-Eight*, No. 1 (Jan. 1948), pp. 104-120.

Josephson, Matthew, *Life Among the Surrealists*, New York: Holt, Rinehart, and Winston, 1962.

Juin, Hubert, *Aragon*, Paris: N.R.F., 1960.

Korg, Jacob, "The Literary Aesthetics of Dada," *Works*, I:3 (Spring, 1968), pp. 43-58.

Kostelanetz, Richard, "Dada and the Future of Fiction," *Works*, I:3 (Spring, 1968), pp. 58-106.

Kreymborg, Alfred, "Dada and the Dadas," *Shadowland*, VII, 1 (Sept., 1922), p. 43.

Kyrou, Ado, *Le Surréalisme au Cinema*, Paris: Le Terrain Vague, 1963.

Lacôte, René, *Tristan Tzara*, Paris: Seghers, 1952.

Langer, Susanne K., *Philosophy in a New Key*, New York: Mentor Books, 1964.

Lautréamont, Comte de, *Les Chants de Maldoror*, New York: New Directions, 1965.

Le Bot, Marc, "Dada et la Guerre," *Europe* (May–June, 1964), pp. 166-173.

Leiris, Michel, "Présentation de 'La Fuite,' " *Labyrinthe*, XV, 7 (Feb. 1946), p. 9.

Lemaître, Georges, *From Cubism to Surrealism in French Literature*, Cambridge, Mass.: Harvard University Press, 1941.

Lemaître, Maurice, *La Lettrisme devant Dada*, Paris: Centre de Créativité, 1967.

Lesage, Laurent, *The French New Novel*, University Park, Penn.: Pennsylvania State University Press, 1962.

Levinson, André, "The Nature of the Cinema," in *Introduction to the Art of the Movies*, New York: Noonday, 1960.

Levy, Julian, ed., *Surrealism*, New York: Black Sun Press, 1936.

MacDonald, Dwight, "Eisenstein, Pudovkin, and Others," in *The Emer-*

gence of the Film Art, New York: Hopkinson and Blake, 1968.

Manvell, Roger, ed., *Experiment in the Film*, London: Grey Walls Press, 1949.

Massat, René, "Tristan Tzara, Poète des Réalités," *Arts* (Nov. 15, 1946), p. 2.

Massot, Pierre de, *De Mallarmé à 391*, Saint Raphael: Au Bel Exemplaire, 1922.

_____, "Theatre and Music-Hall," *The Little Review* (Spring, 1923), pp. 3-6.

Matthews, J. H., *André Breton*, New York: Columbia University Press, 1967.

_____, *An Introduction to Surrealism*, University Park, Penn.: Pennsylvania State University Press, 1965.

Mehring, Walter, *The Lost Library*, New York: Bobbs-Merrill, 1951.

Michaud, Regis, *Modern Thought and Literature in France*, New York: Funk and Wagnalls, 1934.

Middleton, J. C. "Bolshevism in Art: Dada and Politics," *Texas Studies in Literature and Language*, IV (1962), pp. 408-430.

_____, "Dada versus Expressionism or the Red King's Dream," *German Life and Letters*, XV (1961), pp. 37-52.

Miller, Henry, *The Cosmological Eye*, Norfolk, Conn.: New Directions, 1939.

Moholy-Nagy, Laszlo, *Vision in Motion*, Chicago: Theobald, 1961.

Moholy-Nagy, Sibyl, *Experiment in Totality*, New York: Harper, 1950.

Monnier, Adrienne, *Rue de l'Odéon*, Paris: Albin Michel, 1960.

Motherwell, Robert, ed., *The Dada Painters and Poets*, New York: Wittenborn and Schultz, Inc., 1951.

Nadeau, Maurice, *The History of Surrealism*, tr. R. Howard, New York: Macmillan, 1965.

Nash, John R., "Jarry, Reverdy, and Artaud: the Abrupt Path," Unpublished dissertation, Stanford University, 1967.

Ortega y Gasset, José, *The Dehumanization of Art and Notes on the Novel*, Princeton, N. J.: Princeton University Press, 1948.

Pansaers, Clément, *Le Pan Pan au Cul du nu Nègre*, Brussels: Alde, 1920.

Peterson, Elmer R., "The Critical Vision of Tristan Tzara," Unpublished dissertation, University of Colorado, 1962.

Picabia, Francis, *L'Athlète des Pompes funèbres*, Lausanne: s.n.e., 1918.

_____, *Choix de Poèmes*, Paris: G.L.M., 1947.

_____, *Dits, Aphorismes réunis par Poupard-Lieussou*, Paris: Le Terrain Vague, 1960.

_____, *Jésus-Christ Rastaquouère*, Paris: Au Sans Pareil, 1920.

_____, *Poèmes et Dessins de la Fille née sans Mère*, Lausanne: Imprimeries Réunies S.A., 1918.

_____, *Unique Eunuque*, Paris: Au Sans Pareil, 1920.

_____, *391*, Paris: Le Terrain Vague, 1960.

Pierre, José, *Le Futurisme et le Dadaisme*, Paris: Editions Rencontre Lausanne, 1967.

Poggioli, Renato, *The Theory of the Avant-Garde*, Cambridge, Mass.: Harvard University Press, 1968.

Putnam, Samuel, ed., *The European Caravan*, New York: Brewer, Warren, and Putnam, 1931.

——, *Paris was Our Mistress*, New York: Viking, 1947.

Ray, Man, *Self Portrait I*, Boston: Little Brown and Co., 1962.

Raymond, Marcel, *From Baudelaire to Surrealism*, New York: Wittenborn and Schultz, 1950.

Read, Herbert, *The Art of Jean Arp*, New York: Abrams, 1968.

Ribemont-Dessaignes, Georges, "Dadaisme," *Der Sturm* (April 1922), pp. 58-61.

——, *Déjà Jadis ou du Mouvement Dada à l'Espace abstrait*, Paris: René Juillard, 1958.

——, "Tristan Tzara, la Poésie et la Révolte," *Critique*, IV (1948), 779-787.

Richardson, John L., "Dada, Camp and the Mode Called Pop," *The Journal of Aesthetics and Art Criticism*, XXIV, 4 (1966), pp. 149-159.

Richter, Hans, *Dada: Art and Anti-Art*, New York: McGraw-Hill, n.d.

Rivière, Jacques, "Gratitude to Dada," in *The Ideal Reader*, New York: Meridian, 1960.

Robbe-Grillet, Alain, *For a New Novel*, New York: Grove Press, 1965.

Rolland, Romain, *Au-dessus de la Mêlée*, Paris: Albin Michel, 1915.

Rothschild, E. F., *The Meaning of Unintelligibility in Modern Art*, Chicago: University of Chicago Press, 1934.

Roy, Claude, *Aragon*, Paris: Seghers, 1945.

Ryder, A. J., *The German Revolution of 1918*, Cambridge, Eng.: Cambridge University Press, 1967.

Salmon, André, *Souvenirs sans Fin*, Deuxième Epoque (1908-1920), Paris: Gallimard, 1956.

Sanouillet, Michel, *Dada à Paris*, Paris: Pauvert, 1965.

——, ed., *Marchand du Sel: Ecrits de Marcel Duchamp*, Paris: Le Terrain Vague, 1958.

——, *Picabia*, Paris: Les Editions du Temps, 1964.

Satie, Erik, *Le Piège de Méduse*, Paris: Galérie Simon, 1921.

Schinz, Albert, "Dadaism," in *Smith College Studies in Modern Languages*, V, 1 (1923), pp. 51-79.

Schoenberner, Franz, *Confessions of a European Intellectual*, New York: Macmillan, 1946.

Schwartz, Arturo, *Cinquant'anni a Dada*, Milano: Galleria Schwartz, 1966.

Seitz, William C., *The Art of Assemblage*, New York: The Museum of Modern Art, 1961.

Seuphor, Michel, "L'Internationale Dada," *L'Oeil*, No. 24 (1956), pp. 64-75.

——, *Le Style et le Cri*, Paris: Editions du Seuil, 1965.

Shattuck, Roger, *The Banquet Years*, Garden City, N.Y.: Doubleday, 1961.

_____ and S. W. Taylor, ed., *Selected Works of Alfred Jarry*, New York: Grove Press, 1965.

_____ "What is Pataphysics," *Evergreen Review*, IV, 13 (May, June 1960)., pp. 24–187.

Smith, Horatio, ed., *Columbia Dictionary of Modern European Literature*, New York: Columbia University Press, 1947.

Soby, James T., ed., *Arp*, New York: The Museum of Modern Art, 1958.

Soupault, Philippe, *Charlot*, Paris: Plon, 1931.

_____, "Confrontations: Alfred Jarry," *Cahiers Renaud-Barrault*, Nos. 22–23 (May 1958), pp. 174–181.

_____, "Dada's Daddies," *Réalitiés*, No. 112 (March, 1960), p. 16.

_____, *Essai sur la Poésie*, Paris: Eynard, 1950.

_____, *Lautréamont*, Paris: Seghers, 1946.

_____, *Poésies complètes, 1917-1937*, Paris: G.L.M., 1937.

_____, *Profiles perdus*, Paris: Mercure de France, 1963.

Stauffacher, Frank, ed., *Art in Cinema*, San Francisco: Museum of Art, 1947.

Steinke, Gerhardt E., "The Anarchistic, Expressionistic and Dadaistic Phases in the Life and Work of Hugo Ball," Unpublished dissertation, Stanford University 1954.

Taylor, Joshua A., *Futurism*, New York: The Museum of Modern Art, 1961.

Thwaites, John A., "Dada Hits West Germany," *Arts* (Feb., 1959), pp. 30–37.

Tompkins, Calvin, *The Bride and the Bachelors*, New York: Viking Press, 1965.

Tuchman, Barbara, *The Guns of August*, New York: Dell, 1962.

_____, *The Proud Tower*, New York: Macmillan, 1966.

Tzara, Tristan, *Cinema Calendrier du Coeur abstrait*, Paris: Au Sans Pareil, 1920.

_____, *Lampisteries*, Paris: Pauvert, 1963.

_____, *Morceaux choisis*, Paris: Bordas, 1947.

_____, *Le Surréalisme et l'Après-Guerre*, Paris: Les Editions Nagel, 1948.

_____, *13 Poems*, New York: Black Swan Press, 1969.

Vaché, Jacques, *Les Lettres de Guerre*, Paris: K, 1949.

Verkauf, Willy, ed., *Dada: Monograph of a Movement*, New York: Hastings House, 1957.

Wilson, Edmund, *Axel's Castle*, New York: Scribner's, 1931.

Zweig, Stefan, *The World of Yesterday*, New York: Viking Press, 1943.

INDEX

This selective index is limited to the names of people pertinent to the Dada movement and the titles of their works.